Language Change in
English Newspaper Editorials

LANGUAGE AND COMPUTERS: STUDIES IN PRACTICAL LINGUISTICS

No 44

edited by Jan Aarts and Willem Meijs

Language Change in English Newspaper Editorials

Ingrid Westin

Rodopi

Amsterdam - New York, NY 2002

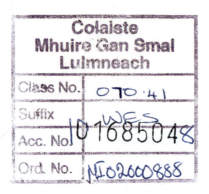
The paper on which this book is printed meets the requirements of
"ISO 9706:1994, Information and documentation - Paper for documents -
Requirements for permanence".

ISBN: 90-420-0863-6 (bound)
©Editions Rodopi B.V., Amsterdam - New York, NY 2002
Printed in The Netherlands

To Maja, Petter, and Robin

Contents

Acknowledgements

I have now reached the point where it is time to write the Preface to my book. Looking back, I realize that many people have, in different ways, contributed to the completion of my work and I would therefore like to take this opportunity to express my gratitude to them.

My first thanks go to Professor Gunnel Tottie, currently at the University of Zürich, formerly Senior Lecturer at Uppsala University, who awakened my interest in English linguistics and my desire to pursue my studies of English, which I interrupted when I started teaching. I am also indebted to Docent Karl Inge Sandred, who opened my eyes for historical linguistics, and to Professor Mats Rydén, my first supervisor, who found a way of combining my interest in language change and newspaper language and who, even after his retirement, followed my work with great interest. Thank you all.

During the last few years, two people have meant more for my research than anyone else: my supervisor, Professor Merja Kytö, and my assistant supervisor, Dr Christer Geisler, who have both given me generously of their time. Professor Kytö introduced me to the fascinating world of corpus linguistics, and Dr Geisler wrote computer programs that facilitated my work. He also provided invaluable help as regards the statistical treatment of my data. My two supervisors were always there for me, sharing with me their knowledge and experience.

Heartfelt thanks are also due to the English Linguistics seminar at the Department of English, Uppsala University. The participants of the seminar discussed the drafts of my thesis and provided constructive criticism and valuable suggestions for improvement through all the stages of my work.

The staff at the newspaper library at Colindale need special mention. They were always ready to help, whether I attended their library to collect material for my corpus or needed support that could be had over the telephone or via e-mail. I would also like to express my gratitude to the staff at Folkbiblioteket in Sandviken who, for several years, supplied me with material from various university libraries thus making it possible for me to carry on my research mainly in my home town. My thanks also go to the staffs of the *Daily Telegraph*, the *Guardian*, and *The Times* for letting me use material from their newspapers and for supplying me with the editorials from the final decades included in my study. They also kindly provided me with background information regarding their newspapers.

I am truly grateful to Dorothy Olsson for scrutinizing my English, and to my colleagues at the University College of Gävle for the interest they have taken in my research.

This study would not have been possible without financial support from different sources. Therefore, I wish to extend my thanks to the University College of Gävle for an in-service development grant enabling both part-time and full-time research. A study period of one year was funded by Riksbankens Jubileumsfond and another six months by a grant from Professor Erik Tengstrand's fund. Furthermore, I thank the Department of English at Uppsala University and their Graduate Student Fund for covering my expenses for research trips and typing assistance.

Finally, my warmest thanks are due to my family for their support and encouragement during all these years. Thoughts of gratitude also go to my parents, who always supported me and encouraged me in my academic work. Unfortunately, they did not live to see the completion of this volume.

Uppsala, June, 2002
Ingrid Westin

Tables and figures

Tables

Figures

1. Introduction

1.1 Aim and scope

The present work shows the results of a corpus-based diachronic study of the language of English up-market newspaper editorials.[1] The investigation is based on samples taken from the *Daily Telegraph*, the *Guardian,* and *The Times,* and describes linguistic variation and change, as well as linguistic continuity, during the 20th century. However, since the language of the editorials mirrors the language used in society, the results of the study can be used in a broader linguistic context in so far as they are also applicable to other types of formal, non-fictional writing.

When texts published within the span of 90 years are compared, linguistic variation is most likely to be found. As far as English up-market newspaper editorials are concerned, my intuitive impression is that a drift towards more informal styles took place during the period studied.[2] The editorials also appear to have lost some of the narrative touch they had at the beginning of the century in favour of a style that is more matter-of-fact. This development towards a more informal and/or less narrative style has been observed in other genres (see, for example, Biber and Finegan 1989, Geisler forthcoming), which makes it reasonable to assume that it has also taken place in newspaper editorials. The reporting and argumentative functions of the editorials today, on the other hand, seem to have been present from the beginning of the century, as this study will

---

1   The term "up-market" as distinguished from "mid-market" and "down-market" was used by, for example, Jucker (1992) in his social stratification of English newspapers. The majority of the "up-market" newspapers (for example, *The Times*, the *Daily Telegraph*, and the *Guardian*) are, mainly, aimed at upper middle-class and middle-class readers, "mid-market" newspapers (for example, the *Daily Express*, the *Daily Mail*, and *Today*) at lower middle-class and skilled working-class readers, and "down-market" newspapers (for example, the *Daily Mirror*, the *Star*, and the *Sun*) at working class readers.

2   In the present study the term *style* is used, more or less, as defined by Crystal and Davy (1969: 10, lines 3–10). *Style*, they say, "may refer to some or all of the language habits shared by a group of people at one time or over a period of time, as when we talk about the style of the Augustan poets, the style of Old English 'heroic' poetry, the style in which civil service forms are written, or styles of public speaking ".

show. The present work aims at giving statistical evidence to support – or refute – the above assumptions through a decade-wise comparison of frequency counts of relevant features. The outcome of this comparison, in turn, serves as the starting-point for a discussion of the development which lies behind the language that meets us in the English up-market editorials of the 1990s.

1.2   Previous research on newspaper language

A great deal of research on media language, written as well as spoken, has been made, especially during the last few decades. Many different aspects have been studied. Content analyses, often with a sociological or ideological emphasis, have been carried out at many university departments, for example, at the Annenberg School of Communications, University of Pennsylvania (see Krippendorff 1980), at the University of Birmingham Centre for Contemporary Cultural Studies (see van Dijk 1988a: 7–8 for references), where research has concentrated on class-dependent news production, and at Glasgow University by the Glasgow University Media Group, who started their research analysing television news contents (*Bad News* 1976, *More Bad News* 1980), but later also investigated press news contents (*Getting the Message* 1993). The sociolinguistic aspects of newspaper language are also treated in the works of individual researchers. Bell (1984, 1991: 104–110) and Jucker (1992), for example, studied the influence by the audience on the linguistic choices that the author of a newspaper text makes, while Kress (1983: 120–138) showed how it is possible for an author to manipulate the audience by choosing the appropriate linguistic variant. Fowler (1991: 91–109) discussed gender and discrimination in British newspapers in general and Fasold et al. (1990: 521–539) gender differences in *The Washington Post*. Closely related to the research mentioned above is the study of news as discourse, a cross-discipline emerging during the 1980s (see, for example, van Dijk 1988a, 1988b, Fowler 1991).

Many researchers have investigated newspaper language from a general stylistic point of view, among others Crystal and Davy (1969: 173–192), who compared two newspaper articles, one from *The Times* and the other from the *Daily Express*, and O'Donnell and Todd (1980: 85–100), who compared a few prominent linguistic features in the *Guardian* and the *Daily Mirror*. Carter (1988: 8–16) made a detailed stylistic analysis of a front page article in the *Daily Mail* to show its shortcomings as to objectivity. Others concentrated on a specific linguistic feature. Rydén (1975: 14–39), Bell (1988: 326–344), and Jucker (1992: 207–250), for example, looked at noun-name appositional phrases, and Axelsson (1998) studied the use of contractions. Newspaper language is also used in comparative studies such as Biesenbach-Lucas (1987), Kikai et al. (1987), Jacobson (1989), and Ljung (1996; 1997). Biesenbach-Lucas (1987: 13–21) and Kikai et al. (1987: 266–277) compared the use of relative pronouns in American newspapers with other written and spoken genres, and Jacobson (1989: 145–154) compared the use of these pronouns in three different American newspapers.

Ljung compared the use of modals (1996: 159–179) and sentence complexity (1997: 75–83) in British and American newspapers.

Special newspaper registers have also attracted attention over the years. Mårdh (1980) investigated the language of newspaper headlines, Ghadessy (1988: 19–51) sports commentary (soccer), and Toolan (1988: 52–64) advertising language, for example. Wallace (1977: 46–78) compared the language of the news section to that of the sports section in the *Chicago Tribune* and the *Champaign-Urbana Courier,* and Floreano (1986) compared written quality and popular media language to spoken. Research on newspaper editorials, the genre chosen for the present study, has also been carried out. Van Dijk (1992: 243–259), studied the argumentative structures and strategies in two British editorials, one from the *Daily Mail* and one from the *Sun,* on the race riots that took place in England during the autumn of 1985. Bolívar (1994: 276-294) also paid attention to the structure of editorials. By using 23 editorials from the *Guardian* (January–March, 1981), she showed that editorials can be analysed in "triads", three-part structures, resembling the two-part or three-part exchange we meet in face-to-face interaction. Hawes and Thomas (1996: 159–170) compared theme types and thematic progression in editorials in *The Times* and the *Sun*, and Hackett and Zhao (1994: 509–541) made a textual analysis of opinion/editorial commentary in the American press (among others editorials from small and medium-sized newspapers throughout the country) during the Gulf War against Iraq in 1991.

The study of newspaper language from a diachronic perspective does not seem to have attracted much attention, however.[3] Diachronic issues have been raised by way of introducing a discussion or giving background information. Otherwise, linguists seem to have preferred other aspects of media research (see above). Laurie Bauer is an exception. In *Watching English Change* (1994: 50–90), he devotes a chapter to the diachronic study of three grammatical features: comparative and superlative marking of adjectives, concord with collective nouns, and relative clauses, using material mainly from editorials published in *The Times* from 1900 to 1985.[4] Still, Bauer's study is not primarily a study of grammatical change in the language of newspaper editorials, but a more general study of grammatical changes that have taken place in the English language during the 20th century. Bauer used editorials from *The Times* to construct a corpus for this part of his study because he wanted to have access to data that he presumed had remained more or less unchanged throughout the century. In the present study, it is the development of the language of English up-market newspaper editorials that is the focus of attention.

---

3 Diachronic studies of late modern (20th century) English, as a whole, are relatively rare (see, for example, Rydén and Brorström 1987: 9). Among those focusing on this period is Övergaard's study of the mandative subjunctive in British and American English (1995).

4 The rest of the book is based on material taken from other sources. For the chapter on lexical change, for example, Bauer uses a sample from the *The Supplement to the Oxford English Dictionary* (*OEDS*).

1.3   Plan of the study

The present study embraces several aspects of linguistic variation and change in English up-market newspaper editorials during the 20th century. The methodological background of the study is outlined in Chapter 2. Chapters 3 through 8 contain a multi-feature/multi-dimensional analysis of 20th century newspaper data based on some of the empirically defined dimensions of linguistic variation presented in Biber (1988). Sets of features that Biber proved to share special communicative functions are compared over the decades and between the newspapers. Thus, such stylistic and pragmatic phenomena as personal involvement (Chapter 3), information density (Chapter 4), narrativeness (Chapter 5), argumentative force (Chapter 6), abstractness (Chapter 7), and explicitness in reference (Chapter 8) are addressed. Chapter 9 analyses the results obtained in Chapters 3 through 8 and shows how the original sets of features can be broken up to form new ones based on the shared communicative functions characteristic of editorials. Chapter 10, finally, contains a summary of the preceding chapters with the emphasis on the results presented in Chapter 9, followed by a conclusion. The Appendix contains the statistics on which the discussion of change and continuity is based.

2. Methodological considerations

2.1   Introduction

The use of machine-readable corpora for diachronic as well as synchronic linguistic analysis started in the 1960s. The size of the corpora and the advent of tools for frequency counts of specific features, or sets of features, made possible large-scale studies of the features in question. Combined with statistical analyses, these frequency counts gave more reliable information on linguistic variation and change than previous research had been able to do.

For the purpose of the present study, the existing corpora were not suitable, however. Even though newspaper texts are included in many of them, such as LOB and Brown and FLOB and Frown (see section 2.2), editorials constitute a very small part. Besides, for a diachronic study as the one at hand, texts covering a time span of some length are needed. It was therefore necessary to compile a new corpus satisfying these needs. Section 2.2 gives some general information on machine-readable corpora and section 2.3 describes the corpus compiled for the present work. The rest of the chapter is devoted to other methodological issues. Section 2.4 presents the multi-feature/multi-dimensional approach and section 2.5 gives a methodological overview of the study.

2.2   Machine-readable corpora

The advent of the two machine-readable language corpora, the Brown University Corpus of Written American English (Brown) in the middle of the 1960s (see Francis and Kučera 1979) and the Lancaster-Oslo/Bergen Corpus of British English (LOB) in the late 1970s (see Johansson, Leech, and Goodluck 1978; Johansson 1986) made quantitative studies of language structure easier and more reliable than before.[1] The new corpora also made possible comparison between

---

1   The text genres in LOB and Brown are: A. Press: reportage; B. Press: editorials; C. Press: reviews; D. Religion;   E. Skills, trades and hobbies; F. Popular lore; G. Bell lettres, biography, and essays; H. Miscellaneous; J. Learned and scientific writing; K. General

different written genres as well as between British and American English usage. At the beginning of the 1990s, FLOB (the Freiburg version of LOB) and Frown (the Freiburg version of Brown), replicas matching their predecessors closely, both as regards size and composition, were compiled at the University of Freiburg under the supervision of Professor Christian Mair (see Hundt, Sand, and Siemund 1998; Hundt, Sand, and Skandera 1999). The texts used for these two corpora were published in 1991 and 1992, respectively, approximately thirty years later than those found in LOB and Brown. When the two new corpora were submitted for international distribution, it was thus possible to make computer-based comparative studies of texts published at a thirty-year interval.

The London-Lund Corpus of Spoken British English (see Svartvik et al. 1982), on the one hand,[2] and projects such as ARCHER, A Representative Corpus of Historical English Registers (see Biber, Finegan, and Atkinson 1994) and the Helsinki Corpus of English Texts (see Kytö and Rissanen 1988; Rissanen, Kytö, and Palander-Collin 1993), on the other, made possible the comparison between written and spoken genres and the study of language change over time, both topics of great interest for my study.

Corpora of newspaper texts have also been compiled, as, for example, the Zurich Corpus of English Newspapers (ZEN) (see Fries 1994: 17–18), containing material covering the period 1671 to 1791, and the Uppsala Press Corpus 1994 (see Axelsson 1998: 226-249), containing material from English up-market as well as mid-market and down-market newspapers printed in 1994. From the 1990s, British national newspapers are also available on CD-ROM.

2.3   The Corpus of English Newspaper Editorials (CENE)

As none of the existing corpora was suitable for my purposes, a new corpus was compiled, the Corpus of English Newspaper Editorials (1900–1993), CENE, for short. In section 2.3.1, a definition of the word *editorial* is given, followed by some background information on the newspapers from which the editorials are taken. The sampling method is described in 2.3.2, the treatment of the sampled texts in 2.3.3, and the size of the corpus in 2.3.4.

---

fiction; L. Mystery and detective fiction; M. Science fiction; N. Adventure and western fiction; P. Romance and love story; R. Humour.

2   The text genres in the London-Lund Corpus are: 1. Spontaneous conversations between intimates and distants;   2. Conversations between intimates and equals; 3. Public conversations between equals; 4. Private conversations between equals; 5. Conversations between disparates; 6. Telephone conversations between personal friends; 7. Telephone conversations between business associates; 8. Telephone conversations between disparates; 9. Spontaneous commentary (sport and non-sport); 10. Spontaneous oration (case in court, dinner speech, radio: 'My word', recordings in the House of Commons); 11. Prepared but unscripted oration (sermons, university lectures, cases in court, political speech, popular lecture).

2.3.1   Background information

CENE, the Corpus of English Newspaper Editorials (1900–1993), comprises editorials from the *Daily Telegraph*, the *Guardian*, and *The Times,* collected at ten-year intervals.[3] An editorial, in British journalism also referred to as a "leading article" or a "leader", is a newspaper article expressing the opinion of the editor or publishers of the newspaper on some topical issue. A distinction is often made between personal editorials, which are by-lined with the writer's name, and institutional editorials, which are not. In the newspapers chosen for the present study, only institutional editorials were found.

Today, the editorials are usually printed on an inside page, sometimes referred to as the "leader page". At the beginning of the century, the editorials were not assigned a special page. They might have started on one page and continued on the next, and they had to share space with, for example, a table of contents, announcements regarding entertainment and commercial markets, brief news bulletins, and reports from the newspaper's London Correspondent. The editorials were easily distinguishable from other pieces of writing, however, since they did not only report on current affairs but also commented on them. To give an idea of what a page with an editorial from the beginning of the century looked like, a copy of the top right hand corner (approximately one sixth of the full page) of the *Daily Telegraph* of January 15, 1900, is shown in Figure 2.1.[4] The editorial starts in the middle of the last column ("No news has been allowed ...") and continues on the next page of the newspaper (not reproduced here). The practice of devoting a page almost exclusively to opinion copy, that is, to editorials and letters to the editor, appears to have started between 1940 and 1950 in the *Guardian*, and between 1950 and 1960 in the other two newspapers, to judge from the material available for the present study.

The oldest of the three newspapers examined is *The Times*, which was founded as early as 1785.[5] It claims to be independent but is usually considered to be right-wing in its reporting. However, its editorials are generally looked upon as sober and unbiased. The second oldest is the *Guardian*, founded in Manchester in 1821, as *The Manchester Guardian.* In 1959, with more than two thirds of its circulation outside Manchester, it changed its name to the *Guardian,* and in 1964 the editorial offices were transferred to London. Politically, it is left of centre and supports the Liberal Party. The *Daily Telegraph* is the youngest of the three newspapers, founded in 1855. It is right of centre and supports the Conservative Party. In 1993 (the last full year before the sampling started), the *Daily Telegraph*

3   In the tables and diagrams in the present study the abbreviations DT (the *Daily Telegraph*), Gua (the *Guardian*), and Ti (*The Times*) are used.

4   The text is reproduced here with the permission of Nicola Chang, the *Daily Telegraph* syndication.

5   Data on the newspapers in the following paragraphs are taken from Burnham (1955) (the *Daily Telegraph*); Mills (1921) and Hetherington (1981) (the *Guardian*); and Howard (1985) (*The Times*).

LARGEST CIRCULATION
IN THE WORLD.

THE SALE OF

The Daily Telegraph

AMOUNTS TO AN AVERAGE WHICH, IF TESTED,
WILL SHOW AN

EXCESS OF HALF A MILLION
COPIES WEEKLY
OVER ANY OTHER MORNING PAPER.

Subscribers and Advertisers are requested to make
their Post-office Orders payable at the Ludgate-circus
Money Order Office to Walter Harvey, of 141, Fleet-
street, London, E.C.
The Editor cannot undertake to be responsible for
the return of rejected manuscripts.

LONDON, MONDAY, JANUARY 15.

THE WEATHER.
THIS MORNING'S SPECIAL FORECAST.

Showery weather is probable.
To-day's forecast is: S.W. winds; dull, some
rain.
Subjoined are the reports from our observing
stations, received at midnight:
VALENTIA.—Bar. 29·55, fall much checked; mist and
rain all day; wind S.W., fresh; clouds inclined to
break; sea rough; temp. 49°.
LIZARD.—Bar. 29·84, falling; temp., max. 51°, min.
42°; wind W., moderate, increasing; rain, overcast.
EDINBURGH.—Bar. 29·50, falling; therm., max.
44·2°, min. 42.2°; wind S.W., gentle; cloudy.,
The highest temperature in the shade was
39°; and the lowest 26°. The sun rises at 8.2
a.m. and sets at 4.18 p.m.

TO-DAY.

The Queen has sent a gracious and touching
message of sympathy to the Hon. Mr. and Mrs.
Vernon, whose son, a captain of the 60th Rifles,
was killed in a recent Mafeking sortie, which
he carried out with great heroism. Her Majesty
has asked for a photograph of the gallant officer.

While little official news of the progress of
the war is published, there is no scarcity of information from other sources. A Durban report of Friday refers to a great battle then pro-
ceeding in the Ladysmith district, fighting being
in progress at three points between General
Buller's force and the enemy. From a Lourenço
Marques telegram it is evident that for several
days past the Boers have been anticipating and
preparing for another great struggle. Sir Charles
Warren is co-operating with Sir Redvers Buller.

for some time as a Professor of Philosophy in
Manchester New College.

On Saturday morning Albert W. Chalfont, a
clerk, who had suffered from melancholia following an attack of influenza, together with his
wife and little child, were found dead at Bassing-
ham-road, Earlsfield, Wandsworth. The child
was suffocated, and the man and woman died from
bullet wounds.

Plumpton January Meeting was concluded in
delightful weather. Mr. E. Hobson's Miss Bur-
naby won the Ashurst Maiden Hurdle Race, Mr.
R. Gore's Ever Deceptive the Hurstpierpoint
Selling Hurdle Race, Mr. R. Buckworth's Brown
Princess the Southover Selling Handicap Steeplechase, Mr. S. E. Barnett's Whitehead the Brook-
side Steeplechase, Mr. Gilbert's Merry Monk II.
the Streat Handicap Hurdle Race, and Lord
Denman's Sheriff's Officer the Barcombe Novices'
Steeplechase.

A strong tone prevailed in the Stock Market
on Saturday, in anticipation of favourable war
news. Consols closed ⅜ up, at 99¾, after touching
99⅞, and English, American, and Canadian railways, as well as some foreign lines, improved.
Foreign Government bonds, too, were rather better. South African and a few Westralian mines
advanced. Rupee Paper closed at 63⅜, and silver
improved to 27₃⁄₁₆d per ounce. Loans ruled at 2,
2¼ per cent., and discount at 3¼, ⅞.

No news has been allowed to come over the
wires from the Tugela River, and we are still
anxiously expecting the issue of General
BULLER's flanking movement. On Saturday
London was full of rumours that the British
had sustained another reverse—subsequently
discovered to be entirely false—while yesterday
it was freely reported that engagements had
taken place at three different points along the
extended Boer lines. As a matter of fact the last
conjecture, for it is nothing more, is likely to be
correct, seeing that Sir CHARLES WARREN
has moved with a flying column " in support of
General BULLER," and there is every reason to
suppose that something was done against
Colenso simultaneously with the seizure of
Potgieter's Drift. It is quite possible that a
double flanking policy may be attempted, both
east and west, except that the ground on the
east is more difficult than towards Springfield,
and it would be necessary to make a wide
détour in the direction of Weenen, inevitably
requiring a large amount of transport. It is
more probable that Hlangwane Mountain may
be attacked, and if this elevation is suc-
cessfully occupied, and our artillery placed in
good position upon it, the Boer trenches at
Colenso will become much more exposed to
our fire. In that case a direct assault
on the enemy's left can be delivered with
far less risk to our men, and General CLERY or
Sir CHARLES WARREN may have the satisfac-
tion of pushing the Boers back northward
towards Ladysmith. If fighting really occurred
at three points yesterday or Saturday, the

Figure 2.1 A copy of the top right hand corner of the "leader page" of the *Daily Telegraph* of January 15, 1900.

had by far the largest circulation of the three newspapers (1,020,908 copies). The circulation figures for the *Guardian* and *The Times* were more modest, 407,508 and 389,365, respectively.[6]

Since the political standpoints of the three newspapers diverge, their readership profiles may also be supposed to diverge. This assumption is confirmed by the statistics compiled by The National Readership Surveys Ltd. In 1993, 27% of the readers representing social grade A chose the *Daily Telegraph*, 15% *The Times,* and 7% the *Guardian* (see Figure 2.2).[7] Among the social grade B and C readers, the *Daily Telegraph* was also the most popular newspaper of the three while the *Guardian* was more popular than *The Times.* Only 1% of the readers from social grades D and E chose one of the up-market papers.

When the readership profiles for 1993 are compared to those for 1970, the earliest available from The National Readership Surveys Ltd., we find an increasing interest in all the newspapers covered by the study among the social grade A and B readers while the number of readers from the other social grades either decreased or remained more or less stable (see Figures 2.3 and 2.4).[8]

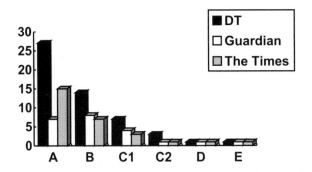

Figure 2.2 Readership profiles for 1993 as percentages (social grades A–E).

---

6   The circulation figures for 1993 for the three newspapers are taken from statistics published by The National Readership Surveys Ltd. The earliest circulation figures obtainable are as follows: *The Times* 157,342 (1941), the *Guardian* 136,366 (1949), and the *Daily Telegraph* 1,305,032 (1963) (source: Audit Bureau of Circulations Ltd.).

7   Grade A refers to the "upper middle class", B to "middle class", C1 to "lower middle class", C2 to "skilled working class", D to "working class", and E to "those at the lowest levels of subsistence" (The National Readership Surveys Ltd.). The readership profiles regard the adult population (ages 15+).

8   To enable comparison, grades A and B and grades D and E of the 1993 data had to be integrated since, for 1970, social grades A and B, as well as D and E, are merged.

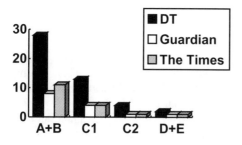

Figure 2.3 Readership profiles for 1970 as percentages .   .

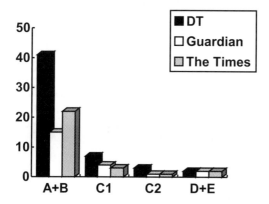

Figure 2.4 Readership profiles for 1993 as percentages.

In 1970, the circulation figures were, for the *Daily Telegraph* 1,409,009, for the *Guardian* 303,717, and for *The Times* 388,406, which means that, between 1970 and 1993, the circulation figures for the *Daily Telegraph* dropped by almost 400,000, those for the *Guardian* increased by more than 100,000, and those for *The Times* remained almost the same. Despite the joint decrease in circulation, the three newspapers increased their share among the social grade A and B readers during the period.

2.3.2 Sampling method

Before compiling a corpus for a diachronic study of newspaper editorials, at least four questions have to be answered: firstly, what newspaper(s) to choose for the study and, secondly, what period to cover. The third and fourth questions concern at what intervals comparisons of the texts samples should be made, and what sampling pattern should be used.

The reason why the *Daily Telegraph*, the *Guardian*, and *The Times* were chosen for my study was two-fold: they were the only newspapers that had been in circulation since the beginning of the century, thus enabling a diachronic study covering a whole century, and, furthermore, they represent a fairly homogeneous group of newspapers, English up-market newspapers. However, since their political standpoints and consequently their readership profiles differ (see section 2.3.1), linguistic variation within the group may also be of some significance for the study.

The fact that the study covers only the 20th century when the youngest of the newspapers concerned had been in circulation since 1855 needs an explanation. It was not until the end of the 19th century that leading articles started to appear more regularly and, from the point of view of content, resemble editorials as we know them today. Starting the investigation at the turn of the century therefore seemed natural. The first texts of the corpus thus date back to 1900. After that, samples from every tenth year follow. Ten-year intervals between the samples compared were considered satisfactory for a thorough observation of the variation over time of the features investigated.[9] However, since 1993 was the last full year before the collection of data started, texts from that year instead of 1990 were chosen to represent the final decade so as to obtain as current material as possible for comparison.

As far as the sampling method is concerned, it is important that the text samples are put together in such a way that they give a representative linguistic picture of the period they cover, in the present case, one year. Choosing editorials from consecutive days of a week, for example, might distort the picture since major political events, such as elections, a new budget, or wars, may, at worst, be the topic of all the editorials during the week, which would probably be reflected in the linguistic choices that the authors make. In choosing the so-called "constructed week" for sampling, that is, a Monday from January, a Tuesday from February, and so on (no Sunday papers were included since they did not exist at the beginning of the period) I hoped to be able to avoid at least some of such pitfalls.[10]

Constructed weeks for each newspaper and year selected for investigation, that is, 1900, 1910, 1920, and so on (henceforth often referred to as "decades") were thus put together. To begin with, the editorials from only one constructed week from each newspaper and year were included in the corpus, but since the editorials from the beginning of the century were usually much longer than those from the latter part of the century, a second constructed week was added to the samples that were comparatively short. The corpus now comprises 864 editorials divided between 44 constructed weeks (see Table 2.1 and 2.2; for statistics, see Appendix, s.v. editorial length).

---

9   In my licentiate thesis (Westin 1997), the intervals between the compared samples were twice
        as long, which, at times, proved to be unsatisfactory.

10   The constructed week is a commonly used design, developed by Jones and Carter (1959) and
        used among others, by Bell (1991: 23).

Table 2.1 Average number of words per editorial.

Year	The Daily Telegraph			The Guardian			The Times		
	Words	Editori-als	Average of words	Words	Editori-als	Average of words	Words	Editori-als	Average of words
1900	11557	11	1050.6	18017	38	474.1	21979	19	1156.8
1910	22410	16	1400.6	17018	29	586.8	21048	18	1169.3
1920	20827	24	867.8	17218	32	538.1	20229	32	632.2
1930	16300	36	452.8	15465	34	454.9	18464	23	802.8
1940	12995	30	433.2	13893	30	463.1	18295	24	762.3
1950	14323	33	434.0	13350	26	513.5	17506	28	625.2
1960	13440	36	373.3	12511	28	446.8	14221	28	507.9
1970	11969	35	342.0	19219	38	505.8	18646	32	582.7
1980	12097	35	345.6	20323	30	677.4	20949	29	722.4
1993	11424	24	476.0	17090	31	551.3	20051	35	572.9
1900–1993	147342	280	526.2	164104	316	519.3	191388	268	714.1

Table 2.2 Average number of words per editorial for the newspapers together.

The newspapers together

Year	Words	Editorials	Average of words
1900	51553	68	758.13
1910	60476	63	959.94
1920	58274	88	662.20
1930	50229	93	540.10
1940	45183	84	537.89
1950	45179	87	519.30
1960	40172	92	436.65
1970	49834	105	474.61
1980	53369	94	567.76
1993	48565	90	539.61
1900–1993	502834	864	581.98

2.3.3   Treatment of data

The texts chosen for sampling were photocopied from the microfilms available at the British Library's Newspaper Library at Colindale, North London and subsequently transferred into machine-readable form, either by the use of a scanner or by manual typing.[11] The texts were proof-read and coded, that is, each editorial was given a special code, providing information about what newspaper the editorial was taken from. Furthermore, each editorial throughout the year was assigned a serial number. The headlines were also marked with a special code (ECH). For illustration, see the beginning of a file cited below:

<Q 1940 GUA E6>
[^The Guardian^]
[^Monday, Jan 8, 1940^]
<P 6>

ECH A Deserved Tribute

The code tells us that this is the sixth editorial in the *Guardian* drawn from 1940; the newspaper was issued on January 8, a Monday, and the editorial was found on page six (<P 6>).[12]

To enable automatic searches, the whole material was 'tagged' by a computer program,[13] the EngCG-2 (see section 2.5.3), which means that each word was assigned 'tags' giving information about morphology and part-of-speech, as in the extract from the tagged version of CENE below:

the_the#DET#SG/PL
treaty_treaty#N#NOM#SG
goes_go#V#PRES#SG3
much_much#ADV#ABS
further_far#ADV#CMP

---

11   Sometimes the quality of the photocopies, as well as of the originals, especially those from the beginning of the century, made it difficult, even impossible, to discern the text. Three asterisks (***) in the text files show that words or phrases have been left out as illegible. Another change that was made when copying the material concerns the use of quotation marks. At the beginning of the century each line of a quotation was preceded by a quotation mark. In the text files, the quotation mark is used only at the beginning and the end of a quotation.

12   This information (except what day of the week) can also be found in Westin 2001, Appendix 1, where details for each editorial included in the corpus are given.

13   In the present work, single quotation marks are used for items having a special meaning in the context where they appear (cf. the use of single quotation marks for philosophical terms as recommended by *The Chicago manual of style* (1993: 213), whereas double quotation marks are used for regular quotations from other sources. Terms commonly used in linguistics are italicized.

2.3.4 The size of the corpus

CENE comprises 864 editorials and contains just above half a million (502,834) words. A corpus of this size may be small compared to the multi-million-word corpora avail-able today, but for the purposes of the present study, it was assumed to be large enough. As seen from Tables 2.1 and 2.2 in section 2.3.2, the sample sizes representing each decade vary, as does the average number of words per editorial, but since all comparisons are made between frequencies normalized to a text length of 1,000 words, this will not affect the results obtained.[14] Only the calculation of sentence length is based on raw data.

2.4   The multi-feature/multi-dimensional approach to linguistic variation

The idea for the treatment of data is taken from the multi-feature/multi-dimensional approach used by Biber in his 1988 study.[15] In his study Biber is able to show that different genres, among others editorials, vary over different dimensions of linguistic variation, such as involved/informational, narrative/non-narrative, explicit/situation-dependent reference, overt expressions of persuasion, abstract/non-abstract information, and on-line informational elaboration.[16] Since this model reflects many aspects of language variation that seemed useful also for my purposes and, besides, had proved to be suitable for diachronic studies (see, for example, Biber 1995; Biber and Finegan 1989, 1992, and 1997; Atkinson 1992; Geisler forthcoming), aspects of this model were applied in the analysis of my material. What distinguishes my study from, for example, Biber's (1988) is that mine is based on frequency counts only. No factor analysis is used (however, an exploratory factor score analysis of the present data is carried out in Westin and Geisler 2002).

With his study Biber wanted to show that we can not simply draw a borderline between written and spoken language as had formerly often been the done. The patterns of variation are much more complex than that. From the 1950s on, researchers had compared the frequency of a selected feature (or sets of features) in the two modes and, on the basis of the results, maintained that the feature was more frequent in one mode than the other, without taking into consideration how text types within the two modes vary. O'Donnell (1974), and Kroll (1977), for example, showed that there are more subordinate clauses in written language; Drieman (1962) that written texts are shorter, have longer words, more attributive adjectives and a more varied vocabulary; Devito (1966,

---

14   From a statistical point of view, however, the fact that some of the samples (=editorials) are very short is a problem (the length of the editorials vary between 116 and 1777 words).

15   For a detailed methodological overview of the study, see Biber (1988: 61–97).

16   The term 'involved' in this context refers to interactive discourse, showing personal involvement.

1967) that written language is more abstract, has fewer quantifiers and hedges, and fewer words that refer to the speaker. However, many of these researchers were probably all aware of the fact that more research, and perhaps other types of research, would be necessary to account for the differences between written and spoken language. Kroll, for example, concludes her article by saying that "[t]here is still much that remains to be said about the distinction and the overlap between which structures are commonly used in speech and writing" (1977: 106).

Towards the end of the 1970s, researchers were able to show that there is no clear-cut borderline between spoken and written genres. Instead, by identifying sets of co-occurring linguistic features and investigating their distribution in written and oral texts, they were able to show that the texts, regardless of medium, are related along functional or situational parameters such as planned/unplanned (Ochs 1979: 51–80, Chafe 1982: 35–45), oral/literate (Tannen 1982a: 1–15, Tannen 1985: 124–147), involved/detached (Chafe 1982: 45–49, Chafe and Danielewicz 1987: 105–112), and formal/informal (Gumpertz et al. 1984: 3–17). A lecture, for example, has more in common with an academic paper and a personal letter with a dinner conversation than the two texts representing the same mode, that is, the lecture and dinner conversation (spoken) on the one hand, and the academic paper and the personal letter (written), on the other (see Chafe 1982: 35–45 and Chafe and Danielewicz 1987: 105–112). A great deal of overlap between written and spoken genres was thus observed, in the sense that some kinds of spoken language are more "writtenlike" and some kinds of written language are more "spokenlike" (Tannen 1982b).

Biber (1985; 1986) went one step further in suggesting that, rather than regarding parameters such as planned/unplanned and oral/literate as discrete poles, we may regard them as dimensions, characterized by sets of co-occurring linguistic features, along which texts vary stylistically. An academic paper, for example, would probably appear far to the 'planned' end of the dimension planned/unplanned while a telephone conversation between friends would appear far to the 'unplanned' end. A lecture and a personal letter would appear in between the two, the lecture closer to the academic paper and the personal letter closer to the telephone conversation. Since its introduction, the multi-feature/multi-dimensional model has frequently been used for the study of synchronic linguistic variation (e.g. Biber 1987, 1988, 1994, 1995, 2001a, 2001b; Besnier 1988, Finegan and Biber 1994; Kim and Biber 1994, Geisler 2001) as well as of diachronic variation (e.g. Biber and Finegan 1988, 1989, 1992, 1997; Biber, Finegan, and Atkinson 1994; Biber and Hared 1994; Atkinson 1992; Geisler forthcoming).

2.5 Methodological overview of the present study

As mentioned in section 1.1, the present work is a corpus-based diachronic study of English newspaper editorials. The approach is mainly quantitative, in so far as the frequencies of sets of linguistic features are compared across time and across newspapers. However, in most cases, the results obtained are accompanied by qualitative interpretations, and Chapter 9 is devoted to a discussion aiming at a synthesis.[17] In the following, I first describe the selection of features (section 2.5.1), then the different steps of the investigation (section 2.5.2), and, finally, the tools used throughout the study (section 2.5.3).

2.5.1   Selection of features

The linguistic features included in the present study were such as Biber (1988) had proved to be markers of the communicative functions I was interested in, that is, personal involvement, information density, narrative discourse, argumentative discourse, abstract discourse, and explicit reference, comprising 42 features, all in all. To these were added four features that, in my opinion, might give supporting evidence: imperatives, as a marker of personal involvement (see section 3.2.4), sentence length and subordination, as markers of information density (see sections 4.5.1 and 4.5.2, respectively), and relative *that*, as a marker of explicit reference (see section 8.2.3).[18]

2.5.2   Frequency counts and data processing

The frequencies of the selected features were obtained through automatic searches (see section 2.5.3).[19] Sometimes, manual screening of the results was necessary, however. When the tagger (see sections 2.3.3 and 2.5.3) cannot decide, from the surrounding words, what tag to assign to an ambiguous form, two or more alternatives are given. In the extract below from the tagged version of CENE, for example, *present* is tagged both as a noun and an adjective and *need* as a noun and a verb.

> on_on#PREP
> present_present#N#NOM#SG_present#A#ABS
> need_need#N#NOM#SING_need#V#PRES-sg3

In such cases, the screening of 'duplicates' in the coded text makes it possible to remove irrelevant instances. Some multi-functional words, such as *general*, *public*, and *cost*, which, at an initial stage of the study, proved to be erroneously labelled, were also screened by hand.[20] The frequency counts of the 46 features were normalized to a text-length of 1000 words,[21] and the means of the normed frequencies compared across the decades and the newspapers. Finally, the

---

17   As so many features are investigated, the qualitative discussions do not, by any means, claim to be exhaustive.

18   Relative *that* was included also in Biber's study, however not as a marker of explicit reference but as a marker of "On-line informational elaboration".

19   Instances from quoted as well as unquoted speech are normally included in the frequency counts. Only when relevant, is special attention given to quoted speech.

variation between decades and newspapers was tested for significance (at 5% significance level) and the results interpreted (see section 2.5.3). The interpretation of the results of the tests is found in the text, together with frequency tables and diagrams, but the statistics for the features are given, in alphabetical order, in the Appendix.

2.5.3 Tools

The tools applied to the material were:

- for the tagging of the corpus: the EngCG-2 tagger (1999)
- for the frequency counts: the WordCruncher program, Version 4.3 (1985–89) and counting scripts in Perl
- for the calculation of sentence length: the TSSA 2.0 (1994)
- for the calculation of variation: one-way Analysis of Variance (ANOVA)
- for the location of statistically significant differences between decades and newspapers: The Newman-Keuls multiple comparison test

EngCG-2 is a program which assigns morphological and part-of-speech tags to words in English text. The present version is an improved version of the original EngCG tagger, which is based on the Constraint Grammar framework designed by a group of computational linguists at the University of Helsinki, Finland (see Karlsson et al. 1995).[22] Before opting for the EngCG-2 tagger, trial runs with other taggers, more precisely, Brill, T-n-T tagger, and Tree Taggers were made to compare the reliability of the different taggers. For my purposes, the EngCG-2 turned out to be by far the most suitable.

The WordCruncher program, developed at the Brigham Young University in Utah, USA, is used for frequency counts of, for example, words and word combinations, of morphological units and of combinations of letters and signs. In the present study, it was mainly used for counting the part-of-speech tags assigned by the Eng-CG2 tagger. To achieve the greatest possible accuracy, these frequency counts were normally followed by manual screening. The counting scripts in Perl, which, like the Word Cruncher program, were applied to the whole

---

20   During trial runs with different taggers (see section 2.5.3), 200-word extracts from each newspaper and decade were tagged and the results scrutinized. Even though the error-rate was the lowest for the EngCG-2 tagger, which was chosen for tagging my data, it turned out that the tagger sometimes gave erroneous labels to some items, most of them adjectives and nouns (approximately 50, all in all).

21   As mentioned in 2.3.4, the calculation of sentence length is based on raw figures, however.

22   The authors of the EngCG-2 are, in alphabetical order, Juha Heikkilä (lexicon), Timo Järvinen (tokenization, lexicon), Pasi Tapanainen (software), and Atro Voutilainen (tokenization, lexicon, grammar). For further information on the EngCG-2 tagger, see http://www.conexor.fi.

data base, were used for, among other things, the calculation of word length and type/token ratios.[23]

The TSSA is a segmentation and sorting program developed at the Department of Linguistics at Uppsala University, Sweden (see Dahlqvist 1994).

The ANOVA test of variance is a statistical tool which is used for the investigation of possible differences between the mean results obtained from several samples (see Woods, Fletcher and Hughes 1986: 194–223).

The Newman-Keuls multiple comparison test is used to locate statistically significant differences between groups of data (see Mendenhall, Mc Clave, and Ramey 1977: 314–319).

---

23   The programs were written by Dr Christer Geisler, The Department of English, Uppsala University, Sweden.

3. Features marking personal involvement

3.1 Introduction

To find out if the language of British up-market newspaper editorials, like many other genres, has changed in the direction of more informal styles (see, for example, Biber and Finegan 1989, 1992, 1997, Geisler forthcoming) the text samples from the different decades of the 20th century were compared, mainly with respect to features that Biber's study (1988) proved to be distinctive in texts marked by personal involvement, for example, personal letters and private conversation. Among these features we find present tense verbs, private verbs (for example *see, believe, think*), and first and second person (personal) pronouns.[1] We also find features characteristic of affective discourse, such as emphatics (for example, *a lot* and *such a*) and adverbial amplifiers (for example, *completely, enormously,* and *very*) and of generalized content, such as the pronoun *it,* demonstrative pronouns, and indefinite pronouns. Other features express uncertainty, for example, 'possibility' modals and hedges.[2] In English up-market editorials, the pattern of development for these features is not unidirectional, however. Some of the features increased in use, which would indicate an increase in personal involvement. Others decreased in use and for still others no statistically significant change was observed during the 20th century (see Table 3.1).

In section 3.2, I deal with the features that, when tested for variance (see sections 2.5.2 and 2.5.3), showed a statistically significant increase over time; in section 3.3, I deal with those which showed a statistically significant decrease and in section 3.4 with those which showed no statistically significant variation over

---

[1]   For brevity, first (second, third) person personal pronouns are referred to simply as 'first (second, third) person pronouns'.

[2]   The term 'possibility' modals is taken from Biber (1988) and corresponds to the modals expressing permission, possibility, and ability (Group 1 in Quirk et al. 1985: 221–223).

time, taken here to mean that they represent linguistic continuity. In section 3.5, finally, I draw some conclusions from what has emerged in sections 3.2 and 3.3.

Table 3.1 The development of features linked with personal involvement.

Statistically significant increase over time	Statistically significant decrease over time	Linguistic continuity
Present tense verbs	Adverbial amplifiers	Demonstrative pronouns
Not-negation	Private verbs	'Possibility' modals
Questions	First person pronouns	Second person pronouns
Imperatives	Pronoun *it*	Indefinite pronouns
Contractions		Causative subordination
		Discourse particles
		General emphatics
		General hedges

3.2   Increase in the use of features indicating personal involvement

Texts characterized by personal involvement are "verbal, interactional, affective, fragmented, reduced in form, and generalised in content" (Biber 1988: 105). In this section I discuss some of the features that have often been mentioned as markers of such discourse, more precisely those which increased in use over time in English up-market editorials and thus indicate an increase in personal involvement, namely, present tense verbs, *not*-negation, questions, imperatives, and contractions. Demonstrative pronouns, showed a statistically significant increase between 1940 and 1960 but no statistically significant difference between the beginning and the end of the century and are therefore discussed together with the features that showed linguistic continuity (see section 3.4.1).

3.2.1   Present tense verbs

Editorials usually deal with topics of 'immediate relevance', and therefore present tense forms (the simple present as well as the present progressive) can be expected to appear with some frequency. Quirk et al. (1985: 179–181) make a distinction between three different meanings of the simple present tense with reference to present time: the state present, the habitual present, and the instantaneous present.[3] State present is used with stative verbs, such as the primary verbs *be* and *have,* and *believe, think, want, like,* and *live,* and the verbs of perception and bodily sensation, such as *see, hear, taste,* and *hurt.* The state present refers to "a single unbroken state of affairs that has existed in the past, exists now, and is likely to continue to exist in the future" (Greenbaum and

---

3   Because of the high frequency of present tense verbs, it would have been too time-consuming to make such a distinction between the different meanings of the feature in this study.

Quirk: 1993: 48). By way of example, see (1). However, the category also includes instances expressing more restricted time spans, such as example (2).

(1)   We now *have a new term for the world we live in*: the data bank society. (GUA70E33)

(2)   *The Dunlop board believe* that the future of their company lies in partnership with a great European company. (TI70E32)

The habitual present is used with dynamic verb forms, such as *eat, drink, talk, write*, and, as the term suggests, refers first and foremost to habitual verbal action, as in example (3).

(3)   But the Lords cannot stand it; *they break off, they talk about anything else; they distract themselves* with exchanges of odd, irrelevant theories, hopes, and illusions. (GUA10E10)

The instantaneous present, finally, is used to report on events of little or no duration. It is found only in some special situations, such as sports commentaries (*She passes the ball to...*) and demonstrations (*We now take a wet sponge...*) and cannot therefore be expected in newspaper editorials.

Three additional, non-present uses are mentioned by Quirk et al. (1985: 179–181): simple present referring to the past, simple present in fictional narrative, and simple present referring to the future. The simple present referring to the past, the so-called historic present, is used in narrative style to make the narrative more thrilling or dramatic. Simple present in fictional narrative resembles the historic present, but whereas the historic present is used in narratives based on real experiences, the fictional 'historic present' is used in imaginary prose. Simple present referring to the future is used in main clauses together with a time adverbial to denote that something is certain to happen, as in example (4). Furthermore, the use appears in subordinate clauses, especially in temporal and conditional clauses. An example of the latter is found in (5).

(4)   What Manchester does today, *all Britain does tomorrow* – was once the proud boast of the cotton capital. (DT80E17)

(5)   *If Mr Churchill keeps up his form of yesterday* the Government will have to be on its toes most of the time. (GUA50E10)

The present study includes the simple present as well as the present progressive. We can assume that most of the simple present forms are used to represent state or habit and, to some extent, to refer to the future. The progressive aspect is not very common in English up-market editorials, only approximately 3.5 per cent (694 out of 20,022) of the instances recorded were present progressives.

The present tense forms given duplicate tags were edited by hand so as to distinguish them from nouns and from other verb forms identical with the base, viz., infinitives, past tense and past participle forms of irregular verbs.[4]

The lines of development for the three newspapers are irregular and divergent. However, between 1900 and 1970, a statistically significant increase was attested for the newspapers together. After 1970, no statistically significant change was noticed (see Table 3.2 and Figure 3.1; for statistics, see Appendix, s.v. present tense verbs).

Table 3.2 Present tense verbs: normed frequencies.

Year	Ti	DT	Gua	All
1900	39.02	32.15	37.04	36.80
1910	44.40	37.94	42.76	42.00
1920	37.56	42.30	38.71	39.27
1930	34.90	38.32	43.65	39.42
1940	32.04	34.62	42.21	36.59
1950	38.18	41.97	43.48	41.20
1960	39.17	44.95	39.45	41.52
1970	43.23	44.83	46.61	44.98
1980	36.78	42.44	41.08	40.26
1993	35.54	42.27	42.87	39.86
1900–1993	37.96	40.95	41.78	40.33

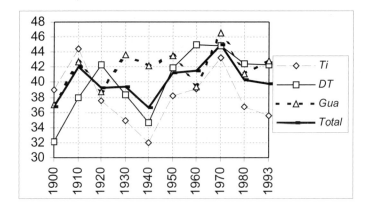

Figure 3.1 The development of present tense verbs.

When the three newspapers were compared, a statistically significant difference was noticed between *The Times,* on the one hand, and the *Daily Telegraph* and

---

4   For duplicates, see section 2.5.2.

the *Guardian* on the other. From 1920 on, the use of present tense verbs is considerably lower in *The Times* than in the *Daily Telegraph* and the *Guardian*. The fact that present tense forms are rarer in *The Times* than in the other two newspapers makes one suspect a more extensive use of past tense forms in this newspaper, but no such result could be verified. Past tense forms are used to approximately the same extent in the three newspapers (see section 5.2). *The Times* is evidently less verbal in style than the *Daily Telegraph* and the *Guardian* and, consequently, its style ought to be more nominal, which is also confirmed by a somewhat more frequent use of nouns, attributive adjectives, and nominalizations (see sections 4.2; 4.3.1; 8.3).

In sum, even though the lines of development for the three newspapers are somewhat divergent, the increase in the use of present tense verbs in the newspapers together suggests a development towards a more 'involved' language.[5]

3.2.2 *Not*-negation

Tottie (1991: 87–88) distinguishes between two morphosyntactic variants of negation: *not*-negation (analytic negation), such as example (6) and *no*-negation (synthetic negation), such as (6a), example (6) rephrased.

(6)   A bankers' mission *cannot do anything* about this; (DT60E11)

(6a)   A bankers' mission *can do nothing* about this;

Not-negation consists of the negative adverb *not* plus the indefinite words *a, an, any, anybody, anyone, anything, one, ever, anywhere,* and *either. No*-negation comprises not only the determiner *no* but also the pronouns *nobody, none, neither, nothing*, and the adverbs *never* and *nowhere* (Tottie 1991: 106; 1988: 245–246). Tottie, among others, found that *not*-negation occurs more often in colloquial texts and *no*-negation in more literary texts (1988: 245–265; 1991: 139–188).

The instances of negations were edited by hand so that the sample analysis should only contain instances where one type of negation can be substituted for the other, such as examples (7) and (7a);[6] indeterminate instances were excluded.

---

5   As mentioned in Chapter 2, note 16, 'involved' language in this context refers to discourse marked by personal involvement.

6   This distinction was not made by Biber (1988), but since it has been shown that the two variants have different uses (see for example Tottie 1988: 245–265; 1991: 139–188), they were treated separately in the present study.

(7)   Their President, Mr Terence Duffy, put it perfectly: "Call it fear if you like, or responsibility, but *we do not see any alternative* to accepting this package." (DT80E10)

(7a)   Their President, Mr Terence Duffy, put it perfectly: "Call it fear if you like, or responsibility, but *we see no alternative* to accepting this package."

The frequency counts showed that *not*-negations are not very frequent in my material. The least frequent of them all is *not* in combination with the compound pronouns *anybody, anyone,* and *anything,* with the '*of*-pronouns' *one* and *either,* and with the adverbs *ever* and *anywhere.* Only 31 instances, altogether, of these *not*-negations appear in my data. *Not* in combination with *a, an, any* is somewhat more frequent.

Up to 1960, the line of development is irregular, but between 1960 and 1980 we observe a statistically significant increase. The decrease that followed is statistically non-significant. No statistically significant differences were attested when the different newspapers were compared (see Table 3.3 and Figure 3.2; for statistics, see Appendix, s.v. *not*-negation).

Not-negation, the more informal of the two forms of negation, is thus not very frequent in English up-market editorials. The increase in the use of this feature, from 1960 onwards, nevertheless, points in the same direction as the increase in the use of present tense verbs, that is, towards greater informality.

Table 3.3 *Not*-negation: normed frequencies.

Year	Ti	DT	Gua	All
1900	0.86	0.36	0.57	0.62
1910	0.61	0.26	0.39	0.42
1920	0.19	0.43	0.38	0.33
1930	0.16	0.46	0.73	0.48
1940	0.15	0.39	0.35	0.31
1950	0.89	0.33	0.23	0.48
1960	0.08	0.39	0.48	0.32
1970	0.36	0.36	0.69	0.48
1980	0.56	0.93	0.88	0.80
1993	0.50	0.50	0.60	0.53
1900–1993	0.42	0.46	0.54	0.48

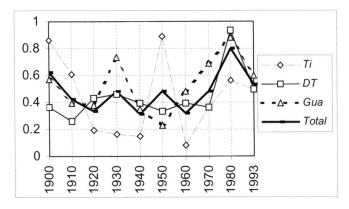

Figure 3.2 The development of *not*-negation.

3.2.3   Questions

Since direct questions, unless they are rhetorical, are used to prompt an answer, they are normally found in discourse where the addressee is physically present, that is, in oral discourse or in written discourse reproducing oral presentation.[7] However, they can also be used in writing to make it possible for the author to enter into a fictive conversation with the reader. Questions appearing in the type of discourse I am studying must thus,   when they are not part of quoted speech, be either rhetorical questions or a device used to involve the reader in a joint communicative venture.[8] My   study comprises direct *wh*-questions, that is, questions starting in *who, whose, whom, what, which, when, where, why* and *how,*[9] as well as *yes/no*-questions, such as example (8), and both rhetorical and regular questions are included.

(8)   *Do the Conservatives want to tear up these principles?* (GUA70E31)

---

7   The definitions of rhetorical questions are many (see Ilie 1994: 42, 216–229). In the present study, I use the terms as applied in Cuddon (1979), Leech (1973), Quirk et al. (1985), *Collins Cobuild English grammar* (1990), and *Longman dictionary of the English language* (1988), among others, where rhetorical questions are characterized as having an interrogative structure but displaying the force of a strong assertion, that is, they are structurally interrogatives but semantically statements. As such, they are questions to which no answer is, generally, expected or to which an answer is at the same time supplied. Another definition, which does not, in any respect, contradict the one above, is given by Beckson and Ganz (1990). They maintain that rhetorical questions are used to produce a stylistic effect.

8   The term 'quoted speech' refers to direct speech indicated by quotation marks in the beginning and the end of an utterance.

9   Some of the question words can be preceded by a preposition, as in *To whom did he send the letter?*

'Alternative' questions, the third group of major question types mentioned by Quirk et al. (1985: 806), that is, questions which give the reader two alternatives to choose between, as in example (9), are rare in my data. Only eight instances were found. However, this is not surprising since they are normally directed to an addressee who is physically present.

(9)   When terrorists throw bombs among tourists and wreck civil aircraft, *is it a matter for airlines or for governments?* (DT70E6)

Only questions ending in a question mark were taken into account for the present study. The questions were collected by hand, so as to exclude questions in quoted speech.[10] Questions in headlines as well as alternative questions were excluded from the frequency counts but will be commented on below. First, the *wh-*questions and *yes/no-*questions were grouped together and dealt with simply as 'questions'. Then each of the categories was treated separately. A statistically significant increase in the use of questions was noticed between 1940 and 1970 (see Table 3.4 and Figure 3.3; for statistics, see Appendix, s.v. questions). After that no statistically significant change was observed. The increase is especially noticeable in the *Daily Telegraph*, where the normed frequency increased from 0.28 in 1940 to 3.18 in 1970.

Also when the three newspapers were compared, a statistically significant difference in the use of questions was noticed. The lines of development for the *Daily Telegraph* and the *Guardian* follow each other fairly closely while *The Times* distinguishes itself by a more infrequent use of this feature.

Table 3.4 Questions: normed frequencies.

Year	Ti	DT	Gua	All
1900	0.32	0.05	1.58	0.98
1910	0.27	0.42	1.10	0.69
1920	0.38	0.98	1.38	0.91
1930	0.46	0.91	0.95	0.81
1940	0.64	0.28	0.73	0.54
1950	0.61	1.71	1.84	1.39
1960	0.90	1.70	2.39	1.67
1970	0.69	3.18	1.81	1.92
1980	1.10	2.17	1.46	1.61
1993	0.84	1.32	2.66	1.59
1900–1993	0.65	1.46	1.58	1.25

10   Normally, no distinction is made between quoted and unquoted speech in the present study. However, as far as questions are concerned, this distinction seems justified as it is the authors' use of questions as a literary device that is of primary interest.

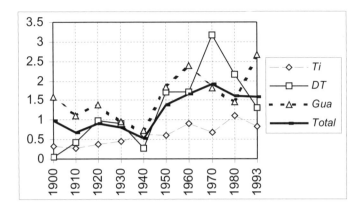

Figure 3.3 The development of questions.

Yes/no-questions are somewhat more frequent than *wh*-questions in my data and more frequent in the *Daily Telegraph* and the *Guardian* than in *The Times* (see Table 3.5 and Figure 3.4; for statistics, see Appendix, s.v. *yes/no*-questions). The normed frequencies attested for *yes/no*-questions in *The Times* vary between 0.49 (1960) and 0.1 (1993), which means that, towards the end of the century, they were almost non-existent. However, the line of development for the newspapers together follows that of 'questions' rather closely, but no statistically significant difference across decades was attested.

Table 3.5 *Yes/no*-questions: normed frequencies.

Year	Ti	DT	Gua	All
1900	0.19	0.05	1.15	0.70
1910	0.18	0.17	0.59	0.37
1920	0.21	0.27	0.55	0.35
1930	0.18	0.32	0.39	0.31
1940	0.30	0.22	0.46	0.33
1950	0.23	1.06	1.42	0.90
1960	0.49	1.12	1.54	1.06
1970	0.34	1.72	0.74	0.94
1980	0.39	1.23	0.87	0.86
1993	0.10	0.69	1.55	0.76
1900–1993	0.26	0.80	0.91	0.67

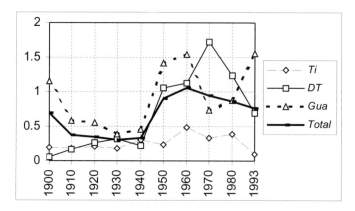

Figure 3.4 The development of *yes/no*-questions.

The lines of development for *wh*-questions also follow those attested for 'questions' fairly closely, and a statistically significant increase, for the newspapers together, was recorded between 1940 and 1970 (see Table 3.6 and Figure 3.5; for statistics, see Appendix, s.v. *wh*-questions). *The Times* showed a substantial increase in the use of the feature over the years, from 0.13 in 1900 to 0.74 in 1993 and a statistically significant difference in the use of the feature was observed between this newspaper, on the one hand, and the *Daily Telegraph* and the *Guardian*, on the other.

Table 3.6 *Wh*-questions.

Year	Ti	DT	Gua	All
1900	0.13	0.00	0.44	0.28
1910	0.10	0.25	0.51	0.32
1920	0.17	0.70	0.83	0.56
1930	0.29	0.59	0.56	0.50
1940	0.33	0.06	0.27	0.21
1950	0.38	0.65	0.42	0.50
1960	0.41	0.57	0.85	0.61
1970	0.35	1.46	1.08	0.98
1980	0.71	0.93	0.59	0.75
1993	0.74	0.63	1.11	0.84
1900–1993	0.39	0.66	0.67	0.58

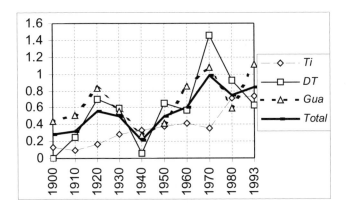

Figure 3.5 The development of *wh*-questions.

Is there, then, a distinction in discourse function between the two question types in the communicative event discussed in the present study? To judge from my data, it seems as if the *wh*-questions, in most cases, were the more genuine rhetorical questions, that is, questions that do not require an answer or are used for stylistic effect (see note 7), such as examples (10) and (11).

(10)   *What again is to be said of the argument that it is wrong to accuse our Government of misconduct, since this lowers us in foreign eyes?* (GUA00E19)

(11)   Here again Mr Churchill showed how muddled is his understanding of economics. *How does he explain the sad fact that free America, whose economic strength enabled it to scrap rapidly all these nasty controls, is even farther off "honest money" than we are?* (GUA50E1)

The *wh*-questions are also used to introduce a topic, as in example (12). Before developing the issue further, the author asks:

(12)   *How then are the local authorities to be protected from loss, as Dr. Addison has promised?* (DT20E6)

Sometimes, the question is followed by the author's own answer, as in examples (13) and (14).

(13)   *Why has the general public reacted so differently from the Government and Parliament?* The first answer must be the depressing one that for many people Afghanistan appears as a small, far-off country of too little direct consequence to Britain ... (TI80E6)

(14)   *What probability is there of predominant association between two entirely independent sets of inherited characteristics?* There are many delicate statistical and technical issues to be resolved before any definite hypothesis can be conclusively asserted. (TI70E19)

Even though *wh*-questions, as in examples (13) and (14) can be used as a device to engage the reader in a joint communicative enterprise, the *yes/no*-questions seem to be such a device to an even greater extent. It is easier for the readers to nod in agreement or shake their heads in disagreement, that is, to react, on a question such as (15) and (16) than to come up with an answer to a *wh*-question.

(15)   *Do the new "shock" posters about drug addiction over-dramatise an already over-dramatised problem?* (DT70E23)

(16)   *Would Mr Eden, Sir John Anderson, or Mr Stanley agree? Does the Conservative Chancellor-designate (whoever he may be) feel the same easy assurance?* (GUA50E1)

By asking questions like (15) and (16), the author has, hopefully, attracted the reader's attention and can proceed to elaborate on the topic chosen.

Towards the end of the century, some of the *yes/no*-questions changed character, especially in the *Guardian.* It seems as if the authors were reasoning with their readers. In an editorial in the *Guardian,* 1993, dealing with the deregulation of nursing and residential homes, we have four questions, the last of them, example (17), in my opinion, of a more 'chatty' nature.

(17)   ...along comes the deregulation letter. The aim is to be "radical". *What was the original purpose of each requirement? Is it still necessary? Are costs to the homes too high?* You don't need to be a political adviser to forecast what happens now. Some time in the near future, a new residential scandal will break out. *Remember the Yorkshire Television documentary on Kent's private residential homes where old people were being dumped, unable to defend themselves or complain about the squalid conditions?* (GUA93E22)

Questions in headlines first turned up in the 1960s. All in all, there are only 24 instances, 15 in the *Guardian,* six in *The Times* and three in the *Daily Telegraph.* Most of them are *wh*-questions, such as (18).

(18)   *When will the food arrive?* (GUA70E1)

However, also sentence fragments, such as (19)–(21), the last of them an alternative question, may be found.

(19)   *Taxpayers' tunnel?* (TI60E14)
(20)   *A needlessly damaging Budget?* (GUA80E7)

(21)   *Saints or scoundrels?* (DT3E2)

Even though the total number of questions is fairly small, the overall increase in use between 1940 and 1970 is, as mentioned above, statistically significant and strengthens the indication of a drift towards more informal styles. The decrease in the use of *yes/no*-questions and the increase of *wh*-questions in *The Times* is conspicuous. It implies an increase in the use of questions for stylistic effect over the years while their use as a conversational feature is minimal throughout the period of study.

3.2.4 Imperatives

Another feature which is often used for rhetorical purposes is imperatives.[11] They are used for a wide range of illocutionary acts, such as advice/recommendation, instruction, invitation, order/command, plea, prohibition, request, suggestion, and warning (see Quirk et al. 1985: 831–832). Imperatives are more common in spoken discourse than in written as they are often intended for an addressee who is physically present. However, they are also found in written discourse in their capacity of representing real illocutionary acts, for example, instructions in manuals or cookery books (*Beat three eggs* ...), orders or prohibitions (*Don't speak with food in your mouth!*), warnings written on a sign, telling us what we should do or should not do (*Walk now!*). When found in other types of written texts, unless in quoted speech, imperatives normally have other meanings. In my data, some of them are used for rhetorical purposes but most of them are employed as a means for the author to enter into a fictive conversation with the reader (cf. questions, section 3.2.3). By way of examples, see the 'suggestion' in (22) and the 'advice' in (23), where the author turns to the reader directly.

(22)   *Consider how little attention has been given by Ministers* to the all-important question of the conservation and use of its resources. (GUA40E1)

(23)   "*Don't lose your temper* with other road users" ... "*Don't drink* if you drive" (DT60E19)

Especially in example (23), in combination with the second person pronoun and the contraction, the imperative gives a 'conversational' impression.

The most common imperative in my data is *let us* as in example (24). Using the imperative together with the pronoun *us,* the author stresses the fact that the communicative enterprise is a joint venture.

---

11   Imperatives were not included in Biber's 1988 study, but, since they have the same discourse function as many of the questions in my material, I found it reasonable also to take this feature into consideration.

(24)   *Let us hope* that his public attitude does not fully reflect his private policy
and the policy of the Government. (GUA60E20).

An unedited automatic search of imperatives was carried out.[12] The prompt #imp
gave all the instances of the feature, which means that even duplicates were
included. The result of the automatic search showed little variation up to 1970,
but between 1970 and 1993, a statistically significant increase in the use of
imperatives was noticed. No statistically significant differences between the three
newspapers were observed (see Table 3.7 and Figure 3.6; for statistics, see
Appendix, s.v. imperatives).

Table 3.7 Imperatives: normed frequencies.

Year	Ti	DT	Gua	All
1900	0.35	0.65	1.11	0.82
1910	0.60	1.06	1.08	0.94
1920	0.89	0.82	0.53	0.74
1930	0.51	0.49	1.02	0.69
1940	0.71	0.70	0.73	0.71
1950	1.36	0.95	0.46	0.94
1960	1.33	1.12	1.01	1.15
1970	0.30	0.94	0.65	0.64
1980	0.62	1.13	1.28	1.02
1993	1.12	1.13	1.96	1.41
1900–1993	0.81	0.91	0.99	0.90

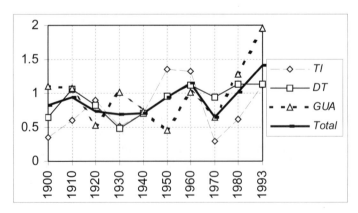

Figure 3.6 The development of imperatives.

---

12   For automatic searches, see sections 2.5.2 and 2.5.3.

The development of imperatives thus follows that of present tense verbs, *not*-negation, and questions even though the increase is manifested somewhat later. The co-occurrence of imperatives with questions strengthens the impression of conversational discourse: the author asks questions and gives advice and suggestions to invite the reader into a fictive conversation.

3.2.5 Contractions

Contractions are usually associated with speech and have so far normally been avoided in formal writing. According to Finegan and Biber (1986: 393), they are distributed as a cline. They are most frequently used in conversations, least frequently in academic prose. Between these extremes we find broadcast speech, speeches, and press reportage, in that order. This is confirmed by Chafe and Danielewicz' findings (1987: 94). In their comparison of two spoken genres, conversations and lectures, and two written genres, personal letters and academic writing, they found, as might be expected, more contractions in the spoken genres than in the written, and more in personal letters than in academic writing, where no contractions at all were found. Chafe and Danielewicz (1987: 94) claim that the use of contractions has much in common with the use of colloquial vocabulary. They see contractions as an example of "innovative spoken vocabulary, innovations which the most formal kind of written language avoids altogether, but which more casual writing is more willing to accept" (1987: 94). This also agrees with the results presented in a doctoral thesis by Axelsson (1998: 190–191, 193), who showed that the frequency of contractions per text was considerably higher in the most popular down-market national daily, the *Sun*, than in the mid-market and up-market newspapers.[13] In my material, only few instances of contractions were found, 65 altogether, distributed as shown in Table 3.8.

To judge from Table 3.8, the use of contractions in up-market newspaper editorials started quite recently. Up to 1980, contracted forms were almost non-existent. In 1993, however, 48 instances were recorded, all of them in the *Guardian*, the newspaper closest to the mid-market papers. The normed frequency per thousand words calculated for the *Guardian*, 1993, is 2.7, a statistically significant increase since 1980 when it was 0.2 (see Appendix, s.v. contractions). The means obtained for the other two newspapers are uninteresting as an indication of frequency; they are interesting, however, as an indication of the firm resistance in these two newspapers against the use of contractions.

---

13   Comparing the three press-text categories in the LOB corpus (1961) with a matched sample from the same categories in 1994 (the Uppsala Press Corpus, UPC (see Axelsson 1998: 226–249)), Axelsson gives a diachronic perspective of the variation between contracted and non-contracted forms found in editorials, reportage, and reviews from a wide spectrum of English newspapers.

Table 3.8 The distribution of contractions over the years: raw frequencies.

	1900-1940	*1950-1970*	*1980*	*1993*	*Total*
Daily Telegraph		2	2		4
Guardian	2	3	7	48	60
The Times			1		1
Total	2	5	10	48	65

The most frequent contractions in my data are contracted negative forms, such as *don't* and *won't,* altogether 37 instances, as Table 3.9 shows. The non-negative contractions are divided between 25 *'s*-contractions, representing a pronoun or an adverb plus *is,* two instances of *they're,* and one instance of *you've.* The most frequent of the non-negative contractions is *there's* (nine instances).[14]

Table 3.9 Contracted forms: raw frequencies.

Negative contractions *n't*		Non-negative contractions *'s*		Non-negative Contractions *'re*		Non-negative contractions *'ve*	
don't	9	there's	9	they're	2	you've	1
didn't	5	it's	6				
won't	4	that's	5				
can't	3	she's	2				
wouldn't	3	what's	2				
hasn't	3	he's	1				
doesn't	2						
aren't	2						
couldn't	2						
ain't	1						
hadn't	1						
shouldn't	1						
wasn't	1						
Total	37		25		2		1

In the following, I will give some examples of contracted forms from my data and discuss what factors might have triggered the use of this feature. Such factors are, for example, quoted speech, special sentence types, and the overall style and subject-matter of the editorials in which the contractions appear (for a definition of the term 'quoted speech', see note 8). The reason why this is discussed in such detail, is the notable increase in the use of the feature in the *Guardian*, 1993, and its infrequency in the other two newspapers.

The earliest contraction in my material, example (25), is found in the introductory sentence in E5 in the *Guardian, 1920.*

14   In Axelsson's study *not*-contractions account for only approximately 40% of the contractions in all the categories (reportage, editorials, and reviews) in the UPC corpus (see Table 2, p. 252). One reason for the discrepancy between her results and mine might be the different sizes of the two samples: 781contractions in the UPC as compared to 65 in mine. A larger sample will, of course, yield a more reliable result.

(25)   There is a vast deal about the Carpentier–Dempsey match appearing in the
        press, but *it hasn't anything to do with boxing*. (GUA20E5)

The match is described as a commercialized happening in a language unusually
informal for the year: "Carpenter ... has become the world's one-man commercial
proposition. He is a superlative athlete and (so the picture-papers say) a Greek
god too ... How much is a super-athletic Greek god worth to a film company
which can 'feature' him on all the movies of the world?" In this editorial, style
and subject matter may be one reason for the appearance of the contraction.
Another reason might be the fact that it is found in the introduction to the
editorial, a position that seems to favour the use of contractions (see Axelsson
1998: 200–205, 212).

    The four contractions attested for the *Daily Telegraph*, two from 1960 and
two from 1980, all appear in texts of a more or less trivial character. Besides,
three of them are found in quoted speech, as in example (26) from an editorial
dealing with Whitsun traffic.

(26)   "*Don't lose your temper* with other road users" ... "*Don't drink* if you
        drive" (DT60E19).

The two contractions in this extract are both negative imperatives, which is
another factor, besides trivial subject-matter and quoted speech, that might have
contributed to the choice of the contracted forms (see also Axelsson 1998: 135
who found that around 90% of *do not* in imperatives were contracted).

    The fourth and last contraction in the *Daily Telegraph*, which is given in
example (27), is also part of a quote, even though not within quotation marks.

(27)   QUESTION: When is a shrimp not a shrimp? Answer: *When it's a prawn.*
        Or so we are told by civil servants from the Ministry of Agriculture and
        Fisheries after nine months of consultation. (DT80E35)

So far the contractions have almost exclusively been found in quoted speech and
in texts of a more or less trivial nature. The only contraction from *The Times* in
my material (see example (28)), which appears in an editorial from 1980, is
distinct from those discussed above in two respects: it is found in unquoted
speech and the subject-matter of the editorial is rather serious (the drawn-out pay
talks at British Leyland).

(28)   Provocative as the suggestion was, it was feebly parried by the unions with
        the threat that they threatened no strike, but *wouldn't answer for the shop
        floor*. (TI80E7)

However, at a closer look we find that the contraction appears in indirect speech
which might have triggered the use of the contraction, but since (28) is the only
contraction in *The Times* over the years, it can also be a slip of the pen.
Supporting this assumption is the fact that *The Times* editor, in an interview by

Reynolds and Cascio (1999), declared that contractions have no place in their leaders and that they would be used only in quoted speech and "more relaxed pieces".

From 1970 on, we observe a steady increase in the use of contracted forms in the *Guardian*, and quoted speech and/or trivial subject-matter are no longer a prerequisite for the appearance of the feature. Only four out of the 58 contractions attested for the *Guardian* 1970, 1980, and 1993 (see Table 3.8) appear in quoted speech and another three in quotes without quotation marks. The subject-matter of the editorials where the contractions are found varies. They may deal with anything from the situation in Bosnia, the new Clinton administration or National Health Service to Mrs Thatcher's greed and Princess Diana's announcement of scaling down her public activities.

When neither subject-matter nor quoted speech can account for the use of contracted forms, other explanations have to be searched for. As mentioned above, Chafe and Danielewicz (1987: 94) are of the opinion that an overall colloquial vocabulary favours the use of contractions. This is confirmed by examples (29) and (30), extracts from E 30 in the *Guardian*, 1993. The editorial, which deals with a meeting between John Major and Albert Reinolds regarding the Irish question, is the text where we find most contractions (10 instances) in my data. The first third of the text is very informal in tone and has a colloquial vocabulary, sentence fragments, and a personal comment in parentheses. In this part of the editorial (see example (29)), we find nine of the ten contractions.

(29)   They *aren't* ideas men. They are get-things-done men ... *It's* a strength because it means the talks process is the hard practical stuff on which both editorials thrive. *It's* a weakness because neither seems quite to understand where the other is coming from ... But *don't* be misled ... *There's* a lot more still going on behind the curtains ... *That's* a warning to Mr Major ... *There's* a pro-talks mood for including Sinn Feinn (which is just as well in the circumstances). But the largest single group in British public opinion about Northern Ireland are the *Don't Knows* ... The danger is that he *won't* be able to sell the result. (GUA93E30)

The rest of the editorial gives a much more formal impression, and here we only find one contraction (see example (30)).

(30)   But the poll shows that this option is favoured by 15 per cent of Ulster voters, with another 18 per cent in favour of joint Dublin–London authority. Together, *that's* only one in three Northern Ireland voters. Even among Catholic voters in the North, only 32 per cent favour union with the Republic, a highly revealing finding. Clearly this is a situation in which nothing is as simple as the old certainties imply, but in which many things are also possible. On the spectrum of possibilities from a united Ireland in the deep green corner (15 per cent) to the restoration of the Stormont *quo ante* (13 per cent) opinion is well scattered. (GUA93E30)

As mentioned above, Axelsson's study (1998: 135; 200–206) showed that sentence type and sentence position are also essential for the appearance of contractions. Imperatives and questions, on the one hand, and introductions, conclusions, and headlines, on the other, turned out to favour the use of contractions. In my data we find five contracted forms in imperatives, as in example (31), and four in questions, as in example (32).

(31)   The sweep of the two messages, though, is consistent. Keep superpower deals out of the equation. Realise that the purpose of peace is to get a Kabul government that we can live with. *Don't make us take sides between Carter and Brezhnev* because that will wreck us within. Give us a sense of common Western purpose, but *don't pull strings*. And remember that the country most virulent in its denunciations of Russian imperialism, the country ready to ferry arms to Afghanistan at the twitch of a beard, is Iran. (GUA80E14)

(32)   In the recent Ashworth hospital inquiry, a consultant psychologist was called to comment on the reliability of patients' evidence. *Why can't courts do the same?* (GUA93E13)

Since questions and imperatives are themselves markers of personal involvement, contractions in these sentence types add to the impression of informal discourse. The author asks questions and gives advice so as to invite the reader to a joint communicative event (cf. sections 3.2.3 and 3.2.4). This 'interaction' with the reader can be further reinforced by the use of second person pronouns, as in example (26) above. The co-occurrence of two or more of these features contributes to giving the text a 'conversational' touch.

Besides being found in a question, the contraction in example (32) appears in the conclusion of the editorial, which would strengthen the possibility for a contracted form to occur (see Axelsson 1998: 205–206). All in all, five instances were found in this position. Two instances were found in introductory sections see examples (25) above and (33) below), another position favouring contracted forms, as mentioned above.[15]

(33)   NEVER has the word railroading been more appropriate. The Railways Bill – *the privatisation that even Nicholas Ridley wouldn't touch* – was conceived in ideological haste, pulled to pieces over long months amid public incredulity, suffered more facelifts than an ageing Hollywood star and has arrived at its legislative destination in almost total disarray amid embarrassing parliamentary scenes. (GUA93E27)

The reason why these positions should promote the use of contractions is, according to Axelsson, that "[i]n these positions ... we find the writer expressing

---

15   In example (33), the reason for a contraction to appear might also be indirect speech.

his own feelings and ideas more immediately, as if addressing the reader directly" (1998: 200).

The third position that proved to promote contracted forms is headlines (Axelsson 1998: 200–203). Two of the contractions in my data were found in that position. The editorials which they introduce are of a non-trivial character: the NATO foreign ministers' meeting in Ankara (see example (34)) and pay comparability for public service (example (35)).

(34)   *At last there's something moving* (GUA80E16)
(35)   *Markets aren't always the best indicators* (GUA80E17)

The fact that the two editorials show no evidence of informal language, besides the headlines, supports Axelsson's suggestion (1998: 203) that the reason for using contractions in headlines is not the same as for using them in introductions and conclusions. Referring to Evans (1974), she mentions that the demand for simplicity and informality in modern headlines, together with "the space-saving advantage" contractions constitute, may further the use of contracted forms.

As mentioned above, in my material, the most common contractions are contracted negative forms. Among the non-negative contracted forms, *there's* is the most frequent. In an editorial in the *Guardian*, 1993, dealing with the Clinton administration, it is the only contraction, used three times. Three more instances of *there is,* which are not contracted, were found in this editorial. The only apparent difference in use between the contracted and non-contracted forms is that the contracted forms were used initially (see example (36)).

(36)   And this week *there is* "national service for young people ... *There's* more
        form than substance here ... But *there is* also a useful flurry ... *There's* a
        broader context of loan repayment ... *There's* a youthful idealism that fits
        ... while his plans stand in stark contrast to the corralling and threatening
        and warning of others (see Kenneth Clarke , above) *there is* a feeling of
        hope ... (GUA93E7)

The sentence initial position and the repetition of the contraction are probably used to create a stylistic effect (cf. the use of questions, note 7). In example (37), taken from the same editorial as (29) above, *it's* is used in the same way.

(37)   JOHN MAJOR and Albert Reynolds are party politicians to their
        bootstraps. The one is a born whip, the other is a parish pumper. They
        aren't ideas men. They are get-things-done men. Or so they hope. This is
        both a strength and a weakness, as yesterday's talks in Dublin seem to
        have shown. *It's a strength* because it means the talks process is the hard
        practical stuff on which both leaders thrive. *It's a weakness* because
        neither seems quite to understand where the other is coming from.
        (GUA93E30)

Summing up the findings, we observe that contractions are still quite infrequent in up-market newspaper editorials. Almost no instances were recorded for the two most up-market newspapers in my data while contracted forms seem to be on the increase in the *Guardian*, the least up-market of them. This could be due to what Bell calls "audience design" (1991: 104 ff.),[16] that is, the newspaper has to adapt its language to the reader group it wants to attract. It might also be due to a change in "house rules", that is, rules as regards language use set up by a newspaper (see, for example, Hicks 1993: 48–73).

Up to 1980, a prerequisite for the appearance of a contraction even in the *Guardian* is quoted speech or more or less trivial subject-matter. After that, neither of the two seems to be necessary. It is clear, however, that contractions are more often chosen in a generally informal context and in combination with an otherwise colloquial vocabulary. Sentence type and the position of the clause where the contraction appears are other important factors for the use or non-use of contracted forms. Used initially and repeated, the contracted forms can also serve stylistic purposes.

3.2.6 Summary

The development of the features dealt with in section 3.2 suggests an increase in personal involvement. Most of the features are such as are associated with conversational discourse, namely, *not*-negation, questions, imperatives, and contractions, something that indicates a drift not only towards more informal language but also towards a more conversational type of informal language. The increase of present tense verbs suggests an increased interest in topics of current relevance.

3.3   Decrease in the use of features indicating personal involvement

As mentioned in section 3.1, the features that Biber (1988) proved to be distinctive in texts marked by personal involvement showed divergent patterns of development in English up-market newspaper editorials (cf. Table 3.1). During the 20th century, four of the features taken into consideration for the present work decreased in use, namely adverbial amplifiers, private verbs, first person pronouns, and the pronoun *it* (see sections 3.3.1–3.3.4).

3.3.1 Adverbial amplifiers

Adverbial amplifiers have a boosting effect and mark not only the presence of certainty but also the degree of certainty in a statement (cf. general emphatics,

---

16   See also Axelsson (1998: 190–193).

section 3.4.7, which only mark the presence of certainty).[17] However, in addition to marking certainty or conviction, they can signal a "heightened feeling" (Biber 1988: 106), and it is in this capacity that they can be regarded as features indicating personal involvement. Quirk et al. (1985: 590–591) divide adverbial amplifiers into two groups, maximizers, "which can denote the upper extreme of the scale", such as *entirely* in example (38) and boosters, "which denote a high degree, a high point on the scale", such as *greatly* in example (39).

(38)   The effect was, briefly, to tie the peasants to a system of ownership and cultivation *which entirely excluded* the possibility of agricultural progress ... (DT20E18)

(39)   Success in this task *would greatly influence* relations between India and Pakistan. (TI50E12)

No such distinction was made in the present study, firstly, because the borderline between the two groups of amplifiers is often difficult to distinguish (see Quirk et al. 1985: 591) and, secondly, because it is as markers of a "heightened feeling" (Biber 1988: 106), in the first place, that they are included in the study.

The amplifiers used in the analysis were the same as those used by Biber (1988: 240), that is, *absolutely, altogether, completely, enormously, entirely, extremely, fully, greatly, highly, intensely, perfectly, strongly, thoroughly, totally, utterly,* and *very*. Only four instances of *intensely* were found in my data, but the other members of the set were rather frequent, especially at the beginning of the century (see Table 3.10). The most frequent of them all was *very*.

The pattern of development for the set is rather consistent, and a statistically significant decrease across the decades was observed. No statistically significant variation between the newspapers was recorded (see Table 3.10 and Figure 3.7; for statistics, see Appendix, s.v. adverbial amplifiers).

The decreased use of adverbial amplifiers, in their capacity of marking "heightened feeling" (Biber 1988: 106), indicates that the language of the editorials became stricter and more matter-of-fact over the years.

---

17   In the following, the term 'amplifier', even when used on its own, refers to adverbial amplifiers only. In other contexts the term may also refer to adjectival amplifiers (see Quirk et al. 1985: 429).

Table 3.10 Adverbial amplifiers: normed frequencies.

Year	Ti	DT	Gua	All
1900	3.45	2.82	3.93	3.62
1910	3.87	2.52	3.35	3.29
1920	2.01	2.53	2.14	2.20
1930	2.01	2.24	1.70	1.98
1940	1.58	2.36	1.48	1.82
1950	2.34	1.16	2.04	1.80
1960	1.50	1.30	1.50	1.42
1970	3.05	1.57	1.18	1.88
1980	1.25	2.12	1.40	1.62
1993	0.77	0.81	1.80	1.14
1900–1993	2.06	1.85	2.07	2.00

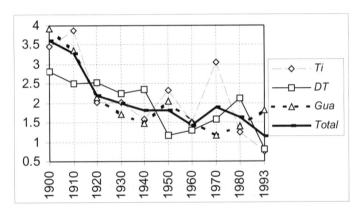

Figure 3.7 The development of adverbial amplifiers.

3.3.2 Private verbs

Private verbs are used to express private thoughts, attitudes and emotions, and are, together with present tense verbs, the most salient feature representing 'involved' discourse in Biber's study (1988: 102) (for the meaning of the term 'involved', as used in this work, see note 5). For the purposes of the present study, I checked the occurrences of the private verbs listed by Quirk et al. (1985: 1181), which include: *anticipate, assume, believe, conclude, decide, demonstrate, determine, discover, doubt, ensure, estimate, establish, fear, feel, find, forget, guess, hear, hope, imagine, imply, indicate, infer, know, learn, mean, notice, observe, prove, realise/realize, recognise/recognize, remember, reveal, see, show, suppose, think,* and *understand.*

The most frequently used private verbs included in the study are *find, know, see,* and *hope,* all with frequencies of around 400 or more. Among the least frequent are *infer, guess, anticipate,* and *doubt* with frequencies varying between four and forty. A comparison of the two sets of verbs indicates the aim and direction of English up-market editorials: they *find, know,* and *see* and only little room is given to *guessing, anticipating,* or *noticing.*

The private verbs were edited by hand to exclude duplicates and words wrongly marked as verbs, for example, nouns such as *doubt, hope,* and *notice.*[18] A statistically significant decrease was observed, for the newspapers together, when the normed frequencies from the beginning and the end of the period were compared. Especially noticeable is the decrease from 1960 on. The patterns of development for the individual newspapers are irregular and divergent and no statistically significant difference between them was attested (see Table 3.11 and Figure 3.8; for statistics, see Appendix, s.v. private verbs).

Table 3.11 Private verbs: normed frequencies.

Year	Ti	DT	Gua	All
1900	15.03	8.87	14.33	13.64
1910	12.59	11.99	11.33	11.86
1920	12.56	13.09	11.01	12.14
1930	12.99	10.62	11.39	11.49
1940	10.18	12.17	12.06	11.56
1950	11.51	10.79	13.94	11.96
1960	12.04	13.00	11.74	12.33
1970	10.63	10.51	10.33	10.48
1980	11.65	10.37	11.13	11.01
1993	9.87	10.67	8.61	9.65
1900–1993	11.72	11.29	11.58	11.53

---

18   For duplicates, see section 2.5.2.

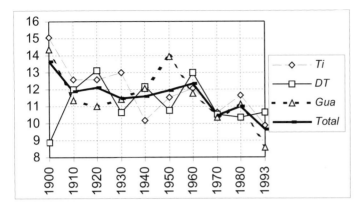

Figure 3.8 The development of private verbs.

3.3.3 First person pronouns

Expressing ego-involvement, first person pronouns are a prominent feature in interactive communicative situations and they have often been used when written and spoken registers are compared (see, for example, Chafe and Danielewicz 1987: 106–107, Biber 1986: 384–414).

In the type of discourse that institutional newspaper editorials represent (for the difference between personal and institutional editorials, see section 2.3.1), the use of first person singular pronouns could hardly be expected. The authors of the editorials are not supposed to speak for themselves but to express the opinions of their newspapers. Therefore, first person pronouns, especially in the singular, need to be avoided. Consequently, it was only what could be expected, when not a single instance of the first person singular, outside quotations, was found in my data. This part of the study will thus deal with the plural forms of the pronoun only, that is, *we, us, our, ours*, and *ourselves*.

We could distinguish between at least five different uses of *we* in my data (cf. Quirk et al. 1985: 346–354), type (a), however, only found in quoted speech:

(a) *we* in the specific sense, that is, with reference directly to the speakers, as in example (40).

(40) And as if to clench the impertinence of this preposterous despatch, the two Presidents add: "*We hesitated to make this declaration* earlier to your Excellency…" (DT00E3)

(b) *we* in the generic sense, that is, with reference to "people in general", as in example (41).

(41) These things will obviously cost no small amount of money, and *we can only hope* that the results will be correspondingly good. (TI00E4)

(c) the 'inclusive authorial *we*', where *we* is used to involve the reader in a joint communicative enterprise, as in example (42).

(42) "An invader," *we find on p. 296* of the Manual, "is said to be in military occupation of so much of a country as is wholly abandoned by the forces of the enemy". (GUA00E33)

(d) the 'editorial *we*', where the plural is used by a single individual because the singular is felt to be somewhat egoistical, as in example (43). In this group I have also included instances where the author speaks for the newspaper, such as *our war correspondent* or *in our opinion*.

(43) *We are aware, and we admit to the full,* that questions of military discipline need be handled very carefully. But common sense is not extinct – except, perhaps, at the War Office ... (TI00E3)

(e) the 'rhetorical *we*' which is used in the collective sense of '*we* – the nation', as in example (44).

(44) Lord Salisbury, speaking at the Guildhall three months ago, explained that by the Samoa agreement *we gave Germany what was useless to us and took what we thought useful.* Count von Bülow, explaining the Treaty to the Reichstag yesterday, argued with equal cogency that *Germany ... made us concessions* which were either nominal, as at Tonga and Zanzibar, or worthless, as in the Solomon Islands and Northern Togoland. (GUA00E14)

To obtain an idea of how the different meanings of the pronoun are distributed in my data and if the use of the pronoun had changed among the editorial authors during the 20th century, I made a closer investigation of the instances, outside quotations, recorded for 1900, the starting point of the present study, and for 1993, the last year included in the study.[19] Since the first person pronouns were sometimes difficult to classify in functional terms, I will only give a rough estimate of their distribution. Excluding *we* in quotations, I found only a dozen instances of *we* used in the generic sense and even fewer instances of the 'inclusive authorial we' in the sample representing the year 1900. Of the remaining 360 to 365 instances of the pronoun, approximately 75 per cent were examples of the 'rhetorical we' and 25 per cent of the 'editorial we'.

In 1993, when the frequency of the pronoun had been considerably reduced (see Table 3.12), only one instance of the 'inclusive authorial *we*' turned up. Of the remaining 80, approximately 80 per cent represent the 'rhetorical *we*' and 20 per cent the 'editorial *we*'. The proportions had remained almost the same; only a slight increase in the use of the 'rhetorical *we*' and a corresponding decrease in the use of the 'editorial *we*' was observed. However, during the

---

19   In this 'close-up' only unquoted speech is taken into consideration, as it is the use among the editorial authors that is of the greatest interest. Normally, no distinction is made between quoted and unquoted speech, however, and in the frequency counts presented in Table 3.13, all the instances of the plural forms of the pronoun are included.

period studied, a shift in the use of the 'rhetorical we' was noticed. In 1900, the 'rhetorical *we*' was almost exclusively used with reference to the nation in warfare while, in 1993, it was more often used with reference to other situations, for example, the nation as a political, social, economic, or sports unity; this is, of course, only natural, as a much larger proportion of the editorials dealt with war affairs in 1900 than they did in 1993.

An automatic search of the plural forms of the first person pronoun (*we, us, our, ours*, and *ourselves*) showed that the pronoun was rather frequent in the editorials at the beginning of the century. However, over the years, a statistically significant reduction was observed, from 9.90 in 1900 to 2.02 in 1993, when the whole sample was taken into account (see Table 3.12; for statistics, see Appendix, s.v. first person pronouns). To begin with, the lines of development are rather irregular, but from 1940 on, the decrease was more consistent (see Figure 3.9). When the three newspapers were compared, a statistically significant difference was noticed between *The Times*, on the one hand, and the other two newspapers, on the other, with considerably lower frequencies attested for *The Times* from 1930 on.

The reason for the obvious decrease in the use of first person pronouns after 1940 can probably be found in subject-matter. Up to and including 1940 a great proportion of the editorials was devoted to war affairs. Since England was involved in most of them, the newspapers felt a responsibility to help in creating a nationalistic feeling by the frequent use of the 'rhetorical *we*'. Even the more frequent use of the 'editorial *we*' at the beginning of the century can be explained by subject-matter as the editorials dealing with war have many references to "*our* war correspondent" or other sources reporting on the war.

Table 3.12 First person pronouns: normed frequencies.

Year	Ti	DT	Gua	All
1900	11.41	6.95	10.00	9.90
1910	8.55	7.86	12.28	10.09
1920	11.42	11.05	6.35	9.48
1930	1.17	7.20	6.30	5.38
1940	4.74	10.39	9.93	8.61
1950	1.36	5.73	7.22	4.77
1960	1.96	4.45	2.43	3.08
1970	1.29	2.50	1.44	1.74
1980	0.21	4.45	3.02	2.69
1993	0.50	4.22	2.02	2.02
1900–1993	3.86	6.19	6.06	5.42

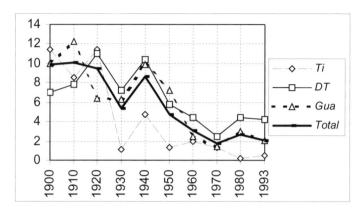

Figure 3.9 The development of first person pronouns.

3.3.4 Pronoun *it*

The pronoun *it* has a wide range of uses (see, for example, Quirk et al. 1985: 348–349; Greenbaum and Quirk 1993: 113). Besides referring to inanimate objects, it may refer to abstract concepts and to noncount substances, to single nouns as well as to phrases, as in example (45), and whole clauses, as in example (46).

(45)   *To prevent unemployment*, he insists, is "the most solemn duty of government". *He puts only one purpose beside it* – "cheap and abundant food ..." (TI50E1)

(46)   Indeed, *if the Labour Party loses this election, it may be* because of its apparent belief that defence is the best form of attack. (TI50E5)

Furthermore, it is used as a "prop", "dummy", or "empty" subject with no or very little meaning as in example (47).

(47)   *It is now a week* since Biafra's dour resistance suddenly collapsed overnight, ... (DT70E3)

No distinction between the different uses of the pronoun was made in present study, as they all, according to Biber, contribute to a "relatively inexplicit lexical content" (Biber 1988: 225–226). The pronoun is frequently used in both speech and writing. It is short and therefore often preferred to repeating the antecedent or trying to find a substitute word or phrase. But a frequent use of the pronoun can result in vagueness (Chafe and Danielewicz 1987: 90–91) since users are not always explicit about what they are referring to. Such vagueness is more easily avoided in writing than in speech, because writers do not normally work under the same strict time constraints as speakers do. Consequently, the pronoun *it* ought to be more frequent in oral discourse than in written.

During the first half of the century an inconsistent pattern of development in the use of the pronoun was noticed, but from 1930 on, a downward tendency was observed. Between 1980 and 1993 the normed frequency for the newspapers together dropped from 15.57 to 12.60, and a statistically significant decrease between 1930 and 1993 could be established. When the three newspapers were compared, a statistically significant difference was observed between the *Guardian*, on the one hand, and the *Daily Telegraph* and *The Times*, on the other, the frequencies attested for the *Guardian* being considerably higher during the first half of the century (see Table 3.13 and Figure 3.10; for statistics, see Appendix, s.v. pronoun *it*).

Table 3.13 Pronoun *it*: normed frequencies.

Year	Ti	DT	Gua	All
1900	13.03	11.21	16.79	14.84
1910	15.92	15.95	19.03	17.36
1920	13.02	14.77	18.94	15.65
1930	17.66	16.36	17.87	17.23
1940	13.71	14.48	16.71	15.06
1950	14.83	15.80	17.64	16.04
1960	14.78	16.63	14.67	15.47
1970	17.82	14.20	15.69	15.84
1980	16.04	15.11	15.66	15.57
1993	11.56	12.61	13.76	12.60
1900–1993	14.76	15.02	16.67	15.54

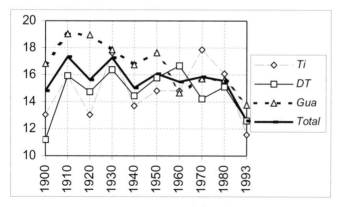

Figure 3.10 The development of pronoun *it*.

Since the pronoun *it* is a marker of inexplicitness, the decrease in the use of the pronoun suggests a development towards a more explicit language in the editorials (cf. Chapter 8). Up to the middle of the century, the language of the *Guardian* seems to have been less explicit than that of the *Daily Telegraph* and *The Times* in so far as the frequencies of the pronoun *it* were considerably higher in the *Guardian* than in the other two newspapers. From 1960 on, the differences between the newspapers in their use of the pronoun were reduced, however.

3.3.5 Summary

The decrease observed as regards the features discussed in section 3.3, that is, adverbial amplifiers, private verbs, first person pronouns, and the pronoun *it*, indicates a development away from a language marked by personal involvement (cf. section 3.2). The reduced use of private verbs, adverbial amplifiers, and the pronoun *it* means increased explicitness and matter-of-factness. The decrease in the use of first person pronouns is, most likely, due to subject-matter.

3.4   Features indicating linguistic continuity

Sections 3.2 and 3.3 show that features which have often been found to co-occur in discourse promoting personal involvement (see, for example, Biber 1988 and Chafe and Danielewicz 1987), do not necessarily follow one and the same pattern of development in newspaper editorials during the period covered by the present study. In section 3.2, such features as had increased in use in my data were discussed and in section 3.3 such as had decreased (cf. Table 3.1). This section presents the features for which no statistically significant change was attested when the frequencies from the beginning and the end of the century were compared. Even such features are of vital interest, as linguistic continuity, as well as linguistic change, may be of importance in the development of a genre, in this case, the English up-market newspaper editorial (see Chapter 9).

The 'involved' features in my material for which no statistically significant change was recorded include: demonstrative pronouns, 'possibility' modals, second person pronouns, indefinite pronouns, causative subordination, discourse particles, general emphatics, and general hedges.

3.4.1 Demonstrative pronouns

When we use the term 'demonstratives', we generally make a distinction between the determiner function, as in *this moment* and the pronoun function, as in *At first sight, this might look like* ... In the present work only demonstratives with the pronoun function were taken into consideration because, more than the demonstratives with determiner function, they are markers of informal discourse. The demonstrative pronouns are often used in speech and in more informal pieces of writing, without explicit reference, like the pronoun *it* (see Chafe and Danielewicz 1987: 90–91).

In written discourse, the demonstrative pronouns normally have definite reference, in so far as they rely on a context shared by the addresser and the addressee. They refer to an extra-linguistic situation (situational, exophoric reference), to an earlier part in the discourse (anaphoric reference), or to a later part in the discourse (cataphoric reference). In English newspaper editorials, owing to the discourse situation, anaphoric reference, as in example (48) and cataphoric reference, as in example (49) are more likely to appear than exophoric reference. However, even cataphoric reference is scarce.

(48)   There is evidence to suggest that price rises now follow quickly on wage increases. *This may be frustrating* for those who have won the increases ... (GUA70E11)

(49)   What exactly is this censure of General Buller, of which people talk with bated breath? *Simply this, that he did not insist* sufficiently on having his own way ... (GUA00E22)

The variation in the use of demonstrative pronouns, across decades as well as across newspapers, was considerable. No statistically significant difference was attested between the beginning and the end of the century. However, an upward tendency was observed in the middle of the century, and a statistically significant increase was recorded between 1940 and 1960, a fact that makes it difficult to decide about change or non-change in the use of this feature (see Table 3.14 and Figure 3.11; for statistics, see Appendix, s.v. demonstrative pronouns).

Table 3.14 Demonstrative pronouns: normed frequencies.

Year	Ti	DT	Gua	All
1900	2.95	3.12	4.51	3.85
1910	3.93	3.96	4.34	4.13
1920	2.34	3.78	3.72	3.23
1930	1.97	4.94	3.09	3.53
1940	2.47	2.59	3.99	3.06
1950	3.74	3.05	4.85	3.81
1960	4.01	6.29	4.15	4.94
1970	4.00	4.52	5.35	4.66
1980	4.85	5.35	3.89	4.73
1993	2.70	5.34	4.40	3.99
1900–1993	3.31	4.44	4.24	4.02

In a comparison between the three newspapers, we observe a statistically significant difference between *The Times*, on the one hand, and the other two newspapers, on the other. The frequencies for *The Times* are lower throughout the period, which suggests a greater awareness, among the authors of the newspaper, of the necessity of avoiding vagueness in reference.

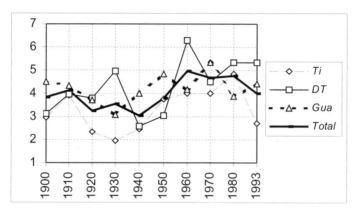

Figure 3.11 The development of demonstrative pronouns.

3.4.2 'Possibility' modals

The English language has a great variety of expressions for uncertainty, or, in terms of linguistics, evidentiality. Chafe and Nichols (1986: vii) state:

> There are some things people are sure of, either because they have reliable evidence for them, or – probably more often, because they have unquestioning faith that they are true. There are other things people are less sure of, and some things they think are only within the realm of possibility. Languages typically provide a repertoire of devices for conveying these various attitudes to knowledge...The term evidential has come to be used for such a device.

The evidentials appear in many shapes, for example as adverbs, such as *probably, possibly, perhaps*, as nouns, such as *possibility, assumption, doubt*, and as verbs, such as *think, believe,* and *presume*. However, the most important set of evidentials is probably the 'possibility' modals (for an explanation of the use of the term 'possibility' modals, see note 2). The reason for including 'possibility' modals among the markers of personal involvement is that they, as markers of generalized or uncertain presentation of information", are characteristic of informal discourse (Biber 1988: 106).[20]

The modal verbs have two different meanings, one representing *intrinsic* modality, involving some kind of human control over events, the other representing *extrinsic* modality, involving human judgement of what is going to happen or not (Quirk et al. 1985: 219–221).[21] As far as the 'possibility' modals, *can/could* and *may/might,* are concerned, they have the meanings of permission (intrinsic), and possibility/ability (extrinsic) (see Quirk et al. 1985: 221–224).

The intrinsic meaning can be paraphrased as "it is possible for ... to" or "circumstances allow ..." (Coates 1983: 141), as in example (50).

(50) The police *can justifiably claim* that both the local and the national misgivings are fed to some extent by prejudice and malice. (TI80E10)

The extrinsic meaning "is concerned with the speaker's assumptions or assessment of possibilities and, in most cases, it indicates the speaker's confidence (or lack of confidence) in the truth of the proposition expressed" (Coates 1983: 18). In these cases, the modals can be paraphrased as "it is possible that ... /perhaps" (Coates 1983: 132), as in example (51).

(51) *It may well be the fact* that hooligans largely develop from children thwarted in affection or ambition. (DT50E14)

Comparing examples (50) and (51), we find that it is only the extrinsic use of the modals that expresses "uncertainty or lack of precision". However, it is often difficult to distinguish between the two meanings, as in example (52). Does the author mean that it is actually possible to do something about corruption and inefficiency or that it is possible, but not certain, that something will be done about it?

(52) Corruption and inefficiency have no doubt plagued Laos as much as other Asian countries and in Laos, too, *these matters may be improved* under military rule. But it is chiefly the international allegiance of Laos which is the point at issue. (TI60E1)

---

20   According to Chafe (1986), however, modals are often used to express uncertainty through deductive reasoning, which is more common in formal discourse, for example, academic writing, than in informal discourse.

21   For further information as regards *intrinsic* and *extrinsic* modality, see Quirk at al. 1985: 219–221. Coates (1983), who uses the terms *root* and *epistemic* for the two modalities, makes no distinction between *intrinsic* modality and *root* modality, on the one hand, and between *extrinsic* modality and *epistemic* modality, on the other. Quirk et al. prefer to regard the *root/epistemic* distinction as a subcategorization of *extrinsic* modality. Other terms for the two modalities are *modulation* and *modality*. For the modality of obligation and permission the term *deontic* is also often used (see Quirk et al. 1985: 220, note).

According to Coates (1983: 145), these intermediate instances, or *mergers* in her terminology, are rather common in formal prose. In such contexts the intrinsic-extrinsic distinction is neutralized. Due to these classificational problems, no distinction between the different uses of the 'possibility' modals was made in the present study. Following Biber, I thus included all the instances of *can, could, may,* and *might.* The normed frequencies for the newspapers together vary between 6.75 and 8.77, but no statistically significant variation was observed, either across decades or across newspapers (see Table 3.15 and Figure 3.12; for statistics, see Appendix, s.v. 'possibility' modals).

Table 3.15 'Possibility' modals: normed frequencies.

Year	Ti	DT	Gua	All
1900	9.44	7.69	7.23	7.92
1910	7.53	7.54	6.83	7.21
1920	6.34	6.40	7.43	6.75
1930	7.60	6.27	7.92	7.20
1940	7.02	8.31	7.11	7.51
1950	7.94	7.15	8.86	7.92
1960	8.24	9.35	8.56	8.77
1970	8.31	8.87	8.20	8.46
1980	7.27	8.71	6.89	7.68
1993	6.97	8.10	6.30	7.04
1900–1993	7.59	7.91	7.52	7.67

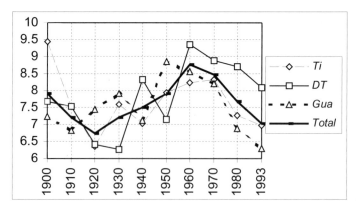

Figure 3.12 The development of 'possibility' modals.

3.4.3 Second person pronouns

Owing to their character, second person pronouns are most frequently used in interactive communicative events. But they can also be used in a generic sense as a more informal equivalent of *one* or of a passive construction. Furthermore, in a discourse situation such as the one described in the present work, they can be used to create a fictive conversation with the reader (cf. questions, section 3.2.3 and imperatives, section 3.2.4).

Only 160 instances of the pronoun were found in my data and no statistically significant variation in use was observed, either between decades or newspapers (see Appendix, s.v. second person pronouns). However, some observations are worth making. The pronouns are distributed across 67 of the 864 editorials that my corpus comprises, with the number of instances per editorial varying between one and 26. Most pronouns, more precisely, 73 instances, turn up in quoted speech. Outside quotations, 48 are used generically, and 37 as a form of address (see Table 3.16).[22] Two instances, both found in *The Times*, 1970, are difficult to classify.

Table 3.16 Second person pronouns: subdivisions.

2nd person pronouns: subdivisions	Different uses Raw Figures				
Year	Generic	Address	Quotation	Indeterminate cases	Total
1900	1		19		20
1910	2		12		14
1920	10		8		18
1930	2		6		8
1940	11	3	4		18
1950			6		6
1960	3		3		6
1970	4	27	2	2	35
1980	6	2	13		21
1993	9	5			14
Total	48	37	73	2	160

More than half of the instances of the second person pronouns were found in the *Guardian*: 88 out of 160, or, 47 out of 87 when the pronouns in quoted speech are disregarded. The figures for the *Daily Telegraph* and *The Times*, outside quoted speech, are 30 and 10, respectively. The number of second person pronouns recorded for the *Daily Telegraph* is somewhat misleading, however, since 26 of them appear in one and the same editorial. An extract from this editorial, which is an attack on Mr Enoch Powell and what he stands for, is reproduced in example (53).

---

22   Only pronouns in unquoted speech are classified since it is the editorial writers' use that is of primary interest in this context.

(53)   Yes, indeed, Mr POWELL, immigration is a terribly important problem. If *you* genuinely feel that what *you* say is going to help to solve it, then *you* have a right, perhaps a duty, to say it. *You* can certainly claim that there was some sense and truth in what *you* said. *You* can also claim that *your* words, chosen presumably with care, will be (or have already been) misrepresented. But *you* are old enough in the political game to know the risks here. Most people go by the general drift of what *you* say: they do not study the text like Biblical scholars. And if *you* have enemies, eager to misrepresent *your* words to *your* disadvantage, that cannot be news to *you*... (DT70E2)

The first time the pronoun is used by way of address is in *The Times,* 1940, in an editorial giving its tribute to the naval forces having landed at Suez, as in example (54).

(54)   The nations of the British Commonwealth are now closely knit in one common endeavour. In their unity lies the certainty of final victory and the assurance of better things to come. *By your action in crossing the seas you have sent the bravest message that the nation's power can give. For this and for the spirit in which you have come*, Britain thanks New Zealand and Australia. (TI40E5)

The use of the pronoun in these two editorials is special. The author turns to a specific addressee, in example (53) to attack and ridicule and in (54) to express gratitude. They are both examples of discourse which could have been written to be spoken. In the *Daily Telegraph* (example (53)), in particular, the pronoun seems to be used for rhetorical reasons.

In the remaining instances, when the pronoun is used by way of address, there is no specific addressee. By using the second person pronoun together with other interactive features, such as contractions and informal vocabulary, the author tries to make the readers feel that they are part of an interactive communicative event. In example (55) from the *Daily Telegraph*, 1980, the new president of the Students' Union is introduced.

(55)   And yet there is a slight snag. *There is no point in keeping it from you any longer*. Mr Aaronovitch is a Communist, moderate, sensible, reasonable – but a Commie withal. (DT80E12)

In example (56) from the *Guardian,* 1993, dealing with nursing home policy, we first meet one instance of the pronoun used generically, and further down two instances addressing the reader.

(56)   *You don't need to be a political adviser* to forecast what happens now. Some time in the near future, a new residential scandal will break out. Remember the Yorkshire Television documentary on Kent's private residential homes where old people were being dumped, unable to defend

themselves or complain about the squalid conditions? ...   Indeed, according to the Royal College of Nursing, one is just "waiting to happen" because of the large number of elderly people who should be in nursing homes but are being placed in the less expensive and less skilled residential homes. *Imagine trying to defend yourself when you've sent a letter* asking whether regulation and inspection are still needed. (GUA93E22)

In example (57) eight instances of the pronoun in a generic sense are found in two consecutive sentences.

(57)   There are two ways of trying to persuade a man or a society to make a great effort. One way is to tell him that the effort will not really exhaust him, and that his success is certain. The other is to tell him that the effort will tax all his strength and willpower, and that success will demand severe sacrifices.... In the first case *you* humour a man; *you* recognise his weakness; *you* coat him into courage; *you* lead him gradually into the presence of danger. In the second case *you* treat a man with respect; *you* recognise his strength; *you* tell him what he has to expect; *you* ask him to match with his spirit the full force of the terrible truth. (GUA40E1)

The extract is found in an editorial which is a summons to the nation in time of war and shows that the generic *you*, like the pronoun addressing the reader, can be used as a rhetorical device.

     In the editorials, second person pronouns were thus used as a more informal variant of *one* or a passive construction and as a means of creating a fictitious conversation with the reader (cf. questions and imperatives, sections 3.2.3 and 3.2.4). They also proved to be used as a rhetorical device. However, only few instances of the feature were recorded in my data and no statistically significant changes across the decades were observed. Nor were there any statistically significant differences between the newspapers.

3.4.4   Indefinite pronouns

According to Biber (1988: 226), indefinite pronouns have not traditionally been used for register comparison. However, Biber included them in his study as markers of "generalised pronominal reference", similar in use to *it* and the demonstrative pronouns. The forms covered by my study are the same as those used by Biber: *anybody, anyone, anything, everybody, everyone, everything, nobody, nothing, none, somebody, someone, something*, and their genitive forms. No forms that could also function as determiners were included, only the compound pronouns and *none*. The indefinite ronouns were not very frequent in my material (see Table 3.17): the normalised frequencies for the whole sample vary between 1.3 (1970) and 1.97 (1980). The lines of development are irregular and diverging and no statistically significant change was noticed, either across decades or across newspapers (see Figure 3.13; for statistics, see Appendix, s.v. indefinite pronouns).

Table 3.17 Indefinite pronouns: normed frequencies.

Year	Ti	DT	Gua	All
1900	1.64	1.61	1.65	1.64
1910	1.14	1.91	1.40	1.45
1920	1.52	1.72	1.91	1.72
1930	1.56	1.51	2.01	1.70
1940	1.60	1.91	1.69	1.74
1950	1.23	1.12	2.06	1.44
1960	1.63	1.88	1.59	1.72
1970	1.39	1.23	1.29	1.30
1980	1.32	2.46	2.04	1.97
1993	1.86	1.80	2.01	1.89
1900–1993	1.50	1.71	1.75	1.66

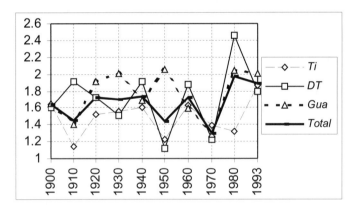

Figure 3.13 The development of indefinite pronouns.

The three pronouns that Biber refers to as markers of "generalised pronominal reference", that is, the indefinite pronouns, the pronoun *it*, and the demonstrative pronouns (1988: 226), thus show different patterns of development in English up-market editorials during the time-period studied. While no change was observed across the years as regards the indefinite pronouns, the demonstrative pronouns showed an increase in the middle of the century (but no difference when the frequencies from the beginning and the end of the period were compared) (see section 3.4.1), and the pronoun *it* decreased in use (see section 3.3.4).

3.4.5 Causative subordination

Opinions seem to diverge as to the use of subordination features. Pool and Field (1976: 308–309) and Halliday (1987: 62–74), for example, associate subordination with the real-time production constraints characteristic of speech while researchers such as O'Donnell (1974: 102–109), Kay (1977: 21–33), and Kroll (1977: 98–99) associate subordination with the greater elaboration that is characteristic of writing. As far as causative subordination is concerned, Tottie (1986) claims that *because* is more common as a causative subordinator in speech while *as* is more common in writing. According to Biber (1988: 107), most researchers who have investigated the use of causative subordination have found more of causative adverbials in speech. Biber himself is of the opinion that causative subordination is associated with production constraints. In a genre like newspaper editorials, however, it can be assumed that causative subordination is used for argumentative purposes; the authors want to explain something, to support an idea, or to defend a view.

As in Biber's study (1988), only *because* was first taken into consideration as a causative subordinator. For comparison, the frequencies of *as* were then also calculated since Tottie (1986) had claimed that this subordinator was more common in written discourse.

Because was relatively rare in the editorials. The normed frequencies vary between 0.52 (1940) and 1.15 (1930) for the newspapers together, but no statistically significant variation across decades was observed (see Table 3.18 and Figure 3.14; for statistics, see Appendix, s.v. causative subordination: *because*).

Table 3.18 Causative subordination: normed frequencies of *because*.

Year	Ti	DT	Gua	All
1900	0.48	0.52	0.83	0.68
1910	0.90	0.50	0.81	0.76
1920	0.52	0.87	0.70	0.68
1930	0.83	0.71	1.82	1.15
1940	0.72	0.21	0.68	0.52
1950	0.51	0.64	1.32	0.80
1960	0.55	1.23	0.92	0.93
1970	0.85	0.80	1.07	0.91
1980	0.61	0.30	1.33	0.73
1993	0.70	0.72	0.87	0.76
1900–1993	0.66	0.67	1.04	0.80

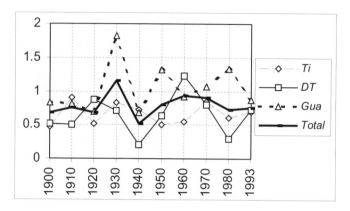

Figure 3.14 The development of causative subordination (*because*).

When the newspapers were compared, a statistically significant difference was noticed between the *Guardian*, on the one hand, and the other two newspapers, on the other. The feature was more frequently used over the years in the *Guardian*, but the line of development is irregular, as are the lines for the other two newspapers, especially for the *Daily Telegraph*.

As, which had to be edited by hand to exclude instances having other functions than causative subordination, proved to be rare in my data. Only 48 instances, evenly spread across newspapers and decades, were found, which suggests that, in written discourse such as English newspaper editorials at least, *because* (405 instances) is preferred to *as* as a causative subordinator.

3.4.6 Discourse particles

Since discourse particles are mainly used in conversation and rarely in writing, it was no surprise that only few instances of them were found in my corpus. *Well, now, anyway, anyhow,* and *anyways* were checked manually. All in all, only 23 instances were recorded for the whole corpus, three of them in quotations. No instances of *anyways* were recorded. The others were distributed as follows:

well	now	anyway	anyhow
2	1	12	5

Outside quotations, the first instance of the feature did not appear until 1940. Most of the discourse particles were found in the texts from the last few decades of the century.

3.4.7 General emphatics

Emphatics are used to mark the certainty of what is said. Such items, for example, *for sure, a lot, such a, just, really, more/most, so* + adjective, *real* + adjective, *do* + verb, which were used in Biber's 1988 study as well as in mine, are frequent in informal, colloquial discourse (Chafe 1982: 47). Due to their colloquial touch, they could hardly be expected to be particularly frequent in editorials.

No instances of *real* + adjective were found and only two instances of *for sure*, both in the *Guardian,* one in 1980 and one in 1993. By way of example, see (58) from 1980.

(58)   And Wall Street is inept at the business of hearts and minds. Wall Street *would have elected John Connally President for sure*, and skipped all the way to the bank: but hearts and minds, in a dozen primaries, humiliated Connally. (GUA 80E29)

Most of the instances of *a lot* were also found in the *Guardian,* as, for example, (59).
(59)   The stock exchange boom has now come to an end, but while it lasted a great many people were able to make themselves *a lot richer*. (GUA60E12)

Only *more* and *most* were rather frequent, with normed frequencies per 1000 words varying between 3.9 (1920 and 1940) and 5.4 (1993).

Great variation in the use of general emphatics was observed, both across decades and across newspapers, but no statistically significant changes were attested (see Table 3.19 and Figure 3.15; for statistics, see Appendix, s.v. general emphatics). Towards the end of the century, the *Guardian* appears to have shown a greater acceptance than the other two newspapers of such colloquial features as emphatics, however (cf. contractions, section 3.2.5).

Table 3.19 General emphatics: normed frequencies.

Year	Ti	DT	Gua	All
1900	6.11	7.31	6.43	6.49
1910	6.98	6.86	6.73	6.84
1920	5.04	4.74	6.88	5.63
1930	4.52	7.00	6.44	6.18
1940	6.41	4.78	5.09	5.36
1950	5.96	6.78	7.02	6.59
1960	6.32	7.71	6.74	6.99
1970	8.14	5.85	6.39	6.74
1980	6.67	5.09	6.58	6.05
1993	5.80	6.53	8.47	6.91
1900–1993	6.20	6.21	6.66	6.37

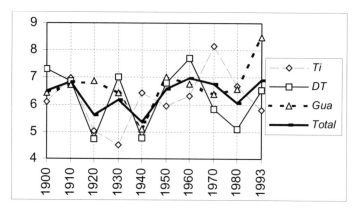

Figure 3.15 The development of general emphatics.

3.4.8 General hedges

Hedges, that is adverbs used to "convey imprecision" (Biber et al. 1999: 557), are employed in 'involved' discourse to mark uncertainty or probability (cf. 'possibility' modals, section 3.4.2, and indefinite pronouns, section 3.4.4). Moreover, according to Chafe and Danielewicz (1987: 89), hedges are used in conversational discourse because of the restricted number of words that are available under the stressed conditions that prevail during speech production. Biber (1986: 384–414) showed that hedges often co-occur with other features marking reduced lexical contents and with interactive features such as first and second person pronouns.

The hedges included in the study are *at about, something like, more or less, almost, maybe, sort of,* and *kind of.*[23] No instances of *sort of* and *kind of* were recorded. The others were distributed as follows:

at about	maybe	something like	more or less	almost
2	8	11	28	210

The alternatives that are normally associated with conversational discourse, such as *sort of, kind of,* and *at about* were thus avoided. Only *almost* is comparatively frequent, probably due to the fact that it is not felt to be as marked as the other hedges. All in all, there were 259 instances of hedges, evenly distributed over the period, the normed frequencies varying between 0.36 (1940) and 0.81 (1980) for the whole sample. No statistically significant variation was attested, either across

---

23   In Quirk et al. (1985: 597–598) these adverbs are found among the "downtoners", more specifically, "approximators" and "compromisers".

decades or across newspapers (see Table 3.20 and Figure 3.16; for statistics, see Appendix, s.v. general hedges).

As markers of conversational discourse, the general hedges have much in common with discourse particles (see section 3.4.6) and general emphatics (see section 3.4.7) and, like these features, they are not very frequent in the editorials.

Table 3.20 General hedges: normed frequencies.

Year	Ti	DT	Gua	All
1900	0.43	0.74	0.76	0.67
1910	0.61	0.81	0.73	0.71
1920	0.71	0.12	0.50	0.48
1930	0.48	0.47	0.28	0.40
1940	0.42	0.35	0.31	0.36
1950	0.60	0.51	0.58	0.56
1960	0.57	1.18	0.52	0.79
1970	0.44	0.46	0.29	0.39
1980	0.39	1.41	0.52	0.81
1993	0.51	0.44	0.81	0.60
1900–1993	0.52	0.67	0.53	0.57

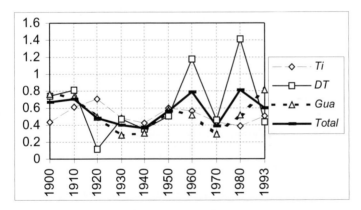

Figure 3.16 The development of general hedges.

3.4.9 Summary

Among the eight features that showed no statistically significant change over the period of study, we observe three that, especially when used in abundance, create vagueness in a text, namely 'possibility' modals, indefinite pronouns, and general hedges. A fourth feature, demonstrative pronouns, can probably also be included among these features (see 3.4.1). Hedges, like discourse particles and general emphatics, are features that are normally associated with conversational discourse. In my data, second person pronouns have much in common with the 'conversational' features in so far as they, besides being used in a generic sense, are used by the editorial authors to create a fictive conversation with their readers. Causative subordination, the last member of the set, seems to have little in common with any of the other members, even though some researchers have found that the feature is more common in spoken than in written discourse.

3.5   Summary and conclusions

As the results obtained in sections 3.2 to 3.4 showed, features that Biber (1988) found to be distinctive in texts marked by personal involvement developed in diverging directions in my material. Some increased in use, others decreased, and for still others no statistically significant change was attested (see Table 3.21, which is identical with Table 3.1 and reproduced here for the sake of clarity). The observed statistically significant changes, whether they are increases or decreases, normally start in the middle of the century. An exception is contractions, for which no change was attested until between 1980 and 1993.

Table 3.21 The development of features linked with personal involvement.

Statistically significant increase over time	Statistically significant decrease over time	Linguistic continuity
Present tense verbs	Adverbial amplifiers	Demonstrative pronouns
Not-negation	Private verbs	'Possibility' modals
Questions	First person pronouns	Second person pronouns
Imperatives	Pronoun *it*	Indefinite pronouns
Contractions		Causative subordination
		Discourse particles
		General emphatics
		General hedges

[a] The frequencies from the beginning and the end of the century showed no statistically significant differences. Between 1940 and 1960, a statistically significant increase was observed, but after 1960 the line of development turns downwards again.

In English up-market editorials, two different 'forces' seem to lie behind the diverging patterns of development among these features: the growing interest among the authors to make the language of their newspapers more 'reader-friendly' on the one hand, and their striving for explicitness and matter-of-factness on the other. Features marking 'involved' and informal discourse, such as present tense verbs and *not*-negation, and conversational features, such as questions, imperatives, and contractions, increased in use while features marking vagueness and implicitness, such as the pronoun *it*, or "heightened feeling", such as adverbial amplifiers, decreased in use. Most of the features representing linguistic continuity can be associated with one or the other of the two sets: discourse particles, general emphatics, and second person pronouns with the former and 'possibility' modals, indefinite pronouns and demonstrative pronouns with the latter. General hedges may be associated with both.

Among the features that have not been mentioned so far, we find first person pronouns and causative subordination. The decrease in the use of first person pronouns is, no doubt, affected by subject matter. Up to and including 1940, when the decrease set in, many of the editorials dealt with war, and a frequent use of the 'rhetorical' *we*, referring to the nation, and the 'editorial' *we*, referring to the newspaper was observed. Causative subordination seems to have little in common with any of the other features discussed in Chapter 3, which may be an indication that this feature has a discourse function other than marking personal involvement in newspaper editorials (see section 3.4.5).

In sum, it is obvious that, during the 20th century, the language of the English up-market editorials developed towards greater informality, primarily due to the fact that the features marking conversational discourse increased in use, but also towards greater explicitness, as most of the features that decreased in use are markers of vagueness and implicitness.

4. Features marking information density

4.1 Introduction

As the results from Chapter 3 showed, features marking personal involvement in Biber's study (1988) developed in diverging directions in English up-market newspaper editorials. Those features that are usually associated with conversational discourse increased in use, which points to increased informality in the editorials. Those marking inexplicit reference, on the other hand, decreased, which indicates a development in the direction of greater explicitness. The features dealt with in the present chapter are such as Biber found to be linked with "high informational focus and a careful integration of information in a text" (Biber 1988: 104). They are therefore normally associated with more formal discourse (see, for example, Chafe 1982, and Chafe and Danielewicz 1987). A decrease in the use of these features would support the findings in Chapter 3 about a development towards greater informality; an increase, on the other hand, would point to a development in the opposite direction.

The markers of information density in the present study can be divided into three groups: first nouns and features marking noun phrase complexity, such as attributive adjectives and adjectival items (past and present participle forms used in attributive position),[1] prepositions, and present participle WHIZ-deletion;[2] then features marking lexical specificity, that is, word length and type/token ratio;[3] and finally, features marking sentence complexity, that is, sentence length and subordination.[4] In Biber's study (1988), agentless passives and past participle

---

1   In the present study the term 'attributive adjectives' is used for items preceding nouns and marked as adjectives by the tagger.

2   Present participle WHIZ-deletions are present participle clauses functioning as reduced relative clauses, such as *the people standing in the corner* for *the people who are standing...* (see section 4.3.3).

3   'Word length' in this context refers to the number of orthographic letters per word. Type/token ratio is the measure obtained when the number of specific words in a text (types) is put in relation to the number of the total of words (tokens). The calculation of the type/token ratio is described in further detail in section 4.4.2.

4   Sentence length and subordination were not included among the markers of information density in Biber's study. However, since sentence complexity (here represented by sentence

WHIZ-deletions were included among the markers of information density as well as among the markers of abstract discourse, but since they proved to play a more important role as markers of abstract discourse in his study (see Biber 1988: 102–103), they will be examined in Chapter 7 in the present work.[5] Most of the markers of information density dealt with in the study proved to have increased in use over time. Prepositional phrases, sentence length, and subordination are exceptions (see Table 4.1).

Table 4.1 The development of features linked with information density.

Statistically significant increase over time	Statistically significant decrease over time	Linguistic continuity
Nouns	Prepositional phrases	(No features)
Attributive adjectives	Sentence length	
Present participle WHIZ-deletion	Subordination	
Word length		
Type/token ratio		

In the following, I first deal with nouns (section 4.2) and the features associated with noun phrase complexity (section 4.3). Section 4.4 is devoted to features associated with lexical specificity and diversity, and section 4.5 to sentence complexity. A summary of the results obtained is given in section 4.6.

4.2   Nouns

Nouns and noun phrases, in their elasticity, incorporate a great deal of information in a compact, integrated form, and they have therefore often been considered as style markers (cf. Varantola 1984, Raumolin-Brunberg 1991, Jucker 1992, and Nilsson 2001). By way of an example, see (1), an extract from *The Times*, 1993, about the privatisation of prisons. All nouns are italicized.

(1)   The *home secretary* must restore *faith* in *prison privatisation*. The *prison privatisation program* is still desperately in *need* of a committed political *champion*. The incompetent *management* of the East *Midlands* and *Humberside prison escort service* by the private *security firm Group* 4 and the *criticisms* levelled at the privately-run *Wolds remand centre* by *Judge Stephen Tumim* last *week* have been seized upon by *opponents* of contracting out. *Ministers* have yet to mount a convincing *counter-attack*. (TI93E25)

---

length and subordination) is also, in my opinion, a measure of the integration of information, the two features were included in the present work.

5   Past participle WHIZ-deletions are past participle clauses functioning as reduced relative clauses, such as *the roses planted in front of the house* for *the roses which are (were) planted...* (see section 7.3.2).

Over the years, the normed frequencies of nouns increased considerably, from 240.59 in 1900 to 271.07 in 1993, for the three newspapers together,[6] and a statistically significant difference between the beginning and the end of the century was recorded (see Table 4.2 and Figure 4.1; for statistics, see Appendix, s.v. nouns). The most conspicuous increase is that between 1980 and 1993 when the frequencies rose from 252.56 to 271.07. When the three newspapers were compared, the use of nouns proved to have increased the most across the decades in *The Times*, which also showed the largest normed frequency of the feature in 1993. However, no statistically significant differences across newspapers were observed.

To judge from these results, the language of English up-market newspapers editorials, especially of those of *The Times,* became more nominal in style during the period studied, which, in turn, points to increased information density.

Table 4.2 Nouns: normed frequencies.

Year	Ti	DT	Gua	All
1900	234.61	249.49	241.00	240.59
1910	228.82	231.91	239.74	234.63
1920	249.25	240.11	234.98	241.57
1930	245.37	246.97	241.83	244.69
1940	251.65	256.49	251.33	253.26
1950	251.11	249.90	237.15	246.48
1960	247.58	240.57	243.24	243.52
1970	247.65	250.87	257.33	252.23
1980	246.66	248.06	263.52	252.56
1993	282.58	265.44	262.42	271.07
1900–1993	250.62	248.37	247.43	248.73

---

6   To obtain more reliable data, the automatic searches of nouns were followed by manual screening. All duplicates and some multi-functional words such as *individual, sovereign,* and *total,* which, at an initial stage of the study (see section 2.5.2) had been found sometimes to be tagged as nouns when they should have been tagged as adjectives and vice versa, were edited by hand to make it possible to remove instances having erroneous labels.

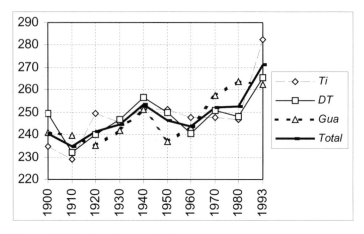

Figure 4.1 The development of nouns.

4.3   Noun phrase complexity

As mentioned in 4.2, a high frequency of nouns in a text indicates a high density of information. The noun phrase can be further elaborated by, for example, the use of attributive adjectives and adjectival items, prepositional phrases, and present participle WHIZ-deletions. Large amounts of information can thus be packed into a single "idea unit" (for an explanation of the term "idea unit", see Chafe 1985: 106–108). Example (2), which is an extract from *The Times*, January, 1993, may serve as an illustration of the information density described above. Nouns, attributive adjectives and prepositional phrases are italicized.

(2)   The *European Community*, after a *year of self-inflicted turmoil* generated *by the over-ambitious Maastricht agenda*, must now end its *dream of "standing up" to America*, as *Jacques Delors* exhorts, and refashion *schemes for better co-operation with Washington*. If it is to reinforce the *humanising and liberating benefits of the collapse of communism*, the *West* cannot afford this *degree of confusion and disunity*. No *purpose* is served *by inflating conflicts of interest with Washington*. The *misery of the Balkans* is a *dreadful warning of the perils of assuming* that *European disorder* can be managed *without American political* and *military participation*. (TI93E1)

For comparison, see example (3), an extract from the *Daily Telegraph*, 1970, with a very low concentration of the features marking information density.

(3)   Yes, indeed, *Mr POWELL, immigration* is a terribly *important problem*. If you genuinely feel that what you say is going to help to solve it, then you

have a *right*, perhaps a *duty*, to say it. You can certainly claim that there was some *sense* and *truth in what you said*. You can also claim that your *words*, chosen presumably *with care*, will be (or have already been) misrepresented. But you are old enough *in the political game* to know the *risks* here. (DT70E2)

Noun phrase elaboration by attributive adjectives is treated in section 4.3.1, by prepositional phrases in section 4.3.2, and by present participle WHIZ-deletions in section 4.3.3.

4.3.1   Attributive adjectives and adjectival items

The fact that adjectives, and especially attributive adjectives and adjectival items, contribute to the information density of a text, was shown by Chafe (1982: 41–42) and Chafe and Danielewicz (1987: 101), among others. Chafe, for example, showed that attributive adjectives were four times as common in his written as in his spoken data. As an example of a text with a frequent use of attributive adjectives in my data, see (4), an extract from the *Guardian,* 1993.

(4)   Clearly the Home Secretary is dutifully responding to the Prime Minister's *inane* call of last week for more condemnation, and less understanding, of *juvenile* crime. Ignoring a mountain of research evidence detailing the failure of *previous special juvenile* units (approved schools, *junior* detention centres and *junior* borstals, all now abandoned), he is plunging ahead with a plan for a network of *new secure* training centres for 12 to 15 year-olds. But changing the name will not change the chances of success. All three *previous* models began with the same *high* hopes and aspirations that Mr Clarke is bestowing on his *latest* project. The emphasis will be on *constructive* regimes aimed to produce *primary* classes in citizenship. Bully for him. But the history of *custodial* institutions is that they quickly generate their *own negative* culture. Putting "really *persistent nasty little* juveniles" into *junior* prisons has one predictable outcome: it turns them, as night follows day, into even *nastier* adult villains. (GUA93E6)

The attributive adjectives were obtained through automatic searches combined with manual editing to eliminate errors. Present and past participle forms used in attributive   position, such as *suffering* humanity and *hurt* feelings were also included in the frequency counts.

The normed frequencies of attributive adjectives showed a statistically significant increase in use over the period studied, from 48.17 in 1900 to 61.90 in 1993 for the newspapers together. The largest increases were those observed between 1900 and 1920 and between 1980 and 1993 (see Table 4.3 and Figure 4.2; for statistics, see Appendix, s.v. attributive adjectives).

Table 4.3 Attributive adjectives: normed frequencies.

Year	Ti	DT	Gua	All
1900	51.56	50.80	45.72	48.17
1910	53.73	59.62	48.26	52.71
1920	55.13	57.52	55.10	55.77
1930	54.16	54.93	53.49	54.21
1940	58.29	54.12	48.47	53.30
1950	56.55	55.21	52.92	54.96
1960	54.41	51.90	58.85	54.78
1970	59.79	55.00	53.41	55.89
1980	56.84	57.12	54.19	56.10
1993	62.08	60.66	62.64	61.90
1900–1993	56.70	55.59	53.14	55.04

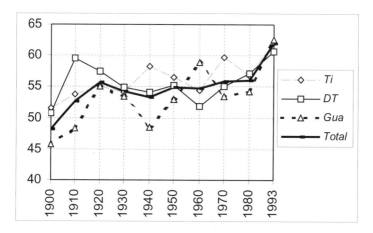

Figure 4.2 The development of attributive adjectives.

When the three newspapers were compared, a statistically significant difference was noticed between the *Guardian* and *The Times*, the frequencies for *The Times* being higher during almost the whole period.

Attributive adjectives thus follow the pattern of development for nouns (see section 4.2). Especially noticeable is the joint increase of the two features between 1980 and 1993, which gives a strong indication that the language of English up-market editorials became more nominal and more compact during the last few decades of the 20th century.

4.3.2 Prepositional phrases

The use of prepositional phrases is an effective way of packing high amounts of information into idea units and of expanding the size of them (see, for example, Chafe 1985: 108–109), which means that the feature is often found in informational discourse, such as example (5), taken from the *Daily Telegraph*, 1930. The prepositions introducing such phrases are italicized.

(5)   *During* the brief interval *before* the meeting *of* the newly elected German Reichstag the prospect *for* the immediate political future *of* the country – *on* which that *of* Europe depends *in* no small degree – will take on clearer outlines. But the probability *of* a drastic and highly unconventional solution *of* the Parliamentary problems is increased *by* the reception given *to* the BRUENING Cabinet's remarkable financial program, details *of* which have been given *by* the Berlin Correspondent *of* THE DAILY TELEGRAPH. (DT30E28)

Chafe (1982: 40–41) and Chafe and Danielewicz (1987: 98–99) showed that prepositional phrases are frequent in all the genres they studied, that is, conversations, lectures, personal letters, and academic writing, but that they are unusually frequent in academic writing, something that was confirmed by Biber's 1988 study.

The automatic search of prepositions was followed by manual editing of duplicates.[7] No analysis was made to distinguish between different types of prepositional phrases, which means that prepositions used in postmodifications such as *the cat in the basket*, in verb complementation such as *walk in the street*, and as part of prepositional and phrasal prepositional verbs such as *look into a problem* and *come up with an idea* were all included. Nor was any distinction made between simple and complex prepositional phrases.[8] Type as well as length and complexity of the prepositional phrase are, of course, of great importance, but for the purpose of this study, the frequency of prepositional phrases as such will suffice as an indicator of information density (cf. Biber 1988: 236–237).

Comparing the feature across decades, we find a large and consistent, statistically significant, decrease over the years, from 134.25 in 1900 to 121.33 in 1993 for the whole sample (see Table 4.4 and Figure 4.3; for statistics, see Appendix, s.v. prepositional phrases). We also notice statistically significant differences between the three newspapers: *The Times* showed the highest normed frequencies over the years and the *Guardian* the lowest.

---

7   Words given duplicate tags (see section 2.5.2) were such as *before*, which was sometimes assigned the two tags #PREP (preposition) and #CS (subordinate conjunction).

8   No such distinctions were made in Biber's study either.

Table 4.4 Prepositional phrases: normed frequencies.

Year	Ti	DT	Gua	All
1900	136.87	139.96	131.29	134.25
1910	137.77	136.48	130.72	134.20
1920	141.36	134.84	136.54	137.83
1930	137.24	136.35	130.99	134.61
1940	136.17	137.58	127.38	133.54
1950	135.98	131.07	120.42	129.47
1960	133.65	119.75	123.94	125.25
1970	119.38	125.74	117.35	120.76
1980	134.67	121.00	114.68	123.20
1993	120.64	125.85	118.62	121.33
1900–1993	132.56	129.60	125.32	128.95

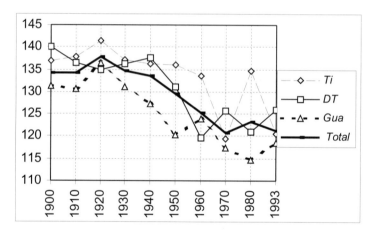

Figure 4.3 The development of prepositional phrases.

Prepositional phrases thus decreased in use over the years at the same time as attributive adjectives increased, which may be difficult to explain since the two features are used for the same purpose, that is, for expanding the noun phrase and for integrating as much information into as few words as possible. However, as mentioned above, prepositional phrases are not only used as postmodifications but also as verb complementation. One cause of the discrepancy may therefore be that it is among prepositional phrases used for other purposes than postmodification, in the first place, that the decrease took place. As the present study makes no distinction between the different uses, it is not possible to tell, but if that should be the case, the decrease has nothing to do with noun phrase complexity.

Another probable reason is that postmodifying prepositional phrases have been replaced by nominal premodifiers adding the same meaning to the noun. Instead of using an *of*-genitive, the authors may have chosen an *s*-genitive such as *the industry's immediate troubles* (DT60E29) and *the House of Commons' efforts* (TI60E6) or a noun in the nominative form, as in *Middle East oil producing countries* (DT60E25), *worker participation* (GUA80E21), and *Treasury approval* (TI93E7) (cf. Rydén 1975 and Bell 1988). Especially proper names in premodifying position, such as *the Bullock report* (GUA80E21) and *Nato secretary general* (GUA80E28) give an impression of having increased during the last few decades studied. Instances where postmodification by prepositions other than *of* has given way to premodifying nouns were also found, as, for example, *the Thatcher years* (DT93E19), *Downing Street Statement*, and *City uncertainty* (TI93E3). Even numerals, which would have been expected to appear as postmodifications occur as premodifiers, as, for example *Peter Walker's 1974 reorganisation* (GUA93E8) and *of the 1940 standard* (DT40E28).

In order to obtain some statistical support, the frequencies per 1000 words attested for *s*-genitives, nouns as premodifiers, and postmodification by prepositional phrases for the period 1900 to1940 were compared to those attested for the period 1950 to 1993. The result of these comparisons supports the above assumption (see Table 4.5).

Table 4.5 Frequencies per 1000 words for *s*-genitives, nouns as premodifiers, and post-modification by prepositional phrases.

Feature	Period 1900–1940	Period 1950–1993
s-genitives	3.67	6.60
Nouns as premodifiers	10.88	15.90
Postmodification by prepositional phrases	82.20	71.07

A considerable increase was noticed as regards *s*-genitives and premodifying nouns while an equally considerable decrease was noticed for postmodifying prepositional phrases. Thus we have at least one possible explanation why the patterns of development for attributive adjectives and prepositional phrases diverge.

4.3.3   Present participle WHIZ-deletion

Participle clauses are generally associated with a high degree of integration of information and are therefore more often found in writing than in speech (see, for example, Carrol 1960, O'Donnell 1974, Chafe 1982, Chafe 1985, Bäcklund 1986, Chafe and Danielewicz 1987, and Greenbaum 1988).[9]

9   Detached (adverbial) present participle clauses are included among the markers of 'narrative' discourse (see section 5.4) and past participle clauses (WHIZ-deletions and detached clauses) among the markers of abstract discourse (see sections 7.3.2 and 7.3.1, respectively).

Present participle WHIZ-deletions, that is, present participle clauses functioning as reduced relative clauses (see example (6)) are more compact than full relative clauses (cf. (6a), example (6) rephrased) and therefore more suitable for highly integrated discourse.

(6)   It has exposed the weakness of one giant, and it has shown the strength of a small and independent people *fighting for existence* and the right. (GUA40E2)

(6a)   a small and independent people *who are fighting for existence* ...

The present participle WHIZ-deletions were edited by hand so as to distinguish them from other present participle forms. Besides introducing non-finite clauses, the present participle is used as the non-finite component of the progressive form (as in *people who are fighting*). It is also used as a nominal amplifier (as in *the fighting troops*), as the head of a noun phrase (as in *the fighting at Tugela*), and as a prepositional complement (as in *by fighting hard*).

No statistically significant change was observed in the use of present participle WHIZ-deletions until between 1970 and 1993, when the normed frequencies for the newspapers together went up from 1.05 to 2.10. Nor was there any statistically significant difference between the three newspapers (see Table 4.6 and Figure 4.4; for statistics, see Appendix, s.v. present participle WHIZ-deletion).

As Figure 4.4 shows, present participle WHIZ-deletions follow the same pattern of development as nouns and attributive adjectives (see sections 4.2 and 4.3.1, respectively), which supports the assumption of increased information density. Especially noticeable is the increase in the use of the three features towards the end of the 20th century.

Table 4.6 Present participle WHIZ-deletion: normed frequencies.

Year	Ti	DT	Gua	All
1900	1.63	1.09	0.83	1.09
1910	1.44	1.18	0.78	1.07
1920	0.78	1.47	1.02	1.06
1930	1.02	1.34	0.89	1.10
1940	1.07	1.29	0.60	0.98
1950	1.75	1.31	0.74	1.28
1960	1.71	1.27	1.91	1.60
1970	1.14	1.23	0.80	1.05
1980	2.08	1.28	1.05	1.45
1993	1.47	2.13	2.79	2.10
1900–1993	1.40	1.36	1.13	1.29

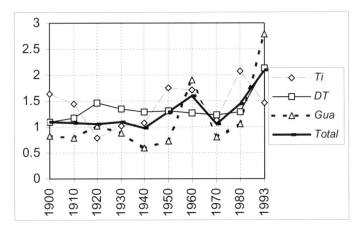

Figure 4.4 The development of present participle WHIZ-deletions.

4.4   Lexical specificity

Not only noun phrase complexity (see section 4.3) but also precise lexical choice is a measure of information density. The most commonly used measures of lexical specificity and diversity are word length and type/token ratio.

Lexical specificity seems to correlate with production circumstances (Chafe and Danielewicz 1987: 87–89). Speakers do not always have the time to choose the best option from their lexical repertoire while writers are usually given the opportunity to ponder over how best to express their thoughts. Therefore, lexical specificity and diversity are more characteristic of writing than of speech. However, even editorials are sometimes composed under fairly strict time constraints. But the authors of the editorials work under another type of constraint as well. They are expected to follow a special model, a "house style", which demands that at least some attention should be given to lexical choice (see, for example, Hicks 1993: 48–73).

4.4.1   Word length

Word length is one way of measuring lexical specificity and diversity. As early as 1927, Bear showed the correlation between the length of a word and its frequency: the longer the word, the less frequent (see Klare 1963: 31–32). The shorter, more general words, are more frequent in spontaneous speech owing to the restrictions of on-line production (Chafe and Danielewicz 1987: 88). The longer and more specific words, on the other hand, are normally found in texts where the author/speaker has had the time to choose their words.

For the calculation of word length, counting scripts in Perl (see section 2.5.3) were used. A straightforward and statistically significant increase was noticed: the word length mean attested for the three newspapers together went up from 4.71 in 1900 to 4.95 in 1993 (see Table 4.7 and Figure 4.5; for statistics, see Appendix, s.v. word length). The average number of letters per word increased the most in *The Times*, from 4.72 in 1900 to 5.01 in 1993, in the *Guardian* slightly less, from 4.62 to 4.88, and in the *Daily Telegraph* the least, from 4.79 to 4.95.[10] However, no statistically significant difference was attested between the three newspapers.

Table 4.7 Word length mean.

Year	Ti	DT	Gua	All
1900	4.72	4.79	4.62	4.71
1910	4.76	4.75	4.70	4.74
1920	4.71	4.71	4.68	4.70
1930	4.77	4.80	4.73	4.77
1940	4.77	4.73	4.66	4.72
1950	4.80	4.87	4.76	4.81
1960	4.76	4.80	4.77	4.78
1970	4.87	4.88	4.87	4.87
1980	4.88	4.88	4.85	4.87
1993	5.01	4.95	4.88	4.95
1900–1993	4.81	4.82	4.75	4.79

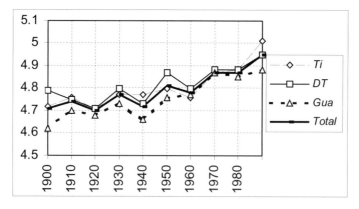

Figure 4.5 The development of word length.

---

10   For comparison it can be mentioned that the figures recorded for official documents in Biber's study were 4.9, for academic prose 4.8, and for editorials 4.7. The lowest figures were those recorded for personal letters and telephone conversations, 3.9 and 4.0, respectively. These figures are to be compared to those attested for 1960 in my study.

The words used in English up-market editorials thus became longer during the 20th century. Since word length and lexical diversity and specificity are associated, it can be assumed that the vocabulary of the editorials became more varied and specific over the 20th century.

4.4.2 Type/token ratio

Besides word length, type/token ratio has often been used as a measure of lexical specificity. When calculating the type/token ratio, the number of specific words in a text (types) are put in relation to the number of the total of words (tokens). Consequently, a high type/token ratio recorded for a text indicates that many different lexical items are used which, in turn, means that a high proportion of the words will have a specific meaning. A low ratio, on the other hand, shows that few specific words are used while the more general ones are frequent. In the 1960s and 1970s, type/token ratios were frequently used by psychologists and researchers in communication in their study of differences between speech and writing (see Biber 1988: 230). Chafe and Danielewicz (1987: 88) found that the type/token ratio was considerably higher in the written genres they investigated than in the spoken, which they suggest is due to differences in production circumstances.

The calculation of type/token ratio in the present study was based on the first 400 words in each text (each editorial) that has 400 words or more and the actual number of words in those that have less.[11] The ratio was calculated with the aid of counting scripts in Perl (see section 2.5.3).

From 1910 on, a consistent and statistically significant increase as regards type/token ratios was observed. The means increased from 54.92 in 1910 to 59.98 in 1993.[12] When the three newspapers were compared, a statistically significant difference between them was observed. The ratios for the *Daily Telegraph* were the highest and those for *The Times* the lowest. The *Guardian* takes an intermediate position (see Table 4.8 and Figure 4.6; for statistics, see Appendix, s.v. type/token ratio).[13]

---

11   The reason for using only 400-word extracts for the calculation of the type/token ratio, and not all the data available, is that, in a comparison of very long and very short texts of the same type, the short texts will have a much higher type/token ratio than the long ones, due to the fact that a large number of *types* (different lexical items) that appear in the first 100 words of a text will be repeated over and over again in a long text thus giving the long texts a lower type/token ratio (see Biber 1988: 239). As mentioned in Chapter 2 note 14, the length of the editorials in the present study vary between 116 and 1777 words.

12   The type/token ratio recorded for editorials in Biber's study was 54.4. The highest mean was that attested for press reviews (56.5) and the lowest for spontaneous speeches (44.9) (to be compared to the means recorded for 1960 in my data).

13   The comparatively low type/token ratio in *The Times* may be the result of the instructions given to the journalists by Sir William Haley, appointed editor of the newspaper in 1952, to avoid many long words (Howard 1985: 120).

Since both type/token ratio and word length, the two foremost markers of precise lexical choice, increased in use over the years, we can conclude that the lexical complexity and diversity of the language of English up-market editorials increased during the period studied.

Table 4.8 Type/token ratio.

Year	Ti	DT	Gua	All
1900	54.34	56.86	58.76	57.22
1910	54.50	56.31	54.42	54.92
1920	55.20	55.60	55.41	55.39
1930	54.25	57.16	57.62	56.61
1940	55.71	59.40	58.91	58.17
1950	55.94	60.76	57.58	58.26
1960	56.78	59.66	57.43	58.10
1970	56.25	61.85	57.22	58.47
1980	55.62	61.59	57.74	58.52
1993	59.58	60.11	60.35	59.98
1900–1993	56.04	59.35	57.57	57.67

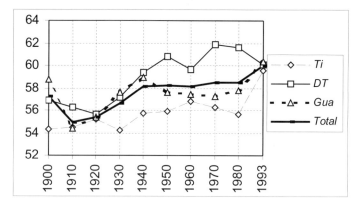

Figure 4.6 The development of the type/token ratio.

4.5   Sentence complexity

Most formulas that have been used over the years to test text complexity include a "word factor" and a "sentence factor" (see, for example, Klare 1963: 162–171). The "word factor" has often been word length (see note 3) or word frequency (Klare 1963: 164–169). As far as the "sentence factor" is concerned, the two most frequently used measures have been sentence length and sentence complexity, usually involving the ratios of simple, complex, and/or compound sentences (Klare 1963: 169–171). More recent research has used other measures of text complexity, such as noun phrase complexity (see, for example, Varantola 1984, Raumolin-Brunberg 1991, Jucker 1992, and Ljung 1997) and subordination (see Poole and Field 1976, Halliday 1987, Ljung 1997). In the following, I concentrate on two of these measures, used in previous research, namely, sentence length, that is, the number of words per sentence, and subordination.

4.5.1 Sentence length

A sentence is normally considered to begin with a capital letter and to finish with a full stop, an exclamation mark or a question mark. Some researchers also consider the colon and semicolon as sentence delimiters. In my earlier research, both these approaches were used (see Westin 1997: 16–17) and the results compared. Since the patterns of development for the two approaches proved to be almost identical, the present study includes only sentences ending in a full stop, an exclamation mark or a question mark. Excluding the colon and the semicolon as sentence delimiters makes some of the sentences, especially in the beginning of the century, very long, as, for example, (7) from the *Daily Telegraph*, 1920.

(7)   There was exaggeration, no doubt, in what was said of the activity of German propaganda throughout the world during the War-years and on the years preceding them; but the visible facts were quite remarkable enough, and of these none was more evident than the immense advantage to the enemy's Government of the presence in foreign countries of devoted and well-organised German communities, willing and prepared to serve the ends of their home Government, and upholding at all times the prestige, the interests, and the culture of their country. (DT20E17)

For the calculation of sentence length, the TSSA, a segmentation and sorting program, was used (see section 2.5.3). The number of sentences in text samples, each comprising the editorials representing one year and newspaper, were segmented and the words in them counted. With that information given, it was possible to calculate the average number of words per sentence for each decade and newspaper, for example, the *Daily Telegraph* of 1900, 1910, 1920 etc. To make it possible to see the general trend among English up-market editorials, the average number of words per sentence was also calculated for samples representing the three newspapers together. During the time-period studied, the average sentence length in English up-market editorials proved to have decreased by approximately 10 words, from 31.4 in 1900 to 20.9 in 1993 (see Table 4.9).

The patterns of development for the three newspapers show very little disagreement even though the figures attested for *The Times,* at most points of comparison, were higher, and those for the *Guardian* lower than those attested for the *Daily Telegraph*. In 1900, the average sentence length was the highest in the *Daily Telegraph* (34.8) and the lowest in the *Guardian* (28.4). The average sentence length attested for *The Times* was 31.0. In 1993, the *Guardian* figures were still the lowest (19.5), but the gap between this newspaper, on the one hand, and the other two, on the other, was reduced. No statistically significant difference between the newspapers was recorded, but the joint decrease across the years is consistent and statistically significant (see Figure 4.7; for statistics, see Appendix, s.v. sentence length).

Table 4.9 Sentence length: average number of words per sentence.

Year	Ti	DT	Gua	All
1900	31.0	34.8	28.4	31.4
1910	29.2	29.7	27.8	28.9
1920	26.8	27.8	26.0	26.9
1930	30.6	27.3	25.8	27.9
1940	29.3	25.6	25.0	26.8
1950	28.0	25.2	22.2	25.2
1960	24.8	22.3	24.8	23.9
1970	22.8	23.0	19.1	21.3
1980	25.8	21.3	22.0	23.2
1993	21.7	21.7	19.5	20.9
1900–1993	27.0	25.9	24.1	25.6

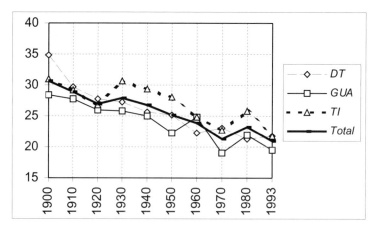

Figure 4.7 The development of sentence length: average number of words per sentence.

Not only sentence length but also sentence length distribution gives important information about a text. Using the information provided by the TSSA program, the sentences representing each decade were split into eight groups according to length (see Table 4.10).

Table 4.10 Distribution of the sentences over the years according to average length.

Year	1-10	%	11-20	%	21-30	%	31-40	%	41-50	%	51-60	%	61-70	%	70+	%	Sentence total
1900	95	5.7	380	22.7	465	27.7	341	20.3	213	12.7	97	5.8	49	2.9	37	2.2	1677
1910	263	12.6	465	22.2	521	24.9	379	18.1	238	11.4	119	5.7	60	2.9	45	2.2	2090
1920	313	14.4	514	23.7	537	24.8	408	18.8	217	10.0	118	5.4	37	1.7	23	1.1	2167
1930	234	13.0	419	23.3	458	25.4	326	18.1	200	11.1	89	4.9	44	2.4	31	1.7	1801
1940	168	9.9	442	26.2	491	29.1	320	18.9	157	9.3	71	4.2	18	1.1	22	1.3	1689
1950	219	12.2	516	28.7	509	28.4	313	17.4	144	8.0	62	3.5	17	0.9	15	0.8	1795
1960	234	13.9	489	29.1	499	29.7	285	17.0	121	7.2	35	2.1	12	0.7	6	0.4	1681
1970	390	16.6	860	36.7	632	27.0	312	13.3	111	4.7	30	1.3	7	0.3	3	0.1	2345
1980	337	14.6	761	33.0	631	27.4	354	15.4	144	6.3	57	2.5	13	0.6	7	0.3	2304
1993	387	16.6	874	37.6	658	28.3	283	12.2	96	4.1	18	0.8	9	0.4	1	0.0	2326
1900–1993	264	13.0	572	28.3	540	27.3	332	17.0	164	8.5	70	3.6	27	1.4	19	1.0	19875

From 1900 up to and including 1940, most of the sentences consisted of between 21 and 30 words. During the next few decades, sentences of 11 to 20 words and those of 21 to 30 words were approximately equally common. From 1970 on, most of the sentences fall within the interval 11 to 20 words per sentence. The shortest sentences, from 1 to 10 words, increased in number, from 5.7% in 1900 to 16.6% in 1993. The sentences consisting of 50 words or more were very rare in 1993.

Provided that there is a relation between sentence length and sentence complexity (see, for example, Klare 1963: 170), it is obvious that the complexity of the sentences in English upmarket newspaper editorials decreased considerably during the 20th century.

4.5.2 Subordination

The term *subordination* may refer to clauses which are immediate constituents of other clauses, often introduced by subordinating conjunctions, but it may also refer to clauses which are constituents of phrases, for example, relative clauses (see Quirk et al. 1985: 44–45). This section treats clauses introduced by subordinating conjunction only (for relative clauses, see section 8.2.1–8.2.3).

Due to its association with structural complexity, subordination has often been used in register comparison as a marker of written discourse (Biber 1988: 229).[14] However, some researchers, for example Poole and Field (1976) and

---

14 Co-ordination, which may also be used as a marker of sentence complexity (see for example Chafe and Danielewicz 1987: 103) was not included in the study since the tagger does not distinguish between co-ordinators as a linking device between clauses, such as *She likes*

Halliday (1987), found that subordination is more common in speech. Biber's study (1988: 106–107; 111–112) showed that different types of subordination are distributed differently. Causative subordination, for example, often proved to co-occur with features marking informal discourse (cf. section 3.4.5) while conditional subordinators and 'subordinators with multiple functions' (in Biber (1988) referred to as "other adverbial subordinators") were found to co-occur with features marking more formal discourse (cf. sections 6.3 and 7.5). Ljung (1997), who compared the frequencies of subordination in editorials, news articles, and sports articles in British and American newspapers, found most instances of the feature in news both in the British and the American papers, while the use differed as to the other two genres. In British English newspapers, subordination was more frequent in editorials than in sports while in American press the situation was reverse. In the British newspapers, at least, subordination thus seems to be associated with the more formal genres; in the American newspapers, the situation is more difficult to interpret.

All the lexical items assigned the tag #CS (subordinate conjunction) by the EngCG-2 tagger were included in the frequency counts.[15] A downward tendency was noticed from the very beginning of the century and a statistically significant decrease was attested between 1900 and 1993. The most noticeable decrease is that between 1960 and 1993. When the three newspapers were compared, a statistically significant difference was noticed between the *Daily Telegraph* and *The Times*, the frequencies for the *Telegraph* being considerably higher during most of the latter half of the period studied (see Table 4.11 and Figure 4.8; for statistics, see Appendix, s.v. subordination).

---

travelling and last year she went to Australia and between "lesser constituents" (see Quirk et al. 1985: 920–29) such as *She went to Australia and New Zealand.* According to Chafe and Danielewicz (1987: 101–103), these uses are distributed differently, and including all the instances of the feature would have led to results difficult to interpret. Manual screening was not within the scope of the present work, taking into consideration that there are 17,820 instances marked as co-ordinating conjunctions, and 12,327 instances of *and*, alone.

15   This means that causative subordination, conditional subordination, and 'subordinators with multiple functions' are also included in the frequency counts even though they are discussed in other contexts (see sections 3.4.5, 6.3 , and 7.5, respectively).

Table 4.11 Subordination: normed frequencies.

Year	Ti	DT	Gua	All
1900	23.84	22.45	24.56	24.02
1910	22.77	22.75	23.85	23.26
1920	21.34	23.28	23.42	22.63
1930	22.69	22.37	25.57	23.62
1940	21.15	21.17	23.14	21.87
1950	20.85	25.13	22.48	22.96
1960	21.10	24.80	23.60	23.31
1970	22.60	22.47	21.97	22.33
1980	21.31	24.01	18.77	21.51
1993	17.12	20.93	16.74	18.00
1900–1993	21.23	23.08	22.47	22.28

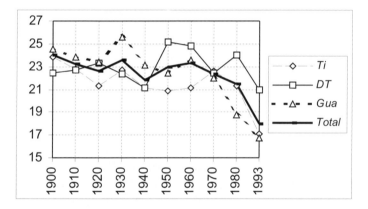

Figure 4.8 The development of subordination.

4.6   Summary and conclusions

The features included in this part of the study are divided into three groups, nouns and markers of noun phrase complexity (sections 4.2–4.3), markers of lexical diversity and specificity (section 4.4), and markers of sentence complexity (section 4.5).

Included in the first group are, besides nouns, attributive adjectives and adjectival items, present participle WHIZ-deletions, and prepositional phrases. The patterns of development for all these features, except for prepositional phrases, are strikingly alike: a noticeable increase is observed, especially during the last few decades of the period studied. Prepositional phrases, on the other hand, decreased in use, which may seem strange, as they, like attributive adjectives and present participle WHIZ-deletions, are used for the integration of information and the expansion of idea units. One reason for the development of these features in diverging directions is that prepositional phrases used as postmodifiers, to some extent at least, seem to have been replaced by premodifications in the form of, for example, *s*-genitives as well as nouns in the common case. The fact that postmodification by prepositions decreased in use, at the same time as genitives and premodifying nouns increased, supports this assumption. Another reason might be that it is mainly among prepositional phrases used as adverbials and/or verb complementation that the decrease took place. Despite the decrease of prepositions, it can therefore be argued that the language of English up-market editorials developed towards greater information density during the 20th century. The increase of the members of the second group, word length and type/token ratio, contributed to this development in so far as the vocabulary used became more specific and varied over the years.

The two members of the third group, sentence length and subordination, in the present study used as markers of sentence complexity, showed a development towards simpler sentence structure: the sentences became shorter and the use of subordination decreased. One of the reasons for the development towards shorter sentences is probably found in the reduced use of subordination. Fewer subordinate clauses ought to contribute to shorter sentences. Another reason is the reduction of relative clauses (see section 8.2).[16] The decrease of subordinate clauses introduced by subordinating conjunctions as well as of relative clauses, in turn, may be due to the increased structural elaboration of the noun phrase. By cramming the information that would otherwise have needed a full clause into a single noun phrase, the number of clauses is reduced and, thereby, the length of the sentence gets cut off. Consequently, it is possible for the editorial authors to give the same amount of information in a smaller space than would otherwise have been needed, which may be an advantage as the space at their disposal is limited. The increased use of shorter sentences may also be the result of an effort among the authors to make the language of the editorials more 'reader-friendly': shorter sentences with few subordinate clauses are normally easier to process than longer ones with many subordinations.

---

16   Yet another reason for the development towards shorter sentences is most likely the increased use of sentence fragments (or fragmentary sentences in Quirk et al.'s (1985: 838) terminology), which is obvious from the middle of the century on. Fragmentary sentences are sentences lacking constituents that are normally obligatory, in my data usually the verb together with one or more other constituents, such as "Apparently she insisted the book be published next week, after Blackpool. *Terribly sporting.*" (GUA93E24); "It is difficult not to conclude that the Milosevic option reflects wishful thinking. *Which brings us back to military intervention ...*" (DT93E8) (see Westin 1997, section 2.3.2). However, since it was beyond the scope of the present study to make any frequency counts of these sentences, no statistical evidence can be produced.

5.   Features marking 'narrative' discourse

5.1   Introduction

A general impression when one compares the editorials from the beginning of the century to those from the end is that the former seem more 'narrative' than the latter.[1] The authors of the editorials often appear to be 'telling a story' rather than trying to influence their readers. Many grammatical and text-linguistic features are generally at work as regards 'narrativeness'. Biber (1988), for example, found that features such as past tense verbs, perfect aspect verbs, third person pronouns, public verbs, *no*-negation and 'detached' present participle clauses often co-occur as markers of 'narrative' discourse.[2] These features were also chosen for the present study to verify a possible drift away from a more 'narrative' style in English up-market newspaper editorials.

To give an idea of the 'narrative' structure of the editorials at the beginning of the century, see example (1), an extract from the *Daily Telegraph*, April, 1900. Features representing 'narrative' discourse, that is, past tense verbs, perfect aspect verbs, third person pronouns, and public verbs, are italicized. No instances of *no*-negation and 'detached' present participle clauses are found in this paragraph.

(1)   *His* Royal Highness the Prince of Wales *has had* the most providential escape from assassination. As the train in which *he* and the Princess *were leaving* Brussels yesterday evening on *their* journey to Copenhagen *was*

---

1   Such a development, that is, away from a more narrative style, has been found also in other genres, as, for example, medical and science texts (see Biber and Finegan 1997) and debates (see Geisler forthcoming).

2   The term 'detached' is taken from Thompson (1983: 43), who explains the choice of the term by referring to Russian grammar, "where intonational criteria are used to distinguish 'detached' and 'nondetached' constituents." For the purpose of the English language, she suggests that "a working definition of 'detached clause' include the criteria of being set off by pauses, of exhibiting a clause-final falling intonation contour characteristic of independent clauses, or of being preceded by a clause ending with a clause-final falling contour. These intonation signals of detachment are virtually without exception marked by commas in writing." In my data, however, quite a few 'detached' participle clauses were found without being marked by commas (see, for example, (9) in section 5.4).

starting, a miscreant who by some unaccountable mischance *had been allowed* access to the platform *stepped* upon the foot board of the carriage and *fired* two shots at the Prince at point-blank range. Mercifully the nerve of these ruffians does not always correspond with *their* wickedness, and, impossible as it seems in the circumstances, both shots *missed their* intended victim. The wretched youth – whose name is Jean Baptiste Sipido – *was* promptly *knocked* down and *secured*, and *their* Royal Highnesses, who *displayed* the traditional intrepidity which at all times commands respectful admiration, *proceeded* at once upon *their* journey. It is stated that the pockets of this youth – *his* age is given as sixteen – *were stuffed* with the usual Anarchist trash written by men who invite the uneducated and half-witted to commit outrages which *they themselves* dare not attempt. Responsibility of the heaviest kind rests upon authorities which permit this pernicious literature to be circulated with impunity. (DT00E5)

The features chosen to support my hypothesis about a drift towards a more 'non-narrative' style in up-market newspaper editorials were found to be no homogeneous group as to change or continuity. A statistically significant decrease was attested for past tense verbs and *no*-negation while no statistically significant difference was observed as regards 'detached' present participle clauses, perfect aspect verbs, public verbs, and third person pronouns when the frequencies from the beginning of the century were compared to those from the end (see Table 5.1). In the following, I first discuss the features showing statistically significant change across time, then those showing linguistic continuity. Finally, some conclusions are drawn from the results obtained.

Table 5.1 The development of features linked with 'narrative' discourse.

Statistically significant increase over time	Statistically significant decrease over time	Linguistic continuity
(No features)	Past tense verbs *No*-negation	'Detached' present participle clauses [a] Perfect aspect verbs Public verbs Third person pronouns

[a] The pattern of development for 'detached' present participle clauses is irregular and difficult to interpret. A statistically significant increase between 1970 and 1993 is worth observing, however.

5.2   Past tense verbs

Past tense verbs are usually considered the primary surface marker of 'narrative' discourse (Biber 1988: 223). As the term suggests, past tense verbs are used with reference to past events. However, they can also refer to present and future time (Quirk et al. 1985: 183–188). They can be used as an alternative to present tense forms in indirect speech or indirect thought, when the past tense verb in the reporting clause 'infects' the tense of the verb in the subordinate clause as in *Did you say you have/had no money?* They can also be used as a more polite variant of the present tense in sentences such as *I wonder/wondered if you could help us*, the so called "attitudinal past" (Quirk et al. 1985: 188). Finally, the past tense is used in certain hypothetical clauses, especially *if*-clauses, to express a hypothetical thought, as in example (2).

(2)   *If the British territories north of the Zambezi were overrun* the enemy could bomb Pretoria and Johannesburg in a couple of hours' flying. (TI40E23)

In the editorials, the past tense verbs refer either to past events or to hypothetical conditions. The other two meanings could hardly be expected in my material due to the discourse situation in question. By way of an example, see (3), the first paragraph of an editorial in *The Times*, April 3, 1930, with a frequent use of verbs referring to past events.[3]

(3)   It is a safe assumption that very few of his fellow-countrymen know the name of HENRY HILL HICKMAN. But his name ought to be known, because as LORD DAWSON of PENN *pointed out* last night, he is the man who first *offered* anaesthesia to the surgeons. They *refused* his offers both here and in France, and he *died* a century ago, at the age of twenty-nine, possibly of a broken heart. He *came* of West Country stock, like his contemporary JENNER, and *was*, like JENNER, a general practitioner. He *worked* in the town of Ludlow and *left* it only to proclaim his discovery to the world. That discovery *included* the uses as anaesthetics of carbonic acid gas and nitrous oxide ("laughing") gas. HICKMAN, however, had not ventured to administer his anaesthetics to human beings; his observations *were carried out* on animals. Dogs and cats in Ludlow *received* painless surgical treatment at his hand, and *made* excellent recoveries from operations to which men and women *were compelled* to submit in full sensitiveness. The modest proposal which he *brought* to London in the third decade of the nineteenth century, and eventually, when London *displayed* no interest, *took* to Paris, *was* that measures which had proved so beneficial to animals *might be given* a trial in the case of human beings by the leaders of his profession. (TI30E14)

---

3   This is the editorial with the highest normed frequency of past tense verbs in my material. The reason for choosing this and other extracts with large frequencies of a feature is that example extracts with lower frequencies would have been rather long and still probably only have illustrated one or two instances of the feature in question.

The automatic search of past tense verbs was followed by manual screening of duplicates.[4] Even though the lines of development for the three newspapers are somewhat irregular and divergent, a downward tendency is noticed, and a statistically significant decrease, between 1900 and 1970, was recorded for the newspapers together (see Figure 5.1 and Table 5.2; for statistics, see Appendix, s.v. past tense verbs). During that period, the normed frequencies dropped from 20.57 to 14.37. After 1970 no statistically significant variation was attested. When the three newspapers were compared, a marginally statistically significant difference between the *Daily Telegraph* and the *Guardian* was observed. From 1940 on, except in 1980, the normed frequencies for the *Guardian* were considerably higher, which gives an indication that, during the latter part of the century, the language of the *Guardian* was more 'narrative' than that of the *Daily Telegraph*. No statistically significant difference between *The Times* and the other two newspapers was observed.

It can thus be confirmed that past tense verbs, one of the foremost surface markers of 'narrative' discourse, were more frequent in English up-market newspaper editorials in 1900 than they were towards the end of the century. Consequently, if only past tense verbs were taken into consideration, the results would point to a decrease as regards 'narrativeness' in English up-market editorials during the 20th century.

Table 5.2 Past tense verbs: normed frequencies.

Year	Ti	DT	Gua	All
1900	16.31	16.60	23.84	20.57
1910	14.96	17.15	17.02	16.46
1920	13.95	19.37	14.66	15.68
1930	22.04	19.56	15.00	18.51
1940	18.59	15.49	20.95	18.33
1950	15.24	13.28	17.98	15.32
1960	17.81	11.37	16.29	14.83
1970	15.91	12.83	14.49	14.37
1980	15.70	17.09	15.90	16.28
1993	16.42	10.62	18.51	15.59
1900–1993	16.58	15.15	17.51	16.45

4   The words given duplicate tags or more, including #PAST, were edited by hand, to distinguish the past tense forms from ambiguous forms, such as the infinitive and past participle of irregular verbs, for example *hit*. For further information as to the need for manual editing, see section 2.5.2.

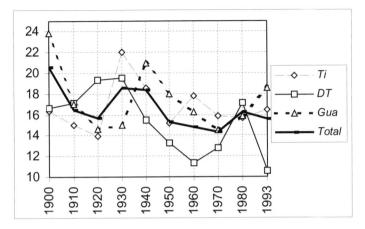

Figure 5.1 The development of past tense verbs.

5.3   *No*-negation

As mentioned in 3.2.2, it is possible to make a distinction between two morphosyntactic variants of negation (see Tottie 1991: 87–88): *no*-negation (synthetic negation) as in *They can do <u>nothing</u> about it*, and *not*-negation (analytic negation), as in *They can<u>not</u> do <u>anything</u> about it*. *No*-negation comprises the determiner *no* as well as the pronouns *nobody, none, neither, nothing*, and the adverbs *never* and *nowhere*. *Not*-negation includes the negative adverb *not* plus an indefinite element such as *a, any, anybody, one, ever, either* (Tottie 1991: 106; 1988: 245–246). In the choice between *no*-negation and *not*-negation, Tottie found that *no*-negation was preferred in more literary contexts (1988: 245–265; 1991: 139–188).

    No-negation as a 'narrative' feature is more difficult to explain than, for example, past tense verbs and third person pronouns. According to Biber (1988: 109), one reason why the feature frequently appears together with other 'narrative' features is "a high frequency of denials and rejections in the reported reasoning process of narrative participants." This can, of course, also be applicable to newspaper editorials even though *no*-negations, in my data, are used in one-way communication, as in example (4).

(4)   The latest news confirms the early impression that the Polish and Bolshevik forces are evenly balanced and that *no early end* to the struggle is to be expected. On the southern front, where Kieff may be regarded as the kernel of the contest, there is *no change*, nor will be any until the Bolsheviks have recreated their front, which will take a considerable time. On the northern section the Poles have just reacted strongly against the first successful Bolshevik attack. The Bolshevik success *was never*

sweeping or decisive even in the limited northern area, and the Poles had sufficient reserves available to win back part. (GUA20E27)

In order to obtain a sample containing only instances where one type of negation could be substituted for the other, the negations were edited by hand (see section 3.2.2, examples (7) and (7a)). A statistically significant change was observed between 1920 and 1970, when the normed frequency for the whole sample decreased from 3.39 to 2.03. The increase that followed is statistically non-significant (see Table 5.3 and Figure 5.2; for statistics, see Appendix, s.v *no-*negation). No statistically significant difference between the three newspapers was noticed.

Table 5.3 *No*-negation: normed frequencies.

Year	Ti	DT	Gua	All
1900	2.64	2.77	3.20	2.97
1910	2.62	2.72	2.50	2.59
1920	2.61	3.35	4.18	3.39
1930	3.28	3.06	1.83	2.67
1940	2.66	2.81	2.90	2.80
1950	2.46	2.92	2.85	2.75
1960	1.85	2.34	2.16	2.14
1970	1.91	1.50	2.61	2.03
1980	1.64	2.81	2.20	2.26
1993	2.16	2.23	2.37	2.25
1900–1993	2.33	2.62	2.69	2.56

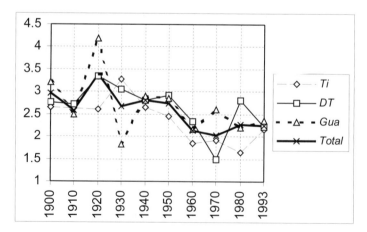

Figure 5.2 The development of *no*-negation.

The decrease in the use of *no*-negation thus follows that of past tense verbs closely (cf. section 5.2), which supports the hypothesis that English newspaper editorials became less 'narrative' over the years.

5.4 'Detached' present participle clauses

In this study a distinction is made between present participle forms, such as (5) and (6), and past participle forms, such as (7) and (8), on the one hand, and between 'detached' (adverbial) participle clauses, as in (5) and (7) and participle clauses functioning as reduced relative clauses, so called WHIZ-deletions as in (6) and (8), on the other.[5] Only 'detached' present participle clauses are dealt with in the present chapter since they alone are considered as markers of 'narrative' discourse in Biber's study (1988: 102).[6]

(5)   *Addressing a nervous people* over the heads of a boisterous, whipped-up crowd, he told them that they were going to war "against the plutocratic and reactionary Democracies of the West". (TI40E22)

(6)   The reconnaissance seems to have been conducted by three bodies *working together on parallel lines*. (TI00E1)

(7)   That is almost certainly the case: and the President has tried to rub it in through his departing days. *Released of the burden of needing to do anything at home*, he has turned his eyes outwards again. (GUA93E2)

(8)   Mr. Stanley wisely gave no total figure yesterday of men under arms; but he did indicate that the strength of the B.E.F. has been practically doubled since last October, and that the figure of volunteers *enlisted since the outbreak of war* (apart from the younger men called up in age groups) had now reached 200,000. (TI40E11)

A 'detached' participle clause may or may not be introduced by a subordinator such as *though, when,* and *while* (see examples (9) – (12)).[7] In my data *while* is the most common subordinator.

---

5   The term 'detached' is explained in note 1. Quirk et al. (1985: 993-994; 1263-1265) refer to 'detached' participle clauses simply as *-ed* and *-ing* participle clauses and to 'WHIZ-deletions' as postmodifying *-ed* and *-ing* participle clauses. O'Donnell (1974), among others, uses the term "adverbial clauses" for 'detached' participle clauses.

6   Present participle WHIZ-deletion is dealt with in Chapter 4 as a marker of information density and past participle clauses, detached as well as WHIZ-deletions, are dealt with in Chapter 7 as markers of abstract discourse (cf. also Biber 1988: 103).

7   Cf. Bäcklund (1986).

(9)   *Turning round in search of security and friends* they have come to feel more urgently their cultural and economic ties with Western Europe ... (GUA50E17)

(10)   The Reservist, *though no longer serving with the colours*, is still a soldier and still subject to military law and discipline. (TI00E3)

(11)   The reflection that our taste for fresh air may, after all, be less due to our own superiority than to that of our climate is not an unwholesome one for English people, especially *when travelling abroad*. (TI10E3)

(12)   *While signalling one step forward in the NHS*, the Government is having to take one step back from its plans for school league tables and the national curriculum. (DT93E16)

Participle clauses are generally associated with a high degree of integration of information or with structural elaboration and are therefore more often found in writing than in speech (see, for example, Carrol 1960, O'Donnell 1974, Thompson 1983, Chafe 1982, Chafe 1985, Chafe and Danielewicz 1987, Bäcklund 1986, and Greenbaum 1988). However, they have also been found to co-occur with 'narrative' features (Biber 1988: 109). Thompson (1983) maintains that 'detached' participle clauses serve as "local" background for the main clause with which they are connected. Furthermore, she associates the use of 'detached' participle clauses with image-evoking, "depictive", discourse. In her study she shows, for example, that there are more than twelve times as many 'detached' clauses per 10,000 words in a novel by Pearl Buck as there are in a text on pharmacology (pp. 50–55).

The 'detached' present participle clauses were edited by hand so as to exclude forms having other functions, such as

-    reduced relative clauses (WHIZ-deletions): "... the rival forces *working within the Socialist party* ..." (DT30E2)
-    verb complements: "An imaginative writer ... claimed to have *seen Otto Skorzeny himself standing* ..." (TI50E16)
-    prepositional complements: "Planning can go ahead *without our resources being thrown into the pool*." (GUA50E23)
-    nouns: "Saving paper is no mere *paper saving*." (DT40E5)
-    premodifiers: "... the price of the tabloids can affect the *pricing* policy ..." (TI70E14)
-    the progressive: "... he *is being* extravagantly funny ..." (DT20E16)

The graphs visualizing the development of the feature across decades show a zig-zag pattern, the lines representing the three newspapers following each other closely. Statistically significant differences were observed between 1910 and

1993, 1920 and 1993, 1950 and 1993, and between 1970 and 1993 (see Table 5.4 and Figure 5.3; for statistics, see Appendix, s.v. 'detached' present participle clauses).

Table 5.4 'Detached' present participle clauses: normed frequencies.

Year	Ti	DT	Gua	All
1900	1.09	1.67	1.03	1.15
1910	0.72	0.80	0.46	0.62
1920	0.32	1.02	0.57	0.60
1930	0.95	0.93	1.13	1.01
1940	1.24	0.88	1.46	1.19
1950	1.00	0.61	0.39	0.67
1960	1.36	1.29	0.87	1.18
1970	0.48	1.06	0.48	0.67
1980	1.01	1.31	0.95	1.10
1993	1.45	1.69	1.43	1.51
1900–1993	0.96	1.09	0.88	0.97

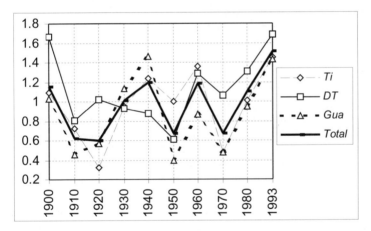

Figure 5.3 The development of 'detached' present participle clauses.

The irregular pattern of development and the fact that no statistically significant difference was attested when the normed frequencies for 1900 and 1993 were compared makes it difficult to draw any safe conclusions about change or continuity. The increase between 1970 and 1993, which was the most noticeable change over the period, needs some attention, however. This increase coincides with statistically significant increases attested for 'detached' past participle clauses (see section 7.3.1) and present participle WHIZ-deletion (section 4.3.3), which suggests that 'detached' present participle clauses have more in common with these two features than with the markers of 'narrative' discourse dealt with in 5.2 and 5.3 (past tense verbs and *no*-negation). Since participle clauses are normally associated with the integration of information and structural elaboration (see above), it is, therefore, reasonable to assume that, in English up-market editorials, 'detached' present participle clauses, are markers of information density rather than of narrativity.

5.5   Perfect aspect verbs

Perfect aspect verb forms normally refer to actions in the past. The present perfect indicates that the action has continued up to the present time and may even continue into the future, as opposed to the simple past which usually indicates that the action is finished. The past perfect has the meaning of "past in the past", and can be regarded as "an anterior version either of the present perfective or of the simple past" (Quirk et al. 1985: 190–196). Perfect aspect verbs have been observed often to co-occur with past tense verbs and third person pronouns as markers of 'narrative' and descriptive discourse, but they have also been associated with certain kinds of academic writing (Biber 1986: 384–414). In this context, however, it is primarily as markers of 'narrative' discourse that they are interesting. By way of example, see (13), an extract from the editorial with the highest frequency of perfect aspect verb forms in my data (for the reason why an example with a very high frequency of the feature is chosen, see note 2).

(13)   Despite the uncompromising attitude of Mr Bonar Law in the House of Commons on Tuesday, the Government *have,* it seems, *wisely decided* to release the hunger-strikers in Mountjoy Gaol. *Had the Government persisted* in their original intention, we have no doubt that a situation of the utmost gravity *must have arisen* in Ireland. In the hush of a general strike the mind of an imaginative people *would have become obsessed* by the drama within the prison walls. Suspense *must have grown* increasingly acute; and if the first fatal news came, only to be followed by that of successive deaths, the depths of national feeling *would have been stirred.* Dubliners *have not forgotten* the cumulative strain of the series of executions which followed the Easter rising of 1916. Few who know Ireland well *have not bitterly regretted* the unwise policy … (TI20E18)

The frequency counts include all the past and present perfect forms shown in Table 5.5. The most frequent forms in my data are the present perfect forms, which appear more than six times as often as the past perfect forms.

Table 5.5 Perfect aspect verbs.

		FINITE	NON-FINITE	
		Infinitive	Present perfect	Past perfect
Active	Simple	*to have tried*	*have/has tried*	*had tried*
	Progressive	*to have been trying*	*have/has been trying*	*had been trying*
Passive	Simple	*to have been tried*	*have/has been tried*	*had been tried*
	Progressive	*to have been being tried*	*have/has been being tried*	*had been being tried*

The perfect aspect verbs were edited by hand to exclude ambiguous forms, such as past tense verbs and infinitives of irregular verbs, for example *put*.[8] Even though the scores point to a decrease in use, no statistically significant change was observed (see Table 5.6 and Figure 5.4; for statistics, see Appendix, s.v. perfect aspect verbs). Nor were any statistically significant differences attested between the three newspapers.

One reason why the use of perfect aspect verbs in my material did not change much during the period studied is the fact that it has always been, and still is, in the nature of editorials to report on past events "with current relevance" (Quirk et al. 1985: 190). As mentioned above, the forms used for this purpose, that is, the present perfect forms, are by far the most frequent of the perfect aspect forms in my data. Consequently, as long as the editorials continue to report on past events "with current relevance" the use of perfect aspect verbs will probably remain similar.

Table 5.6 Perfect aspect verbs: normed frequencies.

Year	Ti	DT	Gua	All
1900	13.71	16.23	12.29	13.32
1910	11.50	13.47	11.47	11.99
1920	13.79	11.52	13.44	13.04
1930	11.74	12.15	10.31	11.38
1940	11.90	12.67	12.21	12.29
1950	10.99	12.04	10.89	11.36
1960	10.69	12.77	12.28	11.99
1970	11.08	8.97	14.00	11.43
1980	12.15	11.95	10.24	11.47
1993	11.56	12.31	9.77	11.14
1900–1993	11.88	12.05	11.76	11.89

---

8   For further information on manual editing, see section 2.5.2.

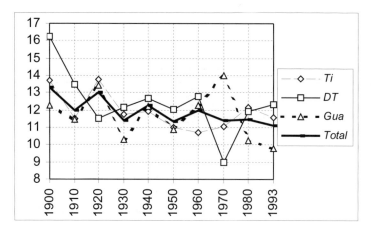

Figure 5.4 The development of perfect aspect verbs.

5.6   Public verbs

Public verbs, a subdivision of factual verbs, also referred to as "reporting verbs" (see, for example, Alexander 1988: 286–288) are speech act verbs normally introducing indirect statements (see Quirk et al. 1985: 1180–1182). This makes them a prominent feature not only in narratives (see, for example, Hue 1984: 601) but also in the kind of 'narrative' discourse that does not only tell a story but retells something that has actually happened or reports on events. It is in this capacity that they are normally used in newspaper editorials. For example, see (14), the beginning of an editorial in the *Guardian*, February 13, 1900, in which we find one of the highest normed frequencies of public verbs in my material.

(14)   Lord Salisbury, speaking at the Guildhall three months ago, *explained* that by the Samoa agreement we gave Germany what was useless to us and took what we thought useful. Count von Bülow, *explaining* the Treaty to the Reichstag yesterday, *argued* with equal cogency that Germany gained very substantial advantages and made us concessions which were either nominal, as at Tonga and Zanzibar, or worthless, as in the Solomon Islands and Northern Togoland. The German Foreign Minister *declared* that he had had no desire to overreach us ... (GUA00E14)

The public verbs used for the frequency count (54 all in all) were taken from Quirk et al. (1985: 1180–81), and include, among others: *acknowledge, admit, agree, argue, assert, claim, comment, complain, confess, declare, deny, explain, hint, insist, mention, proclaim, promise, protest, remark, reply, report, say, suggest,* and *write.*[9] Ambiguous forms, such as *hint, promise,* and *protest,* which can also be nouns, were edited by hand.

Even though the individual newspapers showed diverging and irregular patterns of development in the use of public verbs, no statistically significant changes were observed over the decades for the newspapers together. Nor were there any statistically significant differences between the three newspapers (see Table 5.7 and Figure 5.5; for statistics, see Appendix, s.v. public verbs).

Table 5.7 Public verbs: normed frequencies.

Year	Ti	DT	Gua	All
1900	6.72	5.01	5.32	5.66
1910	5.18	5.65	5.65	5.51
1920	4.61	6.40	4.69	5.13
1930	5.60	5.99	5.14	5.58
1940	4.13	6.92	5.55	5.63
1950	4.75	5.90	5.74	5.48
1960	4.89	4.00	6.16	4.93
1970	5.73	4.35	7.08	5.76
1980	5.03	7.58	6.41	6.42
1993	5.87	5.92	6.70	6.17
1900–1993	5.23	5.79	5.85	5.64

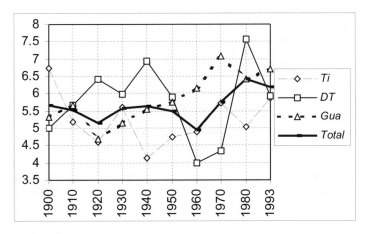

Figure 5.5 The development of public verbs.

However, as we can see from (14), which is a good example of public verb usage in up-market newspaper editorials, these verbs are not primarily markers of

---

9   No instances of *confide* were found in my data.

'narrative' discourse (compare examples (1) in section 5.1 and (3) in section 5.2) but rather of reporting. The reporting function of newspaper editorials did not change during the time-period studied. Thus the use of public verbs also remained stable over the years.

5.7   Third person pronouns

Third person pronouns are used with reference to people, and in the plural also to 'inanimates', outside the direct discourse situation and, because of that, they frequently occur in 'narrative' discourse (see, for example, Hu (1984: 598).[10] Biber (1986: 384–414) showed that they often co-occur with past tense verbs and perfect aspect verbs as markers of 'narrative' discourse.

All the instances of *he, she, they, him, her(s), them, his, their(s), himself, herself,* and *themselves* were included in the frequency count.[11] The editorial where we find the highest frequency of third person pronouns in my data, is reproduced in its entirety in example (15).

(15)   In this free country a man can call *himself* by whatever name *he* pleases. Whether *his* neighbours think *his* reasons for a change respectable or honourable is beside the point. So, if *they* please, the Conservatives can call *their* candidates Liberal-Conservative. *Their* only intent is to deceive, and most people realise this. It is, however, interesting to see that the National Liberals are now on *their* last lap. *They* are giving up the pretence of being an independent party and are admitting that *they* are Conservatives, with merely a hyphenated qualification. Since there will be so many genuine Liberal candidates at the election the voters are not likely to be misled. But *they* will be bound to reflect on the curiosity that a party so superficially powerful as the Conservative has to descend to tricks of name. (GUA50E3)

A downward tendency was noticed in the use of third person pronouns, but no statistically significant variation was observed between the decades. When the feature was compared across newspapers, a statistically significant difference was noticed between *The Times* and the *Guardian*. The *Guardian* scores are considerably lower most of the time (see Table 5.8 and Figure 5.6; for statistics, see Appendix, s.v. third person pronouns).

---

10   The pronoun *it* is not included in the group of third person pronouns but is dealt with separately in section 3.3.4.

11   No distinction is thus made between the pronoun function and the determiner function of the feature.

Table 5.8 Third person pronouns: normed frequencies.

Year	Ti	DT	Gua	All
1900	27.75	25.12	21.38	23.77
1910	33.51	24.48	19.48	24.76
1920	23.09	22.78	17.05	20.81
1930	26.74	20.19	20.47	21.91
1940	25.12	20.41	25.33	23.51
1950	25.68	23.66	21.53	23.67
1960	20.24	16.27	19.75	18.54
1970	20.69	21.78	21.90	21.49
1980	19.36	25.34	16.88	20.79
1993	19.52	19.44	20.91	19.98
1900–1993	23.43	21.56	20.50	21.75

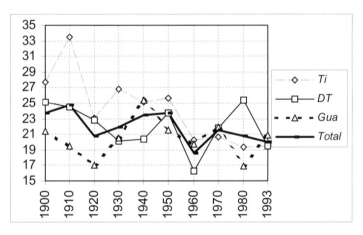

Figure 5.6 The development of third persons pronouns.

5.8   Summary and conclusions

Only two of the surface markers of 'narrative' discourse, that is, past tense verbs and *no*-negation, thus showed a statistically significant decrease in use over the years. The remaining features, 'detached' present participle clauses, perfect aspect verbs, public verbs, and third person pronouns represent linguistic continuity. Still, we can assume that there has been a drift in the language of English up-market newspaper editorials away from a more 'narrative' style since past tense verbs, the primary surface marker of 'narrative' discourse (see Biber 1988: 224), together with *no*-negation, decreased in use during the period (cf. Biber and Finegan 1997 and Geisler forthcoming).

The fact that 'detached' present participle clauses did not follow the pattern of development for past tense verbs and *no*-negation, gives an indication that their function in newspaper editorials is not to signal 'narrativeness' in the first place. Since many researchers (see section 5.4) are of the opinion that participle clauses are, rather, markers of information density and structural elaboration, it is more reasonable to assume that it is in that capacity that we meet them in the editorials (cf. the development of 'detached' past participle clauses, section 7.3.1, and present participle WHIZ-deletion, section 4.3.3).

The linguistic stability that marks perfect aspect verbs and public verbs, can be explained by the nature of editorials as a genre. As certain linguistic features carry important basic functions in different genres, it is unlikely that these features will change much across time.[12] In newspaper editorials, perfect aspect verbs and public verbs carry such basic functions. As far as perfect aspect verbs are concerned, they are usually employed to describe past events "with current relevance" (see section 5.5). Public verbs are used to report rather than narrate. The task of reporting, on the one hand, and of reporting on past events with "current relevance" on the other, is still the same as it was in the beginning of the 20th century. Consequently, no variation in the use of the two features is to be expected. The stability in the use of third person pronouns is probably also related to the reporting function of the editorials. On the basis of these observations, we can assume that, during the 20th century, a drift away from a more 'narrative' style took place in English up-market newspaper editorials while the reporting function remained more or less the same over the years.

---

12   Compare, for example, dialogue in fiction and in drama, which has changed very little since the 17th century, with respect to features representing the Elaborated/Situated Reference Dimension and the Abstract Style Dimension (Biber and Finegan 1992: 698-699). Similar data are found in Geisler (forthcoming).

6. Features marking argumentative discourse

6.1 Introduction

The main purpose of editorials is to contribute to the moulding of public opinion on current affairs. Therefore, they ought to have an argumentative structure. The authors do not need only factual evidence to support their arguments. They also need linguistic means to serve the factual evidence in as convincing a way as possible. Among such means are 'predictive' modals (see example (1)), 'necessity' modals (examples (2) and (3)), suasive verbs (example (4)), and conditional subordination (example (5)).[1]

(1) One way is to tell him that the effort _will not really exhaust him_, and that his success is certain. The other is to tell him that the effort _will tax all his strength_ and willpower, and that success _will demand severe sacrifices_. Those who use the first method are anxious to save the man or the society from anything like shock. (GUA40E1)

(2) The first priority _must now be to persuade_ those nuclear armed parts of the former Soviet Union Ukraine, Kazakhstan and Belarus – to destroy their strategic weapons and become non-nuclear parties to the Non-Proliferation Treaty. At the same time, pressure _must be maintained_... (DT93E1)

(3) Differences of opinion arise not as to the end but only as to the adequacy of the means. They can and _should be voiced_ in a manner inspired solely by a solicitude for the efficacy of our action. (DT50E23)

---

1   The term 'predictive' modals corresponds to modals of volition and prediction together in Quirk et al.'s terminology and 'necessity' modals to modals of obligation and necessity (Quirk et al. 1985: 221). Suasive verbs are verbs suggesting persuasion, such as _demand_ and _insist_.

(4)   Nor would government surrender pave the way to a modus vivendi with the T U C leaders. For they *are demanding* that government should ignore all rational economic considerations and allocate more to everyone in return for less. (DT80E1)

(5)   *If there is deep disagreement between Mr Lamont and Mr Major,* therefore, the Chancellor should go at once. Nothing could be served by his continuing in office and having his views countermanded by his boss. (TI93E3)

According to Biber (1988: 111), infinitives can also serve as markers of persuasion, as they often co-occur with attitudinal adjectives or finite verbs as in examples (6) and (7).[2]

(6)   The clergy accepted this Act without protest, since they were *reluctant to give* any cause for the least suspicion that they were war profiteers ... (TI20E10)

(7)   We Liberals *prefer to look* to the stability of the people. (TI80E32)

Together, these features, which were all included in my study, give the text an argumentative structure, either by marking the author's own persuasion or by building up an argumentative discourse to persuade the reader (Biber 1988: 111).

Below, I first discuss infinitives, the only feature that clearly showed a statistically significant change over time, then those which showed no significant change (see Table 6.1).

Table 6.1 The development of features linked with argumentative production.

Statistically significant Increase over time	*Statistically significant decrease over time*	*Linguistic continuity*
Infinitives	(No features)	Conditional subordination[a] Suasive verbs 'Predictive' modals 'Necessity' modals

[a] Conditional subordination showed an irregular pattern of development: an increase between 1940 and 1960 is followed by an equally substantial decrease between 1960 and 1993, which makes the frequencies attested for the beginning and the end of the century almost the identical.

---

2   Cf., for example, Kiparsky and Kiparsky (1970: 143–173), who maintain that the use of infinitives as adjective and verb complementation is restricted to non-factive predicates and Perkins (1983: 66–71), who gives an account of the meaning of modal infinitives.

6.2   Infinitives

Infinitives have a wide range of discourse functions: "... in addition to reporting speech and cognitive states, they are commonly used to report intentions, desires, efforts, perceptual states, and various other general actions" (Biber et al. 1999: 693). Greenbaum (1988: 4–5) showed that they are a useful device for syntactic compression and are, therefore, more frequent in written than in spoken discourse (see also, for example, Beaman 1984: 64 and Biber et al. 1999: 699).[3] Allerton (1988: 11–20) noticed an overuse of infinitives, "infinitivitis", in written language as well as in formal spoken language. In his opinion, this 'overuse' is due to the fact that the infinitive is chosen in cases where an "unaffected speaker" would have chosen the gerund (*For John to wash the dishes* as compared to *John's washing the dishes* (1988: 11).[4] Biber (1988: 111) states that infinitives, even though they may have other functions (cf. Biber et al. 1999, quoted above), are most frequently used in verb and adjective complementation, as in examples (8) and (9).[5]

(8)   Only by unity can we *hope to survive* and unity begins on the domestic front. (DT50E23)

(9)   It is *satisfactory to be able to add* that in another sphere of the War ... (DT00E1)

Since the head verb or adjective in such constructions often encodes the speaker's or writer's attitude, Biber (1988) found it reasonable to include infinitives among the markers of argumentative discourse.

Between 1920 and 1960, a statistically significant increase in the use of the feature was attested for the newspapers together. The normed frequencies went up from 38.69 in 1920 to 45.58 in 1960. The decrease that followed is non-significant. No statistically significant variation was observed between the three newspapers (see Table 6.2and Figure 6.1; for statistics, see Appendix, s.v. infinitives).

---

3   This is the view commonly held, even though results to prove the opposite, that is, that infinitives are more frequently used in speech, have been put forward (see, for example, O'Donnell 1974: 108).

4   In American English this 'overuse' of infinitives is also found in *informal* spoken language (Allerton 1988: 11).

5   The results shown in Biber et al. 1999 support this statement: infinitives are most frequently used as verb complementation, second most frequent as adjective complementation (1999: 723).

Table 6.2 Infinitives: normed frequencies.

Year	Ti	DT	Gua	All
1900	46.08	35.43	42.25	42.22
1910	40.07	36.97	42.14	40.24
1920	38.78	37.50	39.48	38.69
1930	39.09	36.73	43.41	39.76
1940	39.96	41.49	38.62	40.03
1950	40.46	39.58	44.32	41.28
1960	41.47	48.47	45.97	45.58
1970	45.25	41.89	45.65	44.27
1980	44.07	42.94	45.28	44.03
1993	44.84	44.32	38.88	42.64
1900–1993	42.11	41.18	42.61	41.99

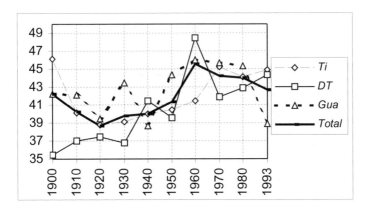

Figure 6.1 The development of infinitives.

Provided Biber's above statement regarding infinitives is correct, English newspaper editorials became more persuasive across the years, at least from 1920 on, in so far as the authors' stance to what is said is more readily shown.

6.3   Conditional subordination

Due to their grammatical structure, conditional sentences are well suited for argumentative discourse: if X happens, (then) Y follows. In the subclause we find the condition that has to be fulfilled before what is stipulated in the main clause can happen. The condition may be either open or hypothetical (Quirk et al.

1985:1087–1092). An open condition leaves open the question if the condition is fulfilled or not, as in example (10).

(10)   It is a doubt large enough to imperil the whole, costly operation. *If it has to be postponed* the Apollo 13 flight cannot be launched again until May 10. (GUA70E13)

A hypothetical condition "conveys the speaker's belief that the condition will not be fulfilled (for future conditions), is not fulfilled (for present conditions), or was not fulfilled (for past conditions) " (Quirk et al. 1985: 1091), as in examples (11–13).

(11)   The gaols are all bursting with delinquents, and many visitors would in any case misunderstand our motives *if we tried to accommodate them in cells.* (TI50E8)

(12)   *If they were aware of the truth* the Patriarchs would assuredly share the resentment expressed by the T.U.C. in a recent circular … (DT50E20)

(13)   *If Mr Khrushchev had really decided to return to Stalinism*, he would surely have returned to that dogma. (GUA60E25)

If and its negative counterpart, *unless,* are the most common conditional subordinators. Others, not so frequently used include, for example, *as long as, in case, on condition* (*that*) and *provided* (*that*). Even conjunctions which we usually regard as temporal, such as *when, whenever,* and *once* can be used to express condition. In the present study, only *if* and *unless* are taken into consideration. Besides introducing full conditional clauses, such as examples (10)–(13) above, they are also used in non-finite clauses, such as examples (14) and (15).

(14)   Such an action (and, as we have said, if report speaks true, these things occur daily in India) is not only a piece of grossly offensive bad manners; it is criminal folly which *if persisted in,* and indeed *if not sternly and immediately checked,* may help to put in peril our Indian dominion. (GUA10E12)

(15)   The present level of taxation, in the words of the President of the Federation of British industries, threatens industry "with a depletion of capital which, *unless corrected*, must make expansion difficult and even prejudice the maintenance of current production". (DT50E9)

The instances of *if* were edited by hand so as to exclude others than conditional subordinators, for example the interrogative *if* in indirect questions. The lines of development observed for conditional subordination showed an irregular and diverging pattern (see Figure 6.2). When the normed frequencies recorded for the newspapers, as a group, are compared, we first notice a statistically significant increase between 1940 and 1960, when the normed frequencies rose from 2.47 to 4.04, then a statistically significant decrease between 1960 and 1993, when the frequencies sank again to 2.53 (see Table 6.3; for statistics, see Appendix, s.v. conditional subordination). Since the increase was followed by a decrease of approximately the same size, no statistically significant difference was attested when the frequencies for 1900 and 1993 were compared, which makes it difficult to draw any conclusions about a possible change in the use of the feature during the period studied.

Table 6.3 Conditional subordination: normed frequencies of *if* and *unless*.

Year	Ti	DT	Gua	All
1900	2.04	1.87	3.37	2.76
1910	1.79	2.50	3.82	2.90
1920	2.77	1.87	3.86	2.92
1930	3.50	2.66	3.49	3.17
1940	2.74	2.10	2.63	2.47
1950	3.39	2.00	2.89	2.71
1960	2.82	5.00	4.04	4.04
1970	3.29	2.63	3.39	3.11
1980	2.74	3.77	3.49	3.36
1993	2.28	2.82	2.58	2.53
1900–1993	2.78	2.86	3.36	3.02

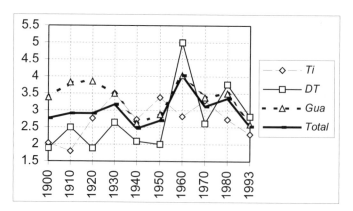

Figure 6.2 The development of conditional subordination (*if* and *unless*).

When the feature is compared across newspapers, we observe a statistically significant difference between the *Guardian*, on the one hand, and the *Daily Telegraph* and *The Times*, on the other. During the first half of the century, the normed frequencies of conditional subordination attested for the *Guardian* were considerably higher than those attested for the *Daily Telegraph* and *The Times*. Apparently, the argumentative structure of the editorials was more prominent in the *Guardian* than in the other two newspapers at the beginning of the century. The high frequency of conditional subordinators recorded for 1960, especially as regards the *Daily Telegraph*, is more difficult to explain. Nothing has so far come up to support an assumption that the subject-matter of the editorials should have promoted a more argumentative style that special year.

The use of conditional subordination, which is a prominent feature in argumentative discourse, thus varied across time. However, no statistically significant differences were noticed for the newspapers together when the normed frequencies attested for 1900 were compared to those recorded for 1993.

6.4   Suasive verbs

Suasive verbs, such as *demand, insist,* and *suggest,* normally introduce indirect directives (Quirk e al. 1985: 1182–1183), which makes them useful in argumentative discourse. The suasive verbs are followed either by a *to*-infinitive, as in example (16), or by a *that*-clause with "putative" *should*, as in example (17), with another modal auxiliary as in example (18), with the "mandative subjunctive" as in example (19), or, especially in British English, with an indicative verb as in example (20) (see Övergaard 1995: 11, 51–54; Quirk et al. 1985: 1182).[6] It is primarily in their capacity of introducing indirect directives that they serve as overt markers of persuasion.

(16)   We *desire to direct the attention* of all our readers to Lord Knutsford's letter to-day on the disaster which overhangs the London Hospital. (TI20E25)

(17)   Mr Roosevelt's program of "invulnerable national defence" *demanded that the American nation should be geared* to the ability of turning out at least 50,000 planes a year. (DT40E13)

(18)   Mr Chamberlain *insisted that there must be no competition* between the municipalities, and concerted action is obviously desirable. (DT20E6)

---

6   For the use of the terms "mandative subjunctive" and "putative" *should*, see Quirk et al. (1985: 156–157 and 1014–1015, respectively). Putative *should* is also discussed in section 6.6.1 and note 10 in the present chapter.

(19)   The commission did not feel strong enough to sweep its broom through so abnormal an annexe, but it did *recommend that a committee be specially appointed* for the purpose and left it the pregnant thought that the press might make a larger contribution to the finances of the university. (TI70E15)

(20)   How can we *ensure that the growing judicial and quasi-judicial functions of Ministers are exercised* better than they have been? (GUA50E24)

The verbs included in the frequency count of the feature (36 all in all) are those listed by Quirk et al. (1985: 1182), among others: *agree, arrange, ask, beg, command, decide, demand, grant, insist, instruct, pledge, pronounce, propose, recommend, request, stipulate, suggest,* and *urge.*[7] A noticeable, though not statistically significant, increase was observed between 1940 and 1993 when the normed frequencies attested for the newspapers together rose from 3.77 to 5.19. No statistically significant difference emerged when the three newspapers were compared between themselves (see Table 6.4 and Figure 6.3; for statistics, see Appendix, s.v. suasive verbs).

Since the increase noticed from 1940 on is not statistically significant, we must draw the conclusion that the use of suasive verbs remained fairly stable during the time-period studied. This, in turn, means that the use of indirect directives, which these verbs normally introduce, remained relatively stable over the years in English up-market newspaper editorials.

Table 6.4 Suasive verbs: normed frequencies.

Year	Ti	DT	Gua	All
1900	3.93	4.18	3.37	3.66
1910	4.03	3.61	5.02	4.38
1920	4.51	3.77	3.84	4.06
1930	3.74	4.10	4.47	4.15
1940	3.40	3.90	3.95	3.77
1950	4.70	3.88	3.13	3.92
1960	3.69	4.42	4.43	4.20
1970	3.55	5.49	3.69	4.25
1980	4.53	4.53	5.12	4.72
1993	5.10	5.49	5.07	5.19
1900–1993	4.17	4.39	4.19	4.25

---

7   No instances of *entreat* were found in my data.

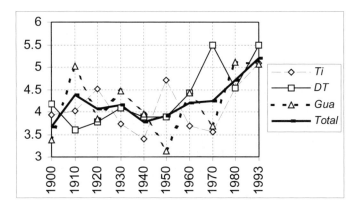

Figure 6.3 The development of suasive verbs.

6.5   'Predictive' modals

As mentioned in 3.4.2, all the modal verbs have two different meanings, one representing intrinsic modality, involving some kind of human control over events, the other representing extrinsic modality, involving human judgement over what is going to happen or not (Quirk et al. 1985: 219–221, Biber at al. 1999: 485–486).[8] As far as the 'predictive' modals *shall* and *will* are concerned, they have the two meanings of volition (intrinsic) and prediction (extrinsic) (Quirk et al. 1985: 228–231, Biber et al. 1999: 495–497). By way of examples, see (21) and (22), respectively.

(21)   Mediation seems virtually at an end. The extremist guerrillas are trying to increase their pressure by insisting that they *will not deal any longer* through the International Red Cross ... (GUA70E26)

(22)   It may be expected that *the task on which this week's conference will concentrate will be that of drawing up a draft convention* on hours of work underground – the creation of an international standard of maximum hours, to which all countries *will be asked to conform.* (GUA30E1)

Since the two meanings are often blurred (see Biber et al. 1999: 495), no distinction between them was made in the present study. The term 'predictive' modals was used as a cover term for both (cf. Biber 1988: 241–242). The forms

---

8   Other terms used for the two modalities are *root – epistemic* (see Coates 1983), *modulation – modality*, and, for the modality of obligation and permission, *deontic* (see Quirk et al. 1985: 220 Note).

110   *Language Change in English Newspaper Editorials*

of 'predictive' modals included in the study are *shall, will, would*, and the negative forms *won't* and *wouldn't*.[9] Only four instances of *won't* and three of *wouldn't* were found in my data (see section 3.2.5). As far as *shall* is concerned, the instances recorded were considerably reduced over the years, which agrees with general tendencies (see, for example, Quirk at al. 1985: 229–230). Between 1900 and 1940, 115 instances were recorded, between 1950 and 1993, only 24. Today *shall* is generally used only with first person pronouns and, outside academic prose, almost exclusively in questions acting as offers or suggestions, such as *Shall I help you?* and *Shall we go now?* (Biber et al. 1999: 496–497). However, all in all, no statistically significant changes in the use of 'predictive' modals were observed, over the years, for the newspapers as a group (see Table 6.5 and Figure 6.4; for statistics, see Appendix, s.v. 'predictive' modals).

When the newspapers were compared, a statistically significant difference was noticed between the *Daily Telegraph* and the *Guardian*. The normed frequencies attested for the *Guardian* were higher throughout the period, except in 1900 and 1993 (cf. the frequencies of conditional subordination (section 6.3) which were also higher in the *Guardian*, especially during the first half of the century). Still, since very little variation was observed when the newspapers were considered as a group, we must assume that the use of 'predictive' modals did not change much across the years.

Table 6.5 'Predictive' modals: normed frequencies.

Year	Ti	DT	Gua	All
1900	6.84	8.65	8.00	7.78
1910	8.15	7.90	9.07	8.51
1920	9.17	7.39	9.43	8.78
1930	7.56	8.26	9.93	8.70
1940	9.71	7.90	9.96	9.15
1950	9.02	7.33	8.90	8.34
1960	9.23	9.07	9.79	9.34
1970	8.69	7.84	9.59	8.73
1980	9.77	7.72	11.84	9.67
1993	9.04	9.97	7.52	8.76
1900–1993	8.83	8.16	9.38	8.81

9   The past tense form of *shall* (*should*) is included among 'necessity' modals (see section 6.6).

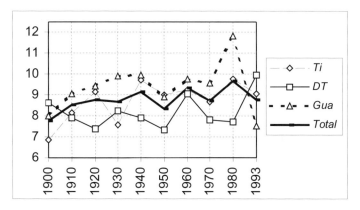

Figure 6.4 The development of 'predictive' modals.

6.6   'Necessity' modals

The most important of the two groups of modals serving as overt markers of persuasion is probably the one marking obligation or necessity (see Quirk et al. 1985: 221, 224–227; Biber et al. 1999: 493–495). This group consists of *must, should* and *ought to* and the marginal modals *need* and *have (got) to*, from now on referred to as 'necessity' modals (cf. Biber 1988: 241–242). In the following, I first discuss *must, should* and *ought to*, then *need* and *have (got) to*.

6.6.1   *Must, should,* and *ought to*

Like the other modals, the 'necessity' modals have both intrinsic and extrinsic uses. The intrinsic use of *must, should* and *ought to* expresses obligation, as in examples (23)–(25).

(23)   Mr Patten *must also ensure* that next year's tests are less vulnerable to disruption. (TI93E13)

(24)   For the motorist who uses a "supplementary" ration for pleasure there is no excuse whatever. He is breaking the law and *should be punished* – if necessary by having all his coupons cancelled. (GUA40E29)

(25)   Long before the exhibition closed the PRINCE CONSORT had settled in his own mind how the money *ought to be spent* – not in any "winter garden" for mere amusement, but in pursuance of the same ends as those of the exhibition. (TI30E10)

The extrinsic use expresses logical necessity, as in examples (26)–(28), that is, the author or speaker makes an assessment of the truth value of what is uttered, based on facts known to them.

(26)   Much of that formidable loss *must be due to general trade depression* and decline of purchasing power ... (DT30E13)

(27)   Scott will restrict cross examination to himself and two colleagues. That looks right. This inquisitorial approach *should be more incisive* than the adversarial style of the past. (GUA93E10)

(28)   Above all, the armed guard *ought to be able to cope with* any hijacker whenever a plane has to land for refuelling, always provided that he has not been overpowered beforehand. (TI70E23)

Two additional meanings may be distinguished as far as *should* is concerned. The modal may be used as a first person alternative of hypothetical *would,* as in (29), and as a marker of the putative meaning (see Quirk et al. 1985: 234), as in example (30).[10]

(29)   If the story which is now told in full had been laid before the British public a couple of months ago, *we should have been better able to understand* the calculated brutality of the German newspapers, and *we should have been spared the trouble* of endeavouring to find out how their savage Anglophobia could be reconciled with the customary assurances of the friendliness of the German Government. (TI00E7)

(30)   The South African Government has declared Seretse a "prohibited immigrant." During the inquiry conducted by Sir Walter Harrigin it was suggested that *permission should nevertheless be obtained* for him to visit the Resident Commissioner at Mafeking. (GUA50E13)

A manual screening of the three modals showed that, in my data, the intrinsic meaning is more common than the extrinsic. As far as *should* is concerned, the putative meaning is also fairly common while only few instances of the

---

10   Putative *should* is found in *that*-clauses after mandative expressions denoting a necessity, plan, intention, or demand. Among those expressions are verbs such as *suggest, demand, consider,* nouns such as *suggestion, principle, desire,* and adjectives such as *natural, important,* and *anxious.* Until recently, putative *should* has been the most common alternant after mandative expressions in British English (see, for example, Quirk et al. 1985: 1013). However, Övergaard (1995) maintains that, by 1990, the putative *should* and other periphrastic alternants (*shall, may, might, must, would,* and *be to*) have decreased in use in favour of the mandative subjunctive, probably due to American influence (Övergaard 1995: 89).

hypothetical meaning were found. However, many indeterminate cases turned up, as, for example, (31) and (32).

(31)   But Lady Thatcher herself *must recognise that the days are gone* when she can be a significant force for good in British politics. (DT93E19)

(32)   To men of all parties *the ultimate consideration should be* the peace and good government of Ireland. (TI20E3)

In these examples it is difficult to tell if the author is giving advice or assessing the possibility of a positive outcome of the proposition given, that is, if we have to do with the intrinsic or the extrinsic meaning of the modals. It need not be a question of either – or, however. In many cases of indeterminacy, the two meanings are merged (see Coates 1983: 77–79), which means that the intrinsic – extrinsic use is neutralized. The intrinsic and putative meanings of *should* are also sometimes merged, as shown by Coates (1983: 68–69).[11] Because of this indeterminacy and the fact that all the meanings of the three modals can be used for argumentative purposes, no distinction between the different uses was made.

When the normed frequencies of the 'necessity' modals were compared, no statistically significant differences were observed, either between decades or between newspapers (see Table 6.6 and Figure 6.5; for statistics, see Appendix, s.v. 'necessity' modals: *must, should,* and *ought to*).

Table 6.6 'Necessity' modals: normed frequencies of *must, should,* and *ought to*.

	Ti	*DT*	*Gua*	*All*
1900	3.62	1.57	3.01	2.95
1910	3.69	3.24	4.09	3.76
1920	5.16	4.18	4.09	4.50
1930	3.11	3.88	3.54	3.57
1940	3.37	5.70	3.48	4.24
1950	3.21	4.80	4.51	4.20
1960	3.55	4.91	4.00	4.22
1970	3.76	4.11	4.76	4.24
1980	3.38	4.67	3.54	3.91
1993	5.64	3.35	4.01	4.47
1900–1993	3.95	4.29	3.89	4.04

---

11   In Coates (1983), the term "quasi subjunctive" is used for putative *should*.

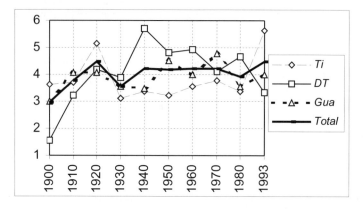

Figure 6.5 The development of 'necessity' modals (*must, should*, and *ought to*).

6.6.2   *Need* and *have (got) to*

Only few instances of the marginal modals *need* and *have (got) to* were recorded in my data: 128 instances of *need* (see Table 6.7) and four of *have got to* in the whole sample. *Have to* was somewhat more frequent, 374 instances, all in all (see Table 6.8).

Table 6.7 *Need to*: normed frequencies.   Table 6.8 *Have to*: normed frequencies

Year	Ti	DT	Gua	All	Year	Ti	DT	Gua	All
1900	0.08	0.29	0.00	0.07	1900	0.65	0.49	0.43	0.50
1910	0.40	0.23	0.17	0.25	1910	0.58	0.82	0.53	0.62
1920	0.36	0.34	0.05	0.24	1920	0.41	0.75	0.86	0.67
1930	0.13	0.13	0.26	0.18	1930	0.93	0.54	0.79	0.73
1940	0.20	0.20	0.06	0.15	1940	0.71	0.64	0.61	0.65
1950	0.08	0.39	0.25	0.25	1950	0.71	0.27	1.03	0.64
1960	0.00	0.44	0.18	0.23	1960	0.79	0.66	0.98	0.80
1970	0.22	0.07	0.81	0.38	1970	1.26	0.48	1.88	1.22
1980	0.24	0.11	0.45	0.26	1980	0.55	0.59	0.64	0.59
1993	0.41	0.09	0.49	0.35	1993	0.87	1.06	0.86	0.92
1900-1993	0.22	0.22	0.28	0.24	1900-1993	0.76	0.61	0.87	0.75

The instances of *need* were edited by hand so as to distinguish the modal from the main verb. No statistically significant change was observed, however, either across decades or across newspapers (see Table 6.7 and Figure 6.6; for statistics, see Appendix, s.v. *need to*).

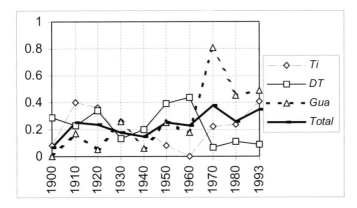

Figure 6.6 The development of *need to*.

As far as *have to* is concerned, a slight but steady increase was noticed up to 1970. However, this increase was followed by a statistically significant decrease, which makes the normed frequency attested for 1980, for the newspapers together, approximately the same as it was in 1900; no statistically significant difference was shown when the normed frequencies recorded for 1900 and 1993 were compared. Nor was there any statistically significant difference between the three newspapers in their use of the feature (see Table 6.8 and Figure 6.7; for statistics, see Appendix, s.v. *have to*).

No important changes in the use of *need* and *have to* were thus attested, which means that these verbs follow the development of the other modals included in the study as markers of argumentative discourse.

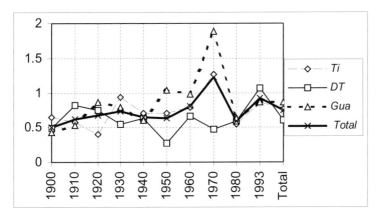

Figure 6.7 The development of *have to*.

6.7   Summary and conclusions

The only feature that showed a straightforward and statistically significant increase over time among the markers of argumentative discourse is infinitives. Since no change was attested for the other markers of persuasion, that is, conditional subordination, 'predictive' modals, and 'necessity' modals, it is reasonable to assume that the argumentative function of the editorials remained more or less the same over the years. It is also reasonable to assume that infinitives, as they do not follow the development of the other markers of the set, are used for other purposes than argumentation in English up-market editorials, perhaps for the integration of information as suggested by researchers such as Chafe (1982).

When the three newspapers were compared, the language of the *Guardian* appeared to be slightly more argumentative, to judge from the more frequent use of conditional subordination and of predictive modals.

7. Features marking abstract discourse

7.1 Introduction

If the language of English up-market editorials should have developed towards a more informal style, a drift away from abstract language would have been expected. Therefore, the present study also includes the investigation of a set of features that previous research has shown to be markers of such discourse. The most important of them and such as have often been used in register comparison to distinguish between oral and written language are passives and participle forms.[1] Svartvik sees passives as distinguishing not between oral and written discourse in the first place, but between informative and imaginative writing (1966: 155). Biber found that passives, 'detached' past participle clauses, past participle WHIZ-deletions, conjuncts, and a group of "subordinators having multiple functions", henceforward referred to as 'subordinators with multiple functions', together, mark "informational discourse that is abstract, technical, and formal ..." (Biber 1988: 112–113).[2] Besides passives and participles, which, as mentioned above, have been found by many researchers to distinguish between different types of discourse, the present work also includes conjuncts and 'subordinators with multiple functions', in accordance with Biber's findings.

As shown in what follows, only one of the features, agentless passives, showed a straightforward decrease in use over the decades. All the other features signal continuity (see Table 7.1).

---

1   See, for example, O'Donnell (1974: 102–110), Poole and Field (1976: 306–311), Chafe (1982: 40–41), Brown and Yule (1983: 14–19), Chafe and Danielewicz (1987: 102; 108–109), Young (1985: 115–127), and Bäcklund (1986: 48–55).

2   For an explanation of the terms 'detached' participle clauses and WHIZ-deletion, see section 5.1, note 2, and section 5.4.

Table 7.1 The development of features linked with abstract discourse.

Statistically significant increase over time	Statistically significant decrease over time	Linguistic continuity
(No features)	Agentless passives	*By*-passives 'Detached' past participle clauses[a] Past participle WHIZ-deletion Conjuncts[b] 'Subordinators with multiple functions'

[a] A statistically significant decrease was observed for 'detached' past participle clauses between 1900 and 1970, but since this decrease was followed by an equally substantial increase between 1970 and 1993, no statistically significant difference was attested when the frequencies for 1900 and 1993 were compared.

[b] Conjuncts showed an upward tendency up to 1980, but then the line of development turned downwards again, and no statistically significant difference was attested when the frequencies for 1900 and 1993 were compared.

7.2   Passives

The frequency of passives varies considerably between text types. According to Svartvik (1966: 152–154), they can be as much as ten times as common in one text as in another. In his investigation of eight text sets, he found that "science" texts were the greatest "consumers" of passives, followed by "news", including editorials, and "arts". The lowest number of passives were found in "advertising", especially television advertising.

Both *by*-passives and agentless passives have, basically, one and the same discourse function: to switch the focus of action in the active clause from subject/actor to object/patient or the action itself. In four out of five passive sentences the actor (agent) is not even mentioned, because it is either irrelevant or unknown (Quirk et al. 1985: 165). Kress (1983: 127–128) showed, by analysing two newspaper articles, how this switch of focus and the possibility of subject/agent deletion can be used for ideological purposes:

> The passive form has a number of features which contribute to its meaning. If we contrast 'someone felt the effects' with 'the effects were felt' we note that the focally significant first position is occupied by the subject of the action in the active, and the object of the action in the passive. That is, the focus has switched from subject/actor to object/goal. In the active form the action seems closely connected with the subject; in the passive form the action has become attached to the object ... These are not all the meanings and effects of the passive but they suffice to indicate the ideological significance of the form: focus on the affected entity; representation of the action as a quality/state, and as an attribute of the affected entity; the possibility of deleting the subject/agent of the sentence.

The passive forms are not always deliberately chosen, however. In fluent English they often come in naturally and spontaneously and would be hard to exchange for their active equivalents (Alexander 1988: 243). A phrase such as *He was killed in a car accident*, for example, is not uncommon in spoken English.

In a passive construction the auxiliary is normally *be,* but also *get* is sometimes used, as in example (1).

(1)   Sometimes they *get killed*. (DT60E14)

In this study, only *be*-passives were considered. *Get*-passives, which are normally avoided in formal style (see Quirk et al. 1985: 161) are rare in my material. Only seven instances, all in all, were found.

7.2.1 Agentless passives

As mentioned above, agentless passives are used when the actor is either irrelevant or unknown (see also Finegan 1994: 214–215). But they are also sometimes deliberately chosen in preference to their active counterparts because the authors/speakers do not want to take on responsibility for actions, opinions etc., which they are not certain about or because they want to avoid a vague word, such as *somebody* or *one*, as the subject of the clause (Alexander 1988: 243–244). In technical and scientific writing, agentless passives are often used to promote object to subject. Choosing the passive alternative makes it possible to avoid the repetition of *I* or *we* and put the emphasis on the processes and experimental procedures, thus giving the writing an objective tone (Greenbaum and Quirk 1993: 45–46). In newspaper editorials, it may be assumed that agentless passives are also used for ideological purposes (cf. above). In some cases, more than one of the above reasons for choosing the agentless passive can apply, as in example (2) from the *Daily Telegraph*, 1950.

(2)   A state of affairs wholly satisfactory to national culture, to domestic life and to the B.B.C. is disclosed by its research into the habits of televiewers. They do not, *it is established*, neglect their reading, letter-writing or social contacts; they *are not chained* to the house, and even their cinema-going *is hardly affected*. The only sacrifice which the home screen claims is one *to be joyfully paid*: in television families less time *is devoted* to domestic duties in the evening. (DT50E6)

Agentless passives are by far the most frequent feature in the set representing abstract discourse in my data, and more than five times as frequent as *by*-passives. Having remained rather stable in use during the first half of the century, agentless passives showed a statistically significant and consistent decrease from 1950 on. No statistically significant difference was noticed between the three newspapers (see Table 7.2 and Figure 7.1; for statistics, see Appendix, s.v. agentless passives).

Table 7.2 Agentless passives: normed frequencies.

Year	Ti	DT	Gua	All
1900	14.97	17.52	15.47	15.66
1910	13.76	14.20	13.73	13.86
1920	14.49	15.09	14.76	14.75
1930	15.90	15.56	13.35	14.83
1940	13.02	16.30	13.23	14.27
1950	15.49	14.09	15.29	14.90
1960	15.62	13.74	13.82	14.34
1970	12.32	10.58	11.76	11.54
1980	13.18	11.70	9.78	11.54
1993	10.98	10.72	10.48	10.74
1900–1993	13.83	13.67	13.16	13.53

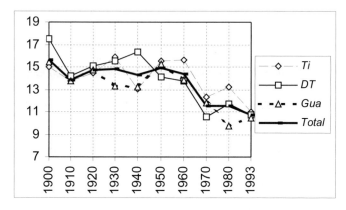

Figure 7.1 The development of agentless passives.

The decrease of agentless passives, with, by far, the largest normed frequencies of the features representing abstract discourse, gives an indication of a drift away from a language that Biber characterizes as "abstract, technical, and formal" (Biber 1988: 112–113).

7.2.2 *By*-passives

When a deliberate choice is made between the active construction and the corresponding passive, including a *by*-agent, one of the reasons for choosing the passive can be that the speaker or writer wants to give the part of the clause that contains new and important information end-focus (see Leech 1986: 21–22; Svartvik and Sager 1983: 419), as in example (3) from the *Guardian,* 1910.

(3)   The French navy suffered yesterday a lamentable disaster by which a
        submarine was lost with all its crew. The boat, which was submerged, *was
        struck by a channel steamer* that had just left Calais harbour ... We do not
        know, however, why it should have been in any way necessary for this
        French submarine to be manoeuvring, as apparently it was, in the direct
        track of the Channel traffic; a submarine travelling with only the periscope
        above water *is scarcely likely to be see*n *by an approaching steamer* unless
        the water is extremely calm. This is a point which *may be cleared up by
        later information.* (GUA10E22)

Therefore, to put the emphasis on the agent rather than the action, *by*-passives are
often found together with verbs such as like *build, damage, destroy, discover,
invent, make,* and *write* (Alexander 1988: 244), as in example (4).

(4)   Some of the critics thought that it would not be a bad thing if the
        "Luxembourg bureaucracy" *were destroyed altogether by newer
        organisations* with a true European spirit. (GUA60E22)

Another reason for using the *by*-passive instead of the active form is, according to
Greenbaum and Quirk (1993: 46), the wish to avoid long subjects, as in examples
(4) and (5), or to keep the same subject throughout the sentence, as in example
(6).

(5)   He has already been obliged to sacrifice not a little of the proposed plan of
        retrenchment, as was shown *by his detailed statement of the Government's
        financial intentions in the House of Representatives on Tuesday last.*
        (DT30E31)

(6)   Savings have not just been achieved *by outhouse contracts, however, but
        by inhouse teams becoming more efficient through the challenge of outside
        bidders.* (GUA93E29)

A noticeable decrease in the use of *by*-passives was observed in the *Guardian*
between 1940 and 1980. However, no statistically significant change was
attested, either across decades or across newspapers (see Table 7.3 and Figure
7.2; for statistics, see Appendix, s.v. *by*-passives). While agentless passives
decreased in use, the use of *by*-passives thus seems to have remained more or less
stable over time, at least when the newspapers are considered as a group.

Table 7.3 *By*-passives: normed frequencies.

Year	Ti	DT	Gua	All
1900	2.82	3.30	2.47	2.70
1910	2.71	2.71	2.82	2.76
1920	2.61	2.54	3.16	2.79
1930	2.91	3.00	2.50	2.79
1940	2.84	2.48	4.24	3.21
1950	2.52	2.95	2.17	2.58
1960	2.32	3.17	1.55	2.42
1970	2.68	3.13	2.09	2.61
1980	3.46	2.31	1.16	2.30
1993	2.70	2.36	1.88	2.33
1900–1993	2.75	2.79	2.41	2.64

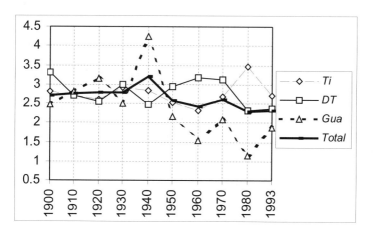

Figure 7.2 The development of *by*-passives.

7.3   Past participle clauses

The basic meaning of 'detached' (adverbial) past participle clauses and past participle WHIZ-deletions corresponds to that of finite passives. The past participle clause normally replaces a finite construction consisting of a form of *be* and the past participle of the verb together with a noun or pronoun subject. The participle clause in (7), for example, replaces the finite construction *when they are taken together* and that in (8) *which was published...* Their close relationship with finite passives is shown by the fact that they can take a *by*-agent, as in example (8).

(7)   All of these are moves in the right direction, but all of them had been previously disclosed, and even *when taken together* they do not amount to a particularly radical package. (TI80E24)

(8)   A survey of married women at work, *published by the Institute of Personnel Management*, records that over the past 20 years the proportion of married women adding a paid job to that of housewife has   doubled. (DT60E3)

As mentioned above, participle clauses have been used in register comparison by, among others, O'Donnell (1974: 102–110), Chafe (1982: 40–41), Chafe and Danielewicz (1987: 102; 108–109), Young (1985: 115–127), and Bäcklund (1986: 48–55). Their studies showed that participle forms are by far more common in written than in oral discourse. However, their results are not quite comparable to mine. Neither O'Donnell (1974) nor Chafe and Danielewicz (1987) makes any distinction between past and present participle forms. Chafe, even though he makes that distinction, does not distinguish between past participles used as premodifiers and those used as WHIZ-deletions or adverbial clauses. Bäcklund (1986) only investigates so-called abbreviated clauses, that is, conjunction-headed non-finite clauses, such as *when taken seriously* or *if found guilty*, and verbless clauses, such as *all people, whether rich or poor*, but as she makes a distinction between the different structural types (past participle, present participle, and verbless clauses) her results are at least to some extent comparable to mine. Biber, whose findings were the starting point for this part of my study, considers it necessary to treat "each of the grammatical functions of participles ... as a separate linguistic feature, since these grammatical functions are likely to be associated with different discourse functions" (Biber 1988: 232). For this reason, the present analysis also distinguishes between the different uses of participles.

7.3.1 'Detached' past participle clauses

'Detached' past participle clauses (adverbial clauses) may or may not be introduced by a subordinator. In example (7) above, the adverbial clause is introduced by *when*. Other common subordinators in my data are *as* and *if*, as in examples (9) and (10). However, most of the past participle clauses are clauses that are not introduced by a subordinator, such as example (11).

(9)   The story of the annexation, *as told in official documents*, demonstrates that the step was taken on the invitation and with the approval of the ruling parties in the Transvaal. (TI00E5)

(10)   Would Labour, *if re-elected*, have been more adventurous? (GUA70E18)

(11)   *Built on the same lines as the international wheat agreement now in force*, it would give each European exporter a definite share of the market and bind each importer to take an agreed annual tonnage. (TI50E24)

The position of the past participle clause may be either initial, as in example (11), medial, as in examples (9) and (10), or final as in example (12).

(12)   The destruction of private property in warfare is always to be lamented, but it is a perfectly legitimate measure *when taken for military reasons*; (TI00E1)

No statistically significant difference was attested in the use of 'detached' past participle clauses when the frequencies for the beginning and the end of the century were compared. However, during the period studied, two statistically significant changes were observed: the decrease between 1900 and 1970 and the increase between 1970 and 1993. No statistically significant difference was recorded when the three newspapers were compared (see Table 7.4 and Figure 7.3; for statistics, see Appendix, s.v. 'detached' past participle clauses).

The fact that, after 70 years of decrease, the line of development turned upwards again needs an explanation. One reason could be the increasing aspiration for information density among the editorial authors: finite passive constructions were replaced by non-finite (cf. the increase, between 1970 and 1993, of 'detached' present participle clauses (see section 5.4) and present participle WHIZ-deletion (see section 4.3.3)).

Table 7.4 'Detached' past participle clauses: normed frequencies.

Year	Ti	DT	Gua	All
1900	0.60	0.97	0.80	0.77
1910	0.51	0.67	0.76	0.66
1920	0.58	0.29	0.65	0.53
1930	0.62	0.48	0.27	0.44
1940	0.63	0.20	0.85	0.56
1950	0.40	0.53	0.35	0.43
1960	0.31	0.75	0.42	0.51
1970	0.20	0.00	0.30	0.17
1980	0.62	0.86	0.81	0.77
1993	0.88	0.61	0.73	0.76
1900–1993	0.54	0.50	0.59	0.55

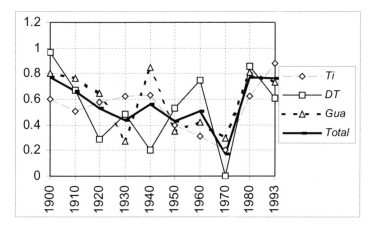

Figure 7.3 The development of 'detached' past participle clauses.

7.3.2 Past participle WHIZ-deletion

Past participle WHIZ-deletions are participle constructions functioning as reduced relative clauses, in so far as the relative pronoun plus a form of *be* are deleted, as in example (13).

(13)   If the women *interviewed for this survey* are representative, the growth in the number of married women at work reflects a sensible desire to make the best of both worlds. (DT60E3)

The WHIZ-deletion in (13), for example, replaces the relative clause *who were interviewed* and that in (14) replaces *which is embedded in ...*

(14)   This power is quite incompatible with the far more important right, *embedded in the 1944 Act*, of each child to the education best suited to his talents. (DT70E27)

In my data, past participle WHIZ-deletions are more than six times as common as 'detached' participle clauses, but the patterns of development for the two participle constructions follow each other fairly closely: a downward tendency between 1900 and 1970 and a noticeable increase between 1970 and 1993. However, as far as past participle WHIZ-deletions are concerned, no statistically significant changes were recorded. Nor were there any statistically significant differences between the newspapers (see Table 7.5 and Figure 7.4; for statistics, see Appendix, s.v. past participle WHIZ-deletion).

Table 7.5 Past participle WHIZ-deletion: normed frequencies.

YEAR	Ti	DT	Gua	Total
1900	3.92	3.94	3.94	3.93
1910	3.56	3.00	2.87	3.10
1920	4.69	2.94	3.22	3.68
1930	3.48	2.88	4.31	3.55
1940	3.21	3.56	3.42	3.41
1950	4.09	3.91	3.17	3.74
1960	4.47	3.10	3.82	3.74
1970	2.31	3.91	2.45	2.89
1980	4.18	3.00	2.95	3.35
1993	3.83	3.45	4.12	3.83
Total	3.78	3.35	3.43	3.51

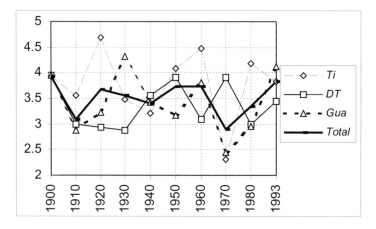

Figure 7.4 The development of past participle WHIZ-deletion.

Apparently, past participle clauses and finite passive constructions developed in different directions in my data during the latter part of the 20th century. It is therefore reasonable to assume that, in English up-market newspaper editorials, past participle WHIZ-deletions and 'detached' participle clauses, have another, shared, function than that of finite passives, such as, for example, the wish for compactness (cf. Chafe 1982: 40–41 and Greenbaum 1988: 3–4). Because of the restricted space given to the editorials (as to other newspaper items), compact language was, as I see it, a necessary prerequisite throughout the time-period studied but especially towards the end of the century.

7.4   Conjuncts

Conjuncts serve as markers of the logical relations between two linguistic units. The units may be "very large or very small: sentences, paragraphs or even larger parts of a text at one extreme …; at the other extreme, they may be constituents of a phrase realizing a single clause element" (Quirk et al. 1985: 632).

According to their semantic roles, the conjuncts can be grouped into seven classes (Quirk et al. 1985: 634–636). The items listed under each heading below are those included in the present study.

A.   LISTING: *furthermore, likewise, moreover, similarly, in addition, in particular,* as in:
Furthermore, those measures proposed by Mr Murray will not strike the unbiased as positive. (DT80E20)

B.   SUMMATIVE: *altogether, therefore, thus, in conclusion, in sum, in summary,* as in:
In sum, we should see what the Islamic Conference can do about Kabul (whilst preparing the arms trails to Jalalabad). (GUA80E14)

C.   APPOSITIVE: *namely, viz., for example, eg, e.g., for instance, i.e., in other words,* as in:
Many, perhaps most, of its most important members were in favour of the general principle of the League, *viz.,* the creation of an international body for the prevention of war and the settlement of international disputes. (DT20E22)

D.   RESULTIVE: *consequently, hence, therefore, thus, as a consequence, as a result, in consequence,* as in:
As a result a fresh crisis developed. (TI50E27)

E.   INFERENTIAL: *else, otherwise, in other words,* as in:
Otherwise, the country will dissolve in chaos. (DT60E32)

F.   CONTRASTIVE: *alternatively, conversely, else, however, nevertheless, nonetheless, notwithstanding, rather, by comparison, by contrast, in comparison, in contrast, on the contrary, on the other hand, in any case, in any event, instead, on the other hand,* as in:
In Parliament, *by contrast*, both Social-Democrats, who provide the present Government, and Agrarians are stronger. (GUA50E4)

G.   TRANSITIONAL: *by the way, incidentally, meantime, in the meantime, meanwhile,* as in:
Meanwhile, Lord Skidelsky and John Marenbon have resigned from SEAC on the grounds that the forthcoming review of the national curriculum has been inadequately planned. (TI93E13)

The most frequently used conjunct in my material is the contrastive *however* (328 instances out of 1,346). *Therefore* (174 instances) and *thus* (123 instances), which can be both summative and resultive, come next. Others are very rare, for example *namely* (four instances), *by the way* (three instances, none of them after 1950), *alternatively* (three instances) and *conversely* (two instances). Two items seem to be on their way out of English up-market editorials: *incidentally* with nine instances of ten and *notwithstanding* with seven instances of eight (five of them in 1900) recorded before 1950. *Likewise*, on the other hand, did not appear in my data until 1950, but, after that, seven instances were recorded. As far as the appositive abbreviations *e.g., i.e.,* and *viz.* are concerned, no instances of *e.g.* or *eg* were found, only two of *viz.* (none after 1930), and eight of *i.e.* (five of them before 1950). Besides the contrastive *however*, the summative and resultive conjuncts are thus the most favoured linking devices in my data. These conjuncts do not only help to link one idea to another in a logical order but also to give the text an argumentative structure.

According to Biber (1988: 239), conjuncts were rarely used in register comparison before the mid-eighties. However, in his study he showed that they often co-occur with passives, prepositions, and nominalizations in highly informative discourse, such as academic prose and official documents, and with passives and past participle clauses in technical texts (Biber 1988: 112–113).

An upward tendency in the use of conjuncts was noticed between 1900 and 1970, but then the line of development turned downwards again and a statistically significant decrease was observed between 1970 and 1993, which means that no statistically significant difference between the beginning and the end of the century was recorded (see Table 7.6 and Figure 7.5; for statistics, see Appendix, s.v. conjuncts).

Table 7.6 Conjuncts: normed frequencies.

Year	Ti	DT	Gua	All
1900	2.90	1.81	2.00	2.22
1910	2.05	2.81	2.37	2.39
1920	2.91	2.03	2.56	2.54
1930	2.40	2.02	2.56	2.31
1940	2.34	4.07	1.38	2.61
1950	2.70	3.15	2.11	2.69
1960	2.80	3.11	2.87	2.94
1970	3.81	4.51	2.30	3.50
1980	3.31	3.51	2.57	3.15
1993	2.48	3.13	0.93	2.12
1900–1993	2.82	3.14	2.16	2.68

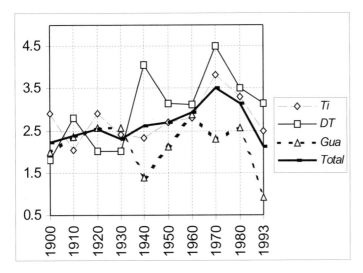

Figure 7.5 The development of conjuncts.

Compared across newspapers, a statistically significant difference was recorded between the *Guardian* as compared to the other two newspapers. From 1940 on (1960 being an exception), the frequencies attested for the *Guardian* were considerably lower than those attested for *The Times* and the *Daily Telegraph,* which suggests that expressing logical reasoning with the aid of conjuncts was of less importance in the *Guardian* than in the other two newspapers.

With the exception of the decrease between 1970 and 1993, only little variation was thus noticed for the newspapers together in their use of the conjuncts investigated, which indicates that the habit of marking logical relations between two linguistic units had not changed much over time.

7.5 'Subordinators with multiple functions'

In his study (1988: 112), Biber showed that a set of subordinators having multiple functions often co-occur with passives and conjuncts. He suggests that the reason for the appearance of the subordinators and conjuncts together with passives is to mark "the complex logical relations among clauses that characterize this type of discourse", that is, abstract discourse (Biber 1988: 112). The subordinators included in this study are the same as those used by Biber (with the exception of *whereupon* and *insomuch as,* which were not found in my data): *since, while, whilst, whereas, whereby, in so far as, inasmuch as, as long as, as soon 'as, so that,* and *such that.* However, these subordinators are not very frequent in the editorials and no statistically significant differences were observed, either between decades or between newspapers (see Table 7.7 and Figure 7.6; for statistics, see Appendix, s.v. 'subordinators with multiple functions').

Table 7.7 'Subordinators with multiple functions': normed frequencies.

Year	Ti	DT	Gua	All
1900	1.29	1.52	1.23	1.29
1910	1.09	0.92	1.15	1.07
1920	1.64	1.09	1.53	1.45
1930	1.01	1.59	1.88	1.55
1940	1.84	1.35	0.83	1.30
1950	1.68	2.08	2.09	1.96
1960	1.48	1.84	1.92	1.76
1970	1.21	1.52	2.18	1.66
1980	1.65	1.29	0.71	1.22
1993	1.71	1.67	1.81	1.74
1900–1993	1.49	1.53	1.54	1.52

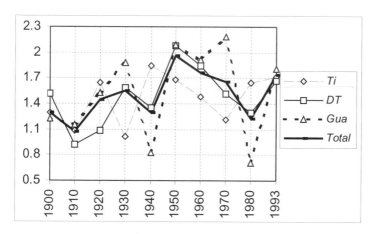

Figure 7.6 The development of 'subordinators with multiple functions'.

The fact that the use of 'subordinators with multiple functions', just as the use of conjuncts, did not change across the years, strengthens the assumption that the need among the authors of English up-market editorials to use these subordinators to organize their material in a logical way remained rather similar during the period covered by the present work.

7.6   Summary and conclusions

Among the features supposed to be markers of abstract discourse, it is only agentless passives that showed a statistically significant change over time. As regards 'detached' past participle clauses, no statistically significant difference was observed when the normed frequencies for 1900 and 1993 were compared, despite two noticeable changes during the period. Conjuncts showed a statistically significant decrease between 1970 and 1993, but since this decrease was preceded by a consistent increase between 1900 and 1970, no statistically significant difference between the beginning and the end of the century was recorded for this feature, either. The use of past participle WHIZ-deletions and 'subordinators with multiple functions' remained more or less stable over the years.

Even though only one of the features marking abstract discourse, that is, agentless passives, decreased in use, it can be argued that a development away from a more abstract style has taken place in English up-market newspaper editorials. Firstly, agentless passives are, by far, the most important of the features representing abstract discourse in my data, with normed frequencies exceeding those of all the other features together. Secondly, the fact that 'detached' past participle clauses and past participle WHIZ-deletions do not follow the development of passives but remain more or less as frequent towards the end of the century as they were at the beginning of the century (the 'detached' past participle clauses even showed a statistically significant increase towards the end of the century), suggests that these features are not primarily markers of abstract discourse in English up-market newspaper editorials. Instead, they are probably a manifestation of the need to compress as much information into as few words as possible due to the limited space allotted for newspaper editorials, as for other newspaper items. As 'detached' past participle clauses give the same information as finite passives, and WHIZ-deletions the same information as full relative clauses even though in both cases fewer words are used, the non-finite variant can be a deliberate choice. This preference for compactness has been encountered in previous chapters (see, for example, present participle WHIZ-deletions, section 4.3.3, and 'detached' present participle clauses, section 5.4). Thirdly, the need to build up logical relations between smaller or larger linguistic units in editorials, which usually have an argumentative structure, must be the same whether the language is abstract or not. This explains the stability in the use of the subordinators included in the study and the development of conjuncts, which, despite the fact that some variation was noticed across the years, showed no big differences in use when the frequencies from the beginning of the century were compared to those from the end. Consequently, a drift away from more abstract discourse is possible even though only the most important of the features in question changed in that direction.

8. Features marking explicit reference

8.1 Introduction

In written discourse it is usually necessary to be more explicit than in oral, as the reader has no possibility of asking for and obtaining additional information if needed, which is feasible with the addresser present. The primary markers of explicit reference, as shown in Biber's study, are relative pronouns, more specifically relative *wh*-pronouns and pied piping constructions (a preposition + *whom* or *which*), which can be regarded as "devices for the explicit, elaborated identification of referents in a text" (Biber 1988: 110).[1] Of lesser importance are nominalizations and phrasal co-ordination. The co-occurrence of these two features with the relative pronouns, Biber states, indicates that "referentially explicit discourse also tends to be integrated and informational" (1988: 110).

To find out to what extent the language of English up-market editorials changed across the years as far as referential explicitness is concerned, the present study concentrates on relative clauses: relative clauses introduced by the *wh*-pronouns,[2] pied piping constructions, and, besides, relative clauses introduced by *that*.[3] The reason why relative *that* is also taken into consideration as a marker of explicit reference is the fact that this pronoun and the *wh*-pronouns, even though they have the same linguistic function, have been found to be distributed differently between oral and written language (see, for example, Beaman (1984: 66), de Haan (1984: 47–58)). A comparison of their uses may give information about whether the more formal or informal variant is preferred in the editorials. Furthermore, some attention is given to nominalizations. Phrasal co-ordination,

---

1   Relative *that* was not included among the markers of explicit reference in Biber's study. Instead, it appeared among the markers of "On-line informational elaboration". This dimension is not dealt with in the present work.

2   Following Quirk et al. (1985: 366), I use the term '*wh*-pronoun' to refer to the relative pronouns *who, whose, whom,* and *which*.

3   Besides relative clauses introduced by *wh*-pronouns and by *that,* there is a third alternative, namely relative clauses lacking a relative pronoun, as in *The book Ø I bought yesterday* or *The people Ø I met.* Such clauses, usually referred to as "zero" constructions, were not included in the present study.

on the other hand, was not included since this feature is not easily retrievable through automatic searches, the basis for the study. Change and continuity in the use of the features dealt with in this chapter are seen in Table 8.1.

Table 8.1 The development of features linked with explicit reference.

Statistically significant increase over time	Statistically significant decrease over time	Linguistic continuity
Nominalizations	who/which	Relative
	Pied piping	that [a]

[a] A statistically significant decrease between 1940 and 1950 was recorded, but no statistically significant difference was observed when the frequencies from the beginning and the end of the century were compared.

8.2   Relative clauses

One way of specifying the identity of a referent in a text, or elaborating on it, is the use of relative clauses (see section 8.1). By way of an example, see (1). Other possibilities are non-finite clauses or prepositional phrases as in examples (1a) and (1b), re-writings of (1).

(1)   Our main interest in the Bolshevik Government is to repress its subterranean machinations in this country, and to concert proper measures to restrain it from shaking and disturbing the communities *which lie beyond its own devastated territories*. (DT20E21)

(1a)   ... from shaking and disturbing the communities *lying beyond its own devastated territories*.

(1b)   ... from shaking and disturbing the communities *beyond its own devastated territories*.

Of these alternatives it is the relative clause that gives the most explicit reference. In non-finite clauses, such as (1a), we have no tense marker, and in prepositional phrases, such as (1b), there is no verb to guide the reader at all. However, it is not only the presence of the finite verb that makes the relative clause more explicit. Part of the specifying power of the relative clause lies in the relative pronoun itself, especially if it is a *wh*-pronoun. In showing referential agreement with the head (countries *which*, people *who*) as well as having a syntactic position in the relative clause (subject, object, adverbial, complement), the relative pronoun facilitates the interpretation of a text.

Many researchers, such as Chafe (1982: 44–45), O'Donnell (1974: 107), Poole and Field (1976: 308), and Finegan and Biber (1997: 65–78), found that relative clauses are more frequent in written discourse than in oral.[4] Others have

---

4   Finegan and Biber's study is based on frequency counts of relative pronouns in a 20-million-word corpus of twentieth-century written and spoken English.

proved that different types of relative clauses are distributed differently. Beaman (1984: 66–67), de Haan (1984: 47–58), Biesenbach-Lucas (1987: 13–21) and Kikai et al. (1987: 266–277), for example, found that relative clauses introduced by *which* are more common in written discourse while those introduced by *that* are more common in spoken.[5] Those introduced by *who* were almost equally common in the two modes in Beaman's study (1984) while they were more common in the written data in de Haan's and Finegan and Biber's studies referred to above. De Haan (1984), Biesenbach-Lucas (1987), Finegan and Biber (1997), and Biber et al. (1999) also showed that there are differences in the choice of relative pronoun not only according to mode but also according to genre. Other factors often taken into consideration in the investigation of the use of relative markers are clause type and the syntactic position of the pronoun. Biber (1988: 110), however, maintains that such differences are minor compared to the "shared function of referential explicitness" among these clauses.

8.2.1 Relative *wh*-clauses

Biber's study shows a high degree of co-occurrence between three different types of relative clauses: relative *wh*-clauses in subject position, as in example (2), relative *wh*-clauses in object position, as in example (3) and pied piping constructions, as in example (4).

(2) A new factory may be an eyesore, the people *who work in it* may have cramped lives, their houses may be as bleak in their own way as the slums which are coming down … (GUA70E6)

(3) No social problem is more disturbing than that of the youthful gangster and the hooligan, *whom modern jargon classifies as "juvenile delinquents"*. (DT50E13)

(4) Secure institutions can, however, remove from the streets a few youngsters *for whom punishment in the community has not worked* and who would otherwise be burgling and joyriding their way around town. (TI93E7)

In the present work, no distinction was made between the first two types. All the instances of relative clauses introduced by *who, whose, whom* and *which*, when not preceded by a preposition, were grouped together. Pied piping constructions were dealt with separately (see section 8.2.2) as they could be expected to show a different pattern of development in so far as they are commonly regarded to appear exclusively in formal language (see Quirk et al. 1985: 1253).

---

5   Biesenbach-Lucas' and Kikai et al.'s studies are based on samples from various written and spoken sources of American English. Biesenbach-Lucas' data are drawn from *The Washington Post* and tape-recorded spontaneous conversations and Kikai et al.'s from, among others, *The New York Times* and other newspapers, television programs, novels, drama, and academic articles.

Between 1900 and 1993 we notice a statistically significant decrease in the use of *wh*-relative clauses. The normed frequencies for the newspapers together sank from 10.95 in 1900 to 7.03 in 1993 (in 1970 the figure was as low as 6.54). It was not until after 1930 that the actual decrease set in, however. No statistically significant differences were observed when the newspapers were compared (see Table 8.2 and Figure 8.1; for statistics, see Appendix, s.v relative *wh*-clauses).

Table 8.2 Relative *wh*-clauses: normed frequencies.

YEAR	Ti	DT	Gua	All
1900	11.03	11.97	10.62	10.95
1910	13.99	10.08	11.87	12.02
1920	10.91	12.60	9.88	11.00
1930	11.45	12.25	9.88	11.19
1940	9.66	8.27	9.50	9.10
1950	8.39	9.08	6.21	8.00
1960	8.16	8.90	8.10	8.43
1970	6.59	7.04	6.05	6.54
1980	7.54	6.59	9.18	7.71
1993	6.19	6.87	8.10	7.03
1900–1993	9.01	9.09	8.95	9.02

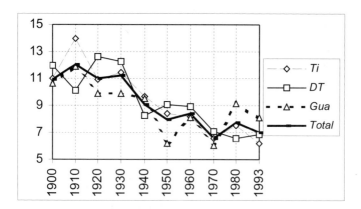

Figure 8.1 The development of relative *wh*-clauses.

8.2.2   Pied piping constructions

As has already been pointed out, pied piping constructions, as distinguished from other relative clauses, are usually associated with formal language. Relative clauses with stranded (post-posed) prepositions, such as example (5) have often been regarded as a more informal variant.

(5)   But when he goes on to assert that his recommendations have helped to assure the public that pay settlements are neither excessively high nor too harsh to the workers, it is legitimate to wonder *whom he has been talking to* in his daily round. (DT80E21)

However, recent research has shown that pied piping, even though it is much more frequent in writing, is more common in oral discourse than was formerly assumed, at least with the relative pronoun *which* (Johansson and Geisler 1998: 67–82). In Johansson and Geisler's data, as many as 79 per cent of all the prepositional relative clauses (pied piping constructions and constructions with stranded prepositions together) in the spoken data proved to be pied piping constructions, compared to 97 per cent in the written. Consequently, preposition stranding is rare in both modes; in writing it is very rare, as is also seen in my data: out of 83 instances of prepositional relative clauses with *whom* as the relative pronoun, for example, 82 are pied piping constructions. The only example of preposition stranding is found in the passage quoted in example (5) above.

The pied piping constructions were edited by hand so as to exclude instances such as the genitive form *of which* (corresponding to *whose*) as in example (6).

(6)   ... an emphatic reply, *the terms of which* have been made public in the Soviet Press ... (DT30E5)

The pattern of development observed for pied piping constructions follows that of relative clauses introduced by *wh*-pronouns closely: a statistically significant decrease between 1900 and 1970 and no statistically significant change after that. No statistically significant differences between the newspapers were found. (see Table 8.3 and Figure 8.2; for statistics, see Appendix, s.v. pied piping).

Relative clauses introduced by *wh*-pronouns as well as pied piping constructions thus decreased in use in English up-market newspaper editorials during the period of study, which suggests a development towards reduced explicitness. Since relative clauses have also been found to be more frequent in written than in oral discourse, the reduced use of them probably means a drift towards more informal styles.

Table 8.3 Pied piping: normed frequencies.

Year	Ti	DT	Gua	All
1900	3.35	2.42	2.81	2.90
1910	3.49	2.04	2.32	2.58
1920	2.91	2.59	2.33	2.61
1930	2.96	2.87	2.09	2.61
1940	2.24	2.21	1.59	2.00
1950	1.88	2.38	1.80	2.05
1960	1.43	2.14	2.64	2.08
1970	1.40	1.09	1.35	1.28
1980	1.75	1.81	0.98	1.52
1993	0.91	1.70	1.60	1.36
1900–1993	2.10	2.10	1.96	2.05

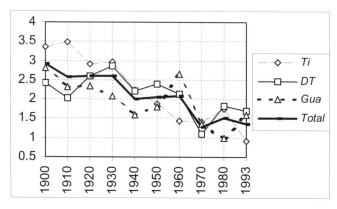

Figure 8.2 The development of pied piping.

8.2.3 Relative *that*-clauses

As mentioned above, previous research has shown that relative clauses introduced by *that* and those introduced by *wh*-pronouns are distributed differently between written and spoken language. In Biber's study (1988), *that*-clauses were included among the markers of "On-line informational elaboration",[6] which means that they, like the relative *wh*-pronouns, are used for the expansion of the noun phrase, but, preferably, in oral discourse. The reason why they are discussed together with the *wh*-pronouns in this study is that I wanted to compare the use of the

---

6   This dimension is not included in my study.

more informal variant (that is, relative *that*) to that of the more formal one (that is, relative *wh*-pronouns) (for the difference as regards formality between the two variants, see, for example, Biber et al. 1999: 616).

That as a relative pronoun has normally been considered to have a more restricted range of application than relative *wh*-pronouns. According to Quirk et al. (1985: 1248–1259), *that* is, by and large, used only in restrictive relative clauses as an alternative to *who*, that is, with a personal antecedent, and to *which,* that is, when the antecedent is a non-personal noun, as in example (7) or one of the non-personal indefinite pronouns *all, anything, everything, nothing little,* and *much,* as in example (8).[7] However, *who* is usually preferred to *that* when the pronoun is the subject of the clause as in example (9) (cf. Geisler and Johansson 2002).

(7)   If he likes to go to a locality where other working men live in numbers, he can get very cheap travelling at the *hours that* suit him. (TI00E16)

(8)   At this moment the sufferings of children in the countries subject to Nazi rule make up a mass of misery greatly exceeding *anything that* was suffered in the years of famine that followed the war. (GUA40E12)

(9)   The authorities could surely afford to take no further measures against *men and women who* have already suffered greatly for conscience's sake.(TI70E1)

Studies carried out by Jacobson (1989) and Biesenbach-Lucas (1987) claimed that, in American newspaper language, a categorical use of the relative pronouns appeared to have developed towards the end of the 20th century. They found that while *who* was used in restrictive as well as non-restrictive clauses, *which* was, almost exclusively, confined to non-restrictive clauses and *that*, competing with "zero" constructions, to restrictive clauses (for the term "zero" constructions, see note 3).[8] However, these results were refuted by the findings presented by Biber et al. (1999: 615–616), whose research of news language is based on 5.4 million words of British English and almost 5.3 million words of American English.[9] They showed that, even though *that* is more than four times as common as *which* in restrictive relative clauses in American newspaper language, *which* is far from rare; in British newspaper language, *which* is even slightly more frequent than *that*. In non-restrictive clauses, *which* is, almost invariably, the only alternative in

---

7   The terms *restrictive* and *non-restrictive* are well established concepts in traditional grammar. For an exhaustive list of references, see Johansson (1995: Introduction, note 2).

8   Biesenbach-Lucas's study was based on a limited amount of relative clauses, just below 300 instances from one newspaper (*The Washington Post*). Jacobson's study comprised almost three times as many, more precisely, 858 instances from two newspapers, the *New York Times* and the *San Francisco Chronicle*. In my material, more than 5,600 relative *wh*-clauses and *that*-clauses were found, distributed between three newspapers and ten decades.

9   The corpus as a whole consists of approximately 40 million words.

newspaper language in both varieties. For comparison it can be mentioned that, in fiction, *that* is more than twice as common as *which* in restrictive relative clauses, while, in academic prose, *which* is almost twice as common as *that*. In both genres *which* is the only alternative in non-restrictive clauses.[10]

In the oral sample of Biesenbach-Lucas's study (see note 5 above), only restrictive relative clauses were found with personal referents. In these clauses *who* was competing with *that*. With non-personal referents, the distribution of the relative pronouns was the same as in the written data: *which* was reduced to non-restrictive relative clauses, and *that*, or "zero", to restrictive.[11] Similar results were shown in a recent study of formal spoken American English carried out at the Department of English at Uppsala University (see Geisler and Johansson 2002).[12] The spoken data in Biber et al. (1999: 610–616), which is based on British English, show a greater variability in the choice of relative pronouns: *who, which, that*, and "zero" constructions are all represented.[13] *That* is the most favoured of the three pronouns (more than twice as common as *who* and *which* together), closely followed by "zero" constructions.

The *that*-clauses in my data were edited by hand in order to distinguish *that* used as a relative pronoun from *that* used as a determiner (*that* day), a demonstrative pronoun (he never did *that* before), or a subordinator (she promised *that* she…). Two things emerged when the frequencies of relative *that* and relative *wh*-pronouns were compared: firstly, that relative *wh*-pronouns were far more frequent than relative *that* (more than five times as frequent), and secondly, that the use of relative *that*-clauses remained more stable across the years. No statistically significant change was attested until between 1940 and 1950 when the frequencies went down from 2.56 to 1.36. After that, the use of the feature remained again more or less stable, and no statistically significant difference was recorded when the frequencies from the beginning and the end of the century were compared (see Table 8.4 and Figure 8.3; for statistics, see Appendix, s.v. relative *that*-clauses).

When the feature was compared across newspapers, a statistically significant difference was recorded between the *Daily Telegraph* and the other two newspapers, with lower frequencies in the former, which suggests a greater resistance among the leader writers in the *Telegraph* against the use of the more informal variant of relative pronouns. The peak observed in the *Guardian*, 1940,

---

10   The data for fiction and academic prose in Biber et al.'s material are based on the British English material only.

11   The instances of relative pronouns and "zero" constructions in Biesenbach's oral data are very few, however, only 40 (compared to 292 in her written data), which makes it difficult to draw any safe conclusions from these results.

12   Geisler and Johansson's data were based on three samples from the Corpus of Spoken Professional American English, together about 2 million words of running text. Altogether, 626 relative clauses were examined. No "zero" constructions were included.

13   No distinction seems to have been made between restrictive and non-restrictive clauses in Biber et al.'s study as far as the spoken data (conversation) are concerned (see 1999: 610).

is difficult to explain. The subject-matter of the editorials in the *Guardian* that year does not distinguish itself from that of the other two newspapers. One reason might be that the leader writers of that year showed a greater acceptance towards the more informal variant of the relative pronouns than those of the other two newspapers.

Table 8.4 Relative *that*-clauses: normed frequencies.

Year	Ti	DT	Gua	All
1900	1.47	1.96	2.53	2.14
1910	1.97	2.24	1.66	1.90
1920	1.27	1.43	2.02	1.59
1930	2.15	1.02	2.95	2.00
1940	2.10	1.49	4.01	2.56
1950	1.67	0.94	1.55	1.36
1960	1.58	1.33	1.07	1.33
1970	2.71	1.41	1.36	1.79
1980	2.10	1.32	0.89	1.42
1993	2.44	1.31	1.21	1.71
1900–1993	1.97	1.35	1.95	1.76

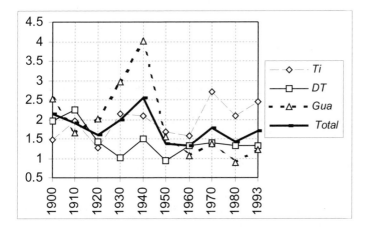

Figure 8.3 The development of relative *that*-clauses.

Relative *wh*-pronouns and relative *that* thus proved to be distributed differently in English up-market newspaper editorials. The *wh*-pronouns were considerably more frequent, which is only what could be expected since they have proved to be the more common variant in written discourse, at least in such discourse as British newspaper language and academic prose (cf. Finegan and Biber 1997: 73; Biber et al. 1999: 610–611). The fact that the patterns of development of the relative *wh*-pronouns and relative *that* do not follow each other more closely is more difficult to explain. One reason could be that the reduction of relative clauses concerned the non-restrictive clauses in the first place, and since *that* is rarely used in that position (see, for example, Geisler and Johansson 2002), it was less affected by the change. Another reason could be that *that* is associated with more informal styles, such as conversation and "contemporary" fiction (see Biber et al. 1999: 616) and therefore needed to be avoided in a genre such as newspaper editorials.

Bauer (1994: 66–83, in his diachronic study of relative pronouns in editorials in *The Times* (see section 1.2) found no evidence of change. However, he was not satisfied with the result since it did not match his expectations. Through "non-systematic but informed observation over a number of years" (p. 71) he was convinced that this was an area where change was going on even though he had not been able to prove it. The present study, which is based on a much larger body of texts than his was, shows that he was right in his assumptions.

8.3   Nominalizations

Nominalizations have often been used in register comparisons. Chafe (1982: 39–40) and Chafe and Danielewicz (1987: 99–100), for instance, found that they are more frequent in written than in oral discourse. Biber (1986) shows that they often co-occur with passives and prepositional phrases and interprets their common function as "conveying highly abstract (as opposed to situated) information" (Biber 1988: 227). In Biber (1988: 110), they are grouped together with phrasal co-ordination and the three relativization features mentioned above. However, according to Biber, a functional difference is observed between the relative *wh*-clauses, on the one hand, and nominalizations and phrasal co-ordination, on the other (see section 8.1). The reason for nominalizations (and phrasal co-ordination) to co-occur with the markers of explicit discourse is, as Biber points out, that explicit discourse is, normally, also integrated and informational (Biber 1988: 110). Consequently, nominalizations are markers of the integration of information in the first place.

Nominalizations are usually connected with texts of high information density. They are used for the expansion of idea units by integrating as much information into as few words as possible:

> A nominalization allows a notion which is verbal in origin to be inserted into an idea unit as if it were a noun. Such an element then plays the role of a noun in the syntax of the idea unit, acting as one of the arguments of the main predication. Thus it adds another, intrinsically predicative, element to the idea unit in the guise of a nominal one. (Chafe 1982: 39)

Semantically, nominalizations are thus usually related to a verb, such as *involvement* to *involve*, but they can also be related to an adjective, such as *darkness* to *dark*. They are usually nominal phrases derived from clauses (Quirk et al. 1985: 1288). Example (10) might be derived from, for instance, an adverbial clause (*when they arrived ...*) and (11) from, for instance, a *that*-clause preceded by *the fact* (*the fact that Mr. Strachey was appointed to the War Office was ...*).

(10)   These civilians whom Bolshevism has ruined, will as Lady Marling states "be absolutely destitute and friendless *on arrival in England*". (TI20E16)

(11)   Mr. Strachey's *appointment to the War Office* was, in any case, lamentable; (DT50E8)

Consequently, most nominalizations can be re-written as a phrase or a clause. Some are more difficult to denominalize, however. Take for example *loan repayment* in (12) from the *Guardian*, 1993.

(12)   The scheme, by 1997, basically offers 100,000 graduates release from college debts in return for one or two years of minimum wage service to the community currently defined as work in schools, the police, immunisation projects and areas of environmental concern. There's a broader context of *loan repayment* for others, but the 100,000 toiling in the community (at an exchequer cost of nearly 3.5 billion dollars) stand at the core. (GUA1993E7)

Due to the fact that so much information is compressed in a single word or phrase, the use of nominalizations can cause ambiguity or obscurity (see, for example, Greenbaum 1988: 9). Kress (1983: 129–134) shows that nominalizations can therefore be used for ideological purposes. To manipulate the reader, central actions are often expressed in nominal form thus omitting the actor and leaving the reader in doubt:

By expressing an event in nominal form it is at once taken out of time, and can therefore be readily assimilated to 'timeless' sets of categories. The event is taken out of the world of the specific, concrete, and placed in the world of the general, abstract ... (Kress 1983: 129)

Halliday agrees that nominalizations may cause ambiguity but maintains that this is a price worth paying because they give "more choice of status in the discourse" (1987: 77).

Only abstract nominalizations, more precisely those ending in *-ity, -ment, -ness*, and *-tion*, and their plural forms, were included in the present study as they are easily retrievable through computer-based searches. Still, the words ending in *-ment* and *-ments* had to be edited by hand since many instances, such as *apartment* or *increment,* have the same ending without being nominalizations.

A statistically significant increase in the use of the feature was observed between 1900 and 1960, but after that no statistically significant changes were noticed. When the feature was compared across newspapers, a statistically significant difference was shown between the *Guardian* and *The Times* (considerably lower frequencies in the *Guardian* over the years) (see Table 8.5 and Figure 8.4; for statistics, see Appendix, s.v. nominalizations).

Table 8.5 Nominalizations: normed frequencies.

Year	Ti	DT	Gua	All
1900	17.12	15.27	12.15	14.04
1910	19.81	15.87	18.94	18.41
1920	18.45	16.42	18.47	17.90
1930	18.88	19.04	16.67	18.14
1940	16.20	18.34	13.65	16.05
1950	17.76	19.68	20.61	19.34
1960	17.92	22.85	21.19	20.85
1970	21.26	18.35	21.37	20.33
1980	22.92	18.94	19.80	20.44
1993	21.59	21.56	17.38	20.13
1900–1993	19.39	19.09	17.89	18.74

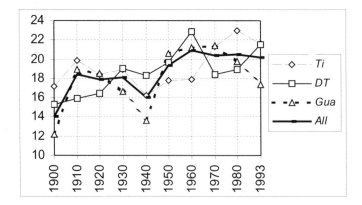

Figure 8.4 The development of nominalizations.

The comparatively low normed frequency attested for the *Guardian* in 1900 is difficult to account for. The contents of the editorials in the three newspapers are almost identical (most of them deal with the Boer wars). The overall style is also very much alike. One reason might, of course, be the idiolects of the authors involved.

From the above results it is apparent that nominalization and relative clauses show different patterns of development. While a substantial decrease was observed, across the years, in the use of relative clauses, the use of nominalizations increased. Hence, it is reasonable to assume, that, as far as English up-market newspaper editorials are concerned, explicitness and informational density are not as closely related as Biber's study indicated (1988: 110).

8.4   Summary and conclusions

The development of relative *wh*-clauses, the foremost marker of explicit discourse in Biber's study (1988), and of relative *that*-clauses, on the one hand, and nominalizations, on the other, thus show divergent patterns of development in English up-market newspaper editorials: the relative *wh*-clauses and, to some extent, also relative *that*-clauses decreased in use while the use of nominalizations increased. The fact that the pattern of development for nominalizations deviates from that observed for the relative pronouns suggests that the feature has more in common with features marking informational and integrated discourse than with those marking explicit reference. Nouns and attributive adjectives, for example, the most important markers of informational density, increased in use over time (see sections 4.2 and 4.3.1) as did present participle WHIZ-deletions (see section 4.3.3). Detached past and present participle clauses, which have also often been used as markers of integrated discourse, showed an increase towards the end of the 20th century, more precisely between 1970 and 1993 (see sections 7.3.1 and 5.4, respectively) even though the lines of development preceding this increase were irregular. On the basis of this, it can be assumed that in English up-market editorials, nominalizations are markers of information density rather than of explicit reference. Finally, it can be argued that the language of the editorials, in its loss of explicitness across the decades, developed towards greater informality.

9. Towards a description of the modern English up-market editorial

9.1 Introduction

To shed light on the development of the modern English up-market editorial, the language of the editorials making up my corpus was investigated with respect to features that previous research, especially Biber's study (1988), had proved to be markers of different types of discourse. The starting point was sets of features associated with the dimensions of linguistic variation presented in Biber (1988), more precisely, personal involvement, information density, narrative discourse, argumentative discourse, abstract discourse and explicit reference. Interestingly, in my data, the members of each set developed in divergent directions. Among the markers of personal involvement, for example, those associated with conversational discourse, such as questions and contractions, were found to have increased in use while most of those associated with inexplicit reference, such as the pronoun *it*, possibility modals, and indefinite pronouns had decreased or showed no statistically significant change over time (see Chapter 3). As far as information density is concerned, nouns, attributive adjectives, present participle WHIZ-deletion, word length, and type/token ratio increased over the years, while prepositions decreased (see Chapter 4). The most important of the markers of narrative discourse, that is, past tense verbs, together with *no*-negation, decreased in use while perfect aspect verbs, public verbs, and third person pronouns showed no statistically significant change (see Chapter 5). As regards argumentative discourse, the infinitive was the only feature that changed over time (see Chapter 6). Among the markers of abstract discourse, we notice an increasing use of agentless passives, the principal marker of such discourse, while no statistically significant change was recorded for, for example, *by*-passives and past participle WHIZ-deletion (see Chapter 7). As to explicit reference, *wh*-relatives and pied piping constructions decreased in use whereas nominalizations increased (see Chapter 8).

Consequently, it was necessary to find new patterns of development, specific for English up-market editorials, based on change and continuity as well as on shared linguistic/stylistic functions among the features involved. Therefore, all the features included in the study were first classified according to increase, decrease, and linguistic continuity, as seen in section 9.2 (Table 9.1). Keeping the change/continuity distinction, the features were then grouped together according to shared linguistic/stylistic functions in English up-market editorials (see section 9.3, Table 9.2). Each group of features was analysed and associations with other groups were established (see sections 9.3.1–9.3.8). The results of this analysis are summarized in section 9.3.9.

It was not only between features representing the same dimension in Biber's study that different patterns of development were noticed, however. Sometimes, one and the same feature also showed different patterns of development in the three newspapers included in the study. In section 9.4, these features are compared across newspapers. The comparison is based on the data presented for each feature in Chapters 3 to 8. The statistics are found in Appendix 1. Section 9.5, finally, aims at a synthesis of the present chapter.

9.2   Classification according to change and continuity

To obtain an overview of the development of the features dealt with in the present study, the features were first grouped together on the basis of 'statistically significant increase', 'statistically significant decrease', and 'linguistic continuity', the last of these groups consisting of the features that showed no statistically significant difference when the normed frequencies attested for the beginning and the end of the 20th century were compared. This means that among the features representing 'linguistic continuity' we also find such as show a statistically significant change over one or more decades, but this change is levelled out by other changes during the period (see, for example, 'detached' present participle clauses, section 5.4, and 'detached' past participle clauses, section 7.3.1). However, these features are given special attention in the contexts where they appear.

The result of the distribution of the features according to change and continuity is shown in Table 9.1.[1] Among the features are also those which were included in the present study without having been included in Biber's (1988), more precisely, imperatives, sentence length, and subordination (see section 2.4.1). In the tables below, they are marked with an asterisk (*).

---

1   The classification of the features into categories showing 'statistically significant increase', 'statistically significant decrease', and 'linguistic continuity' was made on the basis of the results attested for the *Daily Telegraph*, the *Guardian*, and *The Times* together. The statistical tools used for the calculation of statistically significant differences across decades, as well as across newspapers, were the Analysis of Variance (one-way Anova) and The Newman-Keuls multiple comparison test (see section 2.5.3). The probability for a feature to have increased/decreased over time is calculated at the 0.05 significance level (see Appendix 1, introduction).

Table 9.1 Classification of the features analysed according to change and continuity.

Statistically significant increase over time	Statistically significant decrease over time	Linguistic continuity
Attributive adjectives	Adverbial amplifiers	*By*-passives
Contractions	Agentless passives	Causative subordination
Imperatives*	First person pronouns	Conditional subordination
Infinitives	*No*-negation	Conjuncts
Nominalizations	Past tense verbs	Demonstrative pronouns
Not-negation	Pied piping	'Detached' past participle clauses
Nouns	Prepositions	'Detached' present participle
Present participle WHIZ-deletion	Private verbs	clauses
Present tense verbs	Pronoun *it*	Discourse particles
Questions	Relative *wh*-clauses	General emphatics
Type/token ratio	Sentence length*	General hedges
Word length	Subordination: tag #CS*	Indefinite pronouns
		Necessity modals[a]
		Past participle WHIZ-deletion
		Perfect aspect verbs
		Possibility modals
		Predictive modals
		Public verbs
		Relative *that*-clauses
		Second person pronouns
		Suasive verbs
		'Subordinators with multiple functions'
		Third person pronouns

[a] The marginal modals *need* and *have (got) to* are also included among the necessity modals. In Chapter 6, they are dealt with separately, but as they showed the same pattern of development as *must, should,* and *ought to*, they were all grouped together as necessity modals here.

The results presented in Table 9.1 demonstrate that almost half of the features represent linguistic stability. However, as section 9.3 will show, many of these features are linked with sets of features that have either increased or decreased in use, and the disparate patterns of development can be accounted for.

9.3 Classification according to shared linguistic/stylistic functions in English up-market editorials – discussion and interpretation

After being distributed over change and continuity, the features were classified according to shared linguistic/stylistic functions as they appear in English up-market editorials. The results, which are shown in Table 9.2, will be discussed and interpreted in sections 9.3.1 to 9.3.8. Section 9.3.9 summarizes the findings.

Table 9.2 Classification of the features analysed according to shared linguistic/stylistic functions and to change/continuity.

Linguistic/stylistic function	Statistically significant increase over time	Statistically significant decrease over time	Linguistic continuity
1. Informal discourse	Present tense verbs *Not*-negation Questions Imperatives* Contractions		Discourse particles General emphatics Second person pronoun
2. Information density/ lexical specificity	Nouns Attributive adjectives Present participle WHIZ-deletion Word length Type/token ratio Infinitives Nominalizations	Prepositions	'Detached' past participle clauses 'Detached' present participle clauses Past participle WHIZ-deletion
3. Vagueness/ uncertainty		Adverbial amplifiers Private verbs Pronoun *it*	Demonstrative pronoun Possibility modals Indefinite pronouns General hedges
4. Narrative discourse		Past tense verbs *No*-negation First person pronouns	Perfect aspect verbs Public verbs Third person pronouns
5. Explicit reference		Relative *wh*-clauses Pied piping	Relative *that*-clauses
6. Sentence complexity		Sentence length* Subordination: tag #CS*	
7. Abstract discourse		Agentless passives	*By*-passives
8. Argumentative discourse			Suasive verbs Predictive modals Necessity modals Conditional subordination Causative subordination Conjuncts 'Subordinators with multiple functions'

*The features marked with an asterisk were not included in Biber's 1988 study.

9.3.1   Informal discourse

Among the features representing informal discourse we find one set that increased in use and another that showed linguistic continuity. The former comprises such features as proved to have increased in use among the markers of personal involvement discussed in Chapter 3, namely present tense verbs, *not*-negation, questions, imperatives, and contractions. The increasing use of questions, imperatives, and contractions indicates not only increasing informality but also an increasing conversational tone in the editorials over the years (see sections 3.2.3, 3.2.4, and 3.2.5).

The increase in the use of these features, except as regards imperatives and contractions, started in the middle of the century, for most of them in 1940. The increase of imperatives did not set in until 1970 and that of contractions even later. Only few instances of contractions were recorded before 1993, and it was almost exclusively in the *Guardian* that they were found.

In the set that showed no statistically significant change over time we find second person pronouns, discourse particles, and general emphatics. Classifying second person pronouns as markers of informal discourse might need an explanation. One of the discourse functions of the pronoun is that of direct address. In addressing the reader, the author wants to achieve the same effect as using, for example, questions and imperatives, namely, making the readers feel that they are part of a joint communicative event. The use of the pronoun *you* in the generic sense (that is, instead of *one* or a passive construction), may also result in increased informality. The inclusion of second person pronouns among the markers of informal discourse can thus be justified.

The reason why second person pronouns and discourse particles do not follow the pattern of development observed for the other markers of informal discourse could be that, spread out across decades and newspapers (see sections 3.4.3 and 3.4.6, respectively), they were too few to show any pattern of change (cf. contractions, section 3.2.5, which are concentrated to the *Guardian*, 1993 (see section 3.2.5)). Only 23 instances of discourse particles and 85 instances of second person pronouns, outside quoted speech, were found. As to general emphatics, the variation across both newspapers and decades was great, which indicates that there was considerable uncertainty as regards the use of the feature in the editorials. When these aspects are taken into consideration, the fact that the three features showed a deviating pattern of development need not blur the overall picture. It is obvious that, during the 20th century, the language of English up-market editorials developed towards greater informality.

9.3.2 Information density and lexical specificity

The features representing information density and lexical specificity comprise one set that increased in use, one set that showed linguistic continuity, and one single feature that decreased in use. In the first set, we find all the features from Chapter 4 (Features marking information density) that proved to have increased in use: nouns, attributive adjectives, present participle WHIZ-deletion (the markers of information density), and word length and type/token ratio (the markers of lexical specificity). New members are infinitives (see section 6.2) and nominalizations (see sections 8.3). In Biber's study (1988) these two features are associated with argumentative discourse and explicit reference, respectively. However, according to other researchers, infinitives and nominalizations are, rather, markers of integrated discourse (see sections 6.2 and 8.3). Since, in my data, they follow the same pattern of development as the features marking information density, it is reasonable to assume that, in English up-market editorials, they are, primarily, employed for the integration of information.

The increase of attributive adjectives, infinitives, nominalizations, word length, and type/token ratio set in at the beginning of the 20th century while that of nouns and present participle WHIZ-deletion did not begin until the last few decades of the century. Up to 1970, the lines of development observed for some of the features were rather irregular.

New members among the markers of information density are also 'detached' past and present participle clauses and past participle WHIZ-deletions. In Biber's study (1988), 'detached' present participle clauses are included among the markers of narrative discourse and 'detached' past participle clauses and past participle WHIZ-deletions among the markers of abstractive discourse. Normally, these three features, like infinitives and nominalizations, are associated with discourse marked by a high degree of integration of information or with structural elaboration, however (see sections 5.4, 7.3.1, and 7.3.2). In the present study, no statistically significant difference was observed when the frequencies from the beginning and the end of the century were compared. Nevertheless, between 1970 and 1993, a noticeable (for 'detached' past participle clauses and present participle clauses statistically significant) increase was observed, which speaks for their inclusion among the markers of information density and strengthens the assumption about a development in the direction of greater information density in the editorials, especially towards the end of the century (cf. the patterns of development for nouns, section 4.2, and present participle WHIZ-deletion, section 4.3.3).

The only remaining marker of information density, namely prepositional phrases, showed a deviating pattern of development. The decrease in the use of the feature started right from the beginning of the century and continued until the end. The reason why prepositions and prepositional adverbs decreased in use, whereas so many other markers of integrated discourse increased, is difficult to account for. One possible explanation is that postmodification by prepositional phrases, to some extent at least, was replaced by premodifying nouns, such as, *the industry's immediate trouble* (DT60E29) and *City uncertainty* (TI93E3),[2] which proved to have increased during the time-period studied. Another explanation could be that it is mainly among prepositional phrases used for other purposes than postmodification, for example, as adverbials or verb complementation, that the decrease took place (see section 4.3.2). Thus, the decrease of prepositional phrases need not conflict with the general tendency towards a more compact and integrated language.

---

2   In Rydén (1975) such phrases are referred to as "noun-name collocations".

9.3.3   Vagueness/uncertainty

Among the markers of vagueness/uncertainty we find one set that decreased in use and another that showed no change over time.[3] The first set comprises adverbial amplifiers, private verbs, and the pronoun *it*. The pronoun *it* may create referential vagueness since the speakers/writers are not always explicit about what they are referring to (see, for example, Biber 1988: 225–226 and Chafe and Danielewicz 1987: 90–91). Many of the private verbs, such as, *think, believe,* and *assume*, contribute to another type of vagueness in so far as the speakers/writers, in employing them, indicate that they are not certain about the truth value of what is expressed. The reduced use of these features involves reduced vagueness, which, in turn, leads to more precise and exact information. The decrease of adverbial amplifiers might also have contributed to increased explicitness. In Biber's study, adverbial amplifiers, such as, *absolutely, enormously,* and *perfectly*, are linked with personal involvement, marking "heightened feeling" (see section 3.3.1). The decrease in the use of the feature probably led to a language that is of a more matter-of-fact nature.

The decrease of adverbial amplifiers started at the beginning of the century and that of the pronoun *it* as early as the 1930s while the line of development observed for private verbs did not turn downwards until after 1960.

The features marking vagueness/uncertainty that did not change over time include demonstrative pronouns, possibility modals, indefinite pronouns, and general hedges. The demonstrative and indefinite pronouns are often used without explicit reference, like the pronoun *it* (se above). General hedges, such as, *at about, something like,* and *more or less*, as well as the possibility modals are employed to mark uncertainty or imprecision.

The most frequent of the features representing vagueness/uncertainty, that is, the pronoun *it* and the private verbs, and, in addition to these, the adverbial amplifiers thus decreased in use. The rest showed linguistic continuity. It is therefore reasonable to assume that the language of the editorials studied became more precise over the years (cf. the increase of word length, section 4.4.1, and type/token ratio, section 4.4.2).

9.3.4   Narrative discourse

Also among the features associated with narrativity we find one set of features that decreased in use and another that showed no statistically significant change over time. The former includes past tense verbs and *no*-negation, both associated with narrative discourse in Biber's study, and first person pronouns, associated with personal involvement. However, first person pronouns and, more specifically, the plural form of the pronoun, has a very specific range of application in the editorials, which makes it natural to include them among the

---

3   All these features are included among the markers of personal involvement in Biber's study (1988).

features of narrative discourse. Outside quoted speech, *we* is used, almost exclusively, either with reference to the nation (the rhetorical *we*) or with reference to the newspaper (the editorial *we*) (see section 3.3.3). Representing their country or their newspapers, the authors take on the narrator's role, up to and including 1940, mainly giving the readers detailed descriptions from different theatres of war. After that, when the subject-matter of the editorials became more diverse, we see a consistent and noticeable decrease of the pronoun.

Since past tense verbs, by far the most important marker of narrative discourse in Biber's study (1988), as well as *no*-negation and first person pronouns, decreased in use over the years, it is apparent that English up-market editorials became less narrative during the period studied (cf. medical and science texts in Biber and Finegan, 1997, and debates in Geisler, forthcoming). The decrease of past tense verbs and *no*-negation started at the beginning of the century and continued, with some fluctuations, until 1970. After that no statistically significant changes were observed. As to first person pronouns, the decrease started in the middle of the century, as mentioned above.

The reason why no change was attested for perfect aspect verbs, public verbs, and third person pronouns, which are also associated with narrative discourse in Biber's study, is that they carry important basic functions in the editorials and these functions have not changed across the years. From now on, such features will be referred to as 'editorial-inherent' features. Perfect aspect verbs are used to report or comment on past events of current relevance, which is also the aim of the editorials. Public verbs, such as *comment, declare,* and *report,* are often referred to as 'reporting verbs', which reveals their main function in editorials, that is, to report, and the reporting function of the editorials did not change over time. Third person pronouns are also associated with the reporting function of the editorials in so far as they are used for reporting on events with reference to people and, in the plural, also to inanimates.[4]

The decrease of past tense verbs, *no*-negation, and first person pronouns means a development towards a non-narrative style, while the continuity in the use of perfect aspect verbs, public verbs, and third person pronouns shows that the reporting and commenting functions of the editorials have remained the same over the years (cf. the markers of argumentative discourse, section 9.3.8).

9.3.5   Explicit reference

All the features discussed in Chapter 8 except nominalization, that is, relative *wh*-clauses, pied piping, and relative *that*-clauses, are grouped together as markers of explicit reference. The patterns of development attested for relative *wh*-clauses and pied piping are almost identical. The decrease started at the beginning of the century and continued up to 1970. After that no statistically significant changes were noticed. As far as relative *that*-clauses are concerned, no statistically

---

4   The pronoun *it* is not included among the third person pronouns, but is dealt with separately as a marker of vagueness/uncertainty (see section 9.4.3).

significant difference between the beginning and the end of the century was recorded despite the fact that a statistically significant decrease was observed between 1940 and 1950. The fact that relative *that*-clauses do not follow the pattern of development attested for relative *wh*-clauses needs to be accounted for. As suggested in section 8.2.3, the more conspicuous and consistent decrease in the use of the *wh*-clauses might be due to a reduction, over the years, of non-restrictive relative clauses, where *that* seldom appears (see, for example, Geisler and Johansson 2002). Another reason could be that relative *that* is associated with more informal styles (see, for example, Biber et al. 1999: 616) and that the authors of the editorials, therefore, throughout the period studied, suppressed the use of the pronoun.

Relative clauses, as well as, for example, attributive adjectives and participle WHIZ-deletions, are used for the expansion of the noun phrase. The difference between them lies in the fact that, whereas attributive adjectives and participles, even though expanding the noun phrase, compress a great deal of information into comparatively few words, the relative clause normally needs a full finite clause to give the same amount of information.[5] The decrease of the markers of explicit reference (relative *wh*-pronouns, pied piping, and to some extent also relative *that*) and the increase of the markers of information density/lexical specificity (nouns, attributive adjectives, present participle WHIZ-deletion, word length, and type/token ratio) therefore indicate that, during the period studied, the elaborate explicitness of the relative clause had to give way to the demand for more compact language (cf. section 9.3.2). Besides making the language more compact, the decrease of relative clauses might also have been a factor contributing to the reduced sentence length discussed in section 9.3.6.

9.3.6 Sentence complexity

In the present study sentence length and subordination (subordinate clauses introduced by subordinators) are used as a measure of sentence complexity. Since a reduced number of subordinated clauses ought to entail shorter sentences, it is only natural that both these features should have decreased in use across the years. The reduction of words per sentence as well as of subordinations started at the beginning of the century and continued until the end.

The reduced sentence complexity can be interpreted in two ways. It may be the result of the authors' ambition to make the language of the editorials more "reader-friendly" in so far as shorter sentences may be easier to process. It may also be the result of their aspiration for increased information density: the more integrated the language, the shorter the sentences. Subordination, as well as relativization (see section 9.3.5), therefore had to give way to shorter means of expressing an idea. No guidance as to which is the more probable explanation can

---

5   An exception is, of course, relative infinitive clauses, such as *the person to ask* or *something to show* (Geisler 1995).

be had from previous research since scholars have come up with contradictory results (see section 4.5.1 and 4.5.2).

9.3.7 Abstract discourse

The two features representing abstract discourse in Table 9.2, that is, agentless passives and *by*-passives (see sections 7.2.1 and 7.2.2), are found among the markers of abstract discourse also in Biber (1988). In the present study, the agentless passive is the most important feature of the markers of abstract discourse, frequency-wise, with normed frequencies exceeding those attested for all the markers of abstract discourse together and more than five times as frequent as *by*-passives (see sections 7.2–7.5). Lacking an agent NP, the instigator of the action denoted by the verb, the agentless passives are also the most 'abstract' of the markers of abstract discourse. Even though no statistically significant change was attested for *by*-passives, we can thus assume that the language of English up-market editorials became less abstract over time, which, in turn, contributed to making it less formal (cf. section 9.3.1).

9.3.8 Argumentative discourse

The first four features among the markers of argumentative discourse in Table 9.2, that is, suasive verbs, predictive modals, necessity modals, and conditional subordination (see sections 6.3–6.6) were markers of argumentative discourse also in Biber's study (1988) while causative subordination was included among the markers of personal involvement (see section 3.4.5) and conjuncts and 'subordinators with multiple functions' among the markers of abstract discourse (see sections 7.4 and 7.5). The reason for grouping these features together as markers of argumentative discourse in the present study is that even causative subordinators, conjuncts and 'subordinators with multiple functions' are used for argumentative purposes. Causative subordinators, such as *because* and *as,* introduce subordinate clauses giving the reasons for the cause that is argued for or against, thus making the argumentation more forceful. Conjuncts, such as *therefore, consequently,* and *thus,* and 'subordinators with multiple functions', such as *while* and *whereas,* are used for building up the logical relations between different linguistic units, something that is necessary to give the text an argumentative structure. In the present classification of features, conjuncts, causative subordinators, and 'subordinators with multiple functions' were therefore included among the markers of argumentative discourse. As the use of none of these features changed over time, we can conclude that the argumentative structure of English up-market editorials did not change either, which means that these features, as well as perfect aspect verbs, public verbs, and third person pronouns are editorial-inherent features.

9.3.9 Summing-up

From the above discussion, it is obvious that the language of English up-market editorials became more informal during the 20th century. Most of the features marking informal discourse increased in use (see section 9.3.1) while those marking abstract discourse decreased, a fact that also contributed to the development of a less formal language (see section 9.3.7). The increased use of conversational features, such as questions, imperatives, and contractions, is, most certainly, the primary reason for the increased informality of the editorials, however.

At the same time as the language of the editorials moved in the direction of greater informality, a change towards increased information density and precise lexical choice was noticed (see section 9.3.2). The reduced use of finite relative clauses also contributed to increased information density (see section 9.3.5), and the reduced use of features expressing vagueness and uncertainty (see section 9.3.3) led to more precise and exact information.

As mentioned in section 9.3.6, reduced sentence length and fewer subordinations can also be an indication of increased information density in so far as a more compact language results in shorter sentences. However, they can also be the result of the authors' increased endeavour to bring the language of the editorials closer to the readers' everyday language. If so, the features are markers of increased informality rather than information density.

The editorials as narrative pieces of writing became rarer with time, as is understood from the reduced use of the past tense verbs and *no*-negation, and by 1970 the new non-narrative style had established itself. The argumentative and reporting functions of the editorials, on the other hand, did not change over the years (see sections 9.3.8 and 9.3.4, respectively).

9.4 Linguistic/stylistic differences between the three newspapers

The three newspapers, from which the editorials are taken, are all up-market newspapers. Still, some variation between them, as far as language use is concerned, could be expected since their political view and readership profiles diverge.[6] Therefore, the normed frequencies attested for the features discussed in Chapters 3 to 8 were compared not only across time but also across newspapers, and statistical analyses were applied to the results.[7] Consequently, we have evidence for possible differences between the three newspapers in their use of each of the features. However, in most cases no statistically significant differences were observed, which means that the three newspapers constitute a

---

6   For the different political standpoints of the three newspapers and their readership profiles, see section 2.3.1.

7   The probability for statistically significant differences to exist between the three newspapers in their use of a feature is calculated at the 0.05 significance level.

fairly homogeneous group. When the features, for which statistically significant divergences were attested, were distributed over the sets shown in Table 9.2, the results were those presented in Tables 9.3 to 9.8. In these tables, a plus sign (+) in a column indicates that the feature is more frequent (has a higher ratio) and a minus sign (−) that it is less frequent (has a lower ratio) in the newspaper the column represents than in the other newspaper(s). The zero (0) indicates that the feature takes an intermediate position.

As regards informal discourse, statistically significant differences between the newspapers were attested for three features, namely, present tense verbs, questions, and contractions (see Table 9.3).

Table 9.3 Informal discourse.

Feature	The Times	The Daily Telegraph	The Guardian
Present tense verbs	−	+	+
Questions	−	+	+
Contractions	−	−	+

+ = more frequent than in the other newspaper(s)
− = less frequent than in the other newspaper(s)

From the distribution of these features across newspapers it is apparent that the language of the *Guardian* is the most informal and that of *The Times* the least informal. The *Daily Telegraph* takes an intermediate position.

In Table 9.4, we find four markers of information density and precise lexical choice that showed statistically significant differences across newspapers, namely, attributive adjectives, nominalizations, prepositions, and type/token ratio; the fifth, subordination, is a marker of sentence complexity (see Table 9.4).

Table 9.4 Information density and lexical specificity/sentence complexity.

Feature	The Times	The *Daily Telegraph*	The *Guardian*
Attributive adjectives	+	0	−
Nominalizations	+	0	−
Prepositions	+	0	−
Type/token ratio (mean)	−	+	0
Subordination*	−	+	0

+ = more frequent than in the other newspaper(s)
− = less frequent than in the other newspaper(s)
0 = intermediate position

A clear pattern emerges: the language of *The Times* shows the highest information density and that of the *Guardian* the lowest. Once again, the *Daily Telegraph* takes an intermediate position. The highest rate of lexical specificity and diversity, on the other hand, is found in the *Daily Telegraph* and the lowest in *The Times*, as the result of the comparison of type/token ratios showed. The ratio of subordination is also higher in both the *Daily Telegraph* and the *Guardian* than it is in *The Times* (the highest in the *Daily Telegraph*), which points to greater sentence complexity in these two newspapers. The fact that lexical specificity and sentence complexity are lower in *The Times* than in the *Guardian* is surprising when their readership profiles are taken into consideration. Since the *Guardian* is normally associated with an audience closer to the mid-market newspapers than the other two newspapers, its language and vocabulary would have been expected to be the least complex of the three (see, for example, Bell 1991: 104–125, where "audience design" is discussed). However, even though the vocabulary is the least specific in *The Times,* the authors of this newspaper seemed to be those who cared the most for avoiding vagueness in reference, as shown in Table 9.5. In this respect, the *Guardian* scored the highest while the *Daily Telegraph* took the intermediate position, to judge from their uses of the pronoun *it* and demonstrative pronouns.

Table 9.5 Vagueness in reference.

Feature	The Times	The *Daily Telegraph*	The *Guardian*
Pronoun *it*	–	–	+
Demonstrative pronouns	–	+	+

+ = more frequent than in the other newspaper(s)
– = less frequent than in the other newspaper(s)

As far as narrative discourse is concerned, it seems as if the language of the *Guardian*, with the highest normed frequencies of first person pronouns and past tense verbs, were the most narrative and that of *The Times* the least narrative, with the *Daily Telegraph* in an intermediate position (see Table 9.6).

Table 9.6 Narrative discourse.

Feature	The Times	The *Daily Telegraph*	The *Guardian*
First person pronouns	–	+	+
Past tense verbs	0	–	+

+ = more frequent than in the other newspaper(s)
– = less frequent than in the other newspaper(s)
0 = intermediate position

Three features marking argumentative discourse, namely, predictive modals, conditional subordination, and causative subordination, are more frequent in the *Guardian* than in the other two newspapers (see Table 9.7). Even though conjuncts are more frequent in *The Times* and the *Daily Telegraph*, it is reasonable to assume that the editorials of the *Guardian* are the most argumentative of the three.

Table 9.7 Argumentative discourse.

Feature	The Times	The Daily Telegraph	The Guardian
Predictive modals	0	–	+
Conditional subordination	–	–	+
Causative subordination	–	–	+
Conjuncts	+	+	–

+ = more frequent than in the other newspaper(s)
– = less frequent than in the other newspaper(s)
0 = intermediate position

Two features showing differences across newspapers remain, namely, relative *that* (explicit reference) and third person pronouns, the latter one of the editorial inherent features (see Table 9.8).

Table 9.8 Other features.

Feature	The Times	The Daily Telegraph	The Guardian
Relative that	+	–	+
Third person pronouns	+	0	–

+ = more frequent than in the other newspaper(s)
– = less frequent than in the other newspaper(s)
0 = intermediate position

The more frequent use of relative *that* in *The Times* and the *Guardian* indicates that these two newspapers were more willing to accept the more informal variant of relative pronouns (see section 8.2.3). The fact that third person pronouns, one of the editorial-inherent features, was the most frequent in *The Times* and the least frequent in the *Guardian* is difficult to account for since no differences between the newspapers were recorded for the other features associated with the reporting function of the editorials, that is, perfect aspect verbs and public (reporting) verbs (see section 9.3.4).

9.5 Conclusion

From the results obtained in the present chapter, we can conclude that the language of the English up-market editorials, during the period covered by the study, became more informal but at the same time more compact and precise, in so far as the complexity of the noun phrase increased and the use of markers of vagueness and uncertainty decreased. Besides, the vocabulary used became more varied and specific. The sentences became shorter and the instances of subordination fewer, which is either the result of the authors' increasing striving for reader-friendliness or of their striving for information density. Furthermore, we notice that the editorials became less narrative but that their reporting and argumentative functions remained the same over the years.

When the features were compared across the newspapers analyzed, a clear distinction was noticed between *The Times* and the *Guardian*. The language of the *Guardian* is the most informal and the most narrative while that of *The*

Times is the least so. The information density is the highest in *The Times*, and the lowest in the *Guardian*. In these respects the *Daily Telegraph* thus takes an intermediate position. The editorials of the *Guardian* are the most argumentative. As far as vocabulary is concerned, that of the *Daily Telegraph* is the most varied and specific. Besides, the sentence structure is the most complex. Both as regards lexical specificity and sentence complexity *The Times* scores the lowest and the *Guardian* takes the intermediate position, which is surprising, considering the readership profiles of the three newspapers. However, as far as *The Times* is concerned, this might be an indication that the authors of the newspaper, in their competition for readers, try to adjust the language of the editorials to a broader audience, as a compensation for the over-all compact and integrated (complex) style.

10. Summary, conclusions, and discussion

10.1 Summary

The primary aim of the present study was to describe linguistic change and continuity in the language of English up-market editorials during the 20th century. The study is based on a corpus of 864 editorials, comprising just above 500,000 words, from the *Daily Telegraph*, the *Guardian* and *The Times*. To make a systematic diachronic study possible, the editorials were chosen to represent periods at ten-year intervals. The method used was basically quantitative in so far as statistical tools were applied to compare the frequencies of the features chosen for investigation, across decades as well as across newspapers. However, for an interpretation of the results arrived at, a qualitative perspective was necessary.

In Chapters 3 to 8, sets of features that previous research has proved to be representative of different types of discourse were investigated. As the patterns of development for the features within each set were often divergent, a reinterpretation of the functions of the features was necessary. In Chapter 9, the old sets were reanalysed and new ones established on the basis of shared development patterns as well as shared linguistic/stylistic functions, characteristic of the editorials.

10.2 Linguistic change and continuity as reflected in the editorials

From the results obtained, it is evident that the language of the editorials became more informal over the years but at the same time more integrated and lexically more specific and diverse. Interactional features, such as questions and imperatives, increased in use. The sentences became shorter and the subordinate clauses fewer, which can be interpreted in two ways. The reduced sentence complexity can either be the result of the authors' striving for greater information density, or it can be the result of their striving for increased informality since shorter sentences are easier to process and therefore more "reader-friendly".

The reduced use of passives during the second half of the century can also be explained in different ways. It can be the result of the authors' ambition to make the language as compact as possible by using abbreviated participle clauses instead of clauses with a finite verb, but it can also be the result of their ambition to distance themselves from too impersonal and abstract language. Consequently, two conflicting linguistic paradigms are at work in the editorials: the aspiration for informality and the aspiration for information density and lexical specificity, the former probably the result of an adjustment to a new and broader reading public and the latter the result of an adjustment to the special "house styles" that developed over the years. In addition to changes relating to formality and information density, we also notice a change as regards narrativity. The 'narrativeness', which was a prominent feature in the editorials at the beginning of the century, gradually decreased, and by 1970 the new, non-narrative style had established itself.

Linguistic history is not only a matter of change, however, but a matter of change and continuity, which is also shown in the present study. As a matter of fact, almost half of the features investigated showed linguistic continuity. Many of them were linked with sets of features that either increased or decreased in use, and, in most cases, a plausible reason could be given for the diverging patterns of development. However, there were also features for which no such links were discernible, namely those associated with argumentative discourse and with reporting, which indicates that these features carry important basic functions inherent in the editorials and therefore did not change over time.

10.3 Differences between the newspapers

A comparison of the three newspapers reveals a clear linguistic/stylistic difference between the *Guardian*, on the one hand, and *The Times* and the *Daily Telegraph*, on the other. The language of the *Guardian* was the most informal, with the highest frequencies of conversational features such as questions, imperatives, and contractions, whereas that of *The Times* was the most compact and integrated. The *Daily Telegraph* showed the greatest lexical diversity and specificity and also the greatest sentence complexity of the three newspapers. As far as narrativity is concerned, the *Guardian* scored the highest and *The Times* the lowest. The fact that the conversational and narrative tone is more conspicuous in the *Guardian* editorials than in those of the other two newspapers gives an indication that the *Guardian* authors direct themselves to a readership that is somewhat broader than that of *The Times* and the *Daily Telegraph*. While keeping their position as an up-market newspaper, they are approaching the domain of the mid-market ones, such as the *Daily Mail,* the *Daily Express*, and *Today*. The editorial writers of the *Daily Telegraph* and *The Times*, on the other hand, in using less informal language and in paying more attention to the presentation of information than does the *Guardian*, wish to emphasize the position of their newspapers as up-market newspapers.

However, even though there are linguistic/stylistic differences between the editorials of the three newspapers investigated, a joint pattern of development can be observed. Towards the end of the period studied, the language used in English up-market newspaper editorials, as represented by the *Daily Telegraph*, the *Guardian*, and *The Times* together, is more informal but at the same time more compact and more lexically specific and varied. Furthermore, the narrative aspect of the editorials has largely disappeared whereas the argumentative and reporting functions are still the same as they were at the beginning of the 20th century.

10.4 Aspects on the methodology employed

When investigating linguistic change it is possible to use either a quantitative or a qualitative approach or a combination of both. Since my aim in this study was to present statistical evidence for such changes as I had intuitively felt were underhand in the editorials, a quantitative approach was necessary. Using aspects of the multi-feature/multi-dimensional approach (see section 2.4) enabled me to give an objective account not only of the development of isolated features but also of sets of features representing different types of discourse. However, a qualitative interpretation of the results was necessary to gain a deeper insight into the linguistic/stylistic development of language use specific for the editorials. In the present case, the combination of a qualitative and a quantitative approach was thus a prerequisite to reach the goal aimed at. Factor score analysis, which gives a more objective but less detailed description of linguistic change, was later applied to the material (see Westin and Geisler 2002), but no major differences were observed.

10.5 Editorial language as an agent of language change

No other printed matter has such a broad reading public as newspapers. Since the language used in the newspapers reflects language use in the society where it appears (see section 10.1), it must be assumed that linguistic change in newspaper language mirrors linguistic change in society. Some of the results obtained in the present study, that is, those which are not genre-specific, can therefore give a hint of changes in the norms of formal written usage that the English language went through during the 20th century.

What is most conspicuous is the growing acceptance of informal language, as for example, contractions, questions, and imperatives, which supports the assumption of a "colloquialisation" of the written language as put forward in, for example, Mair (1997: 195 – 209) and Mair and Hundt (1997: 71 – 82). Other aspects indicating a development in the same direction are the reduced use of passive constructions, rendering a more personal style, and the preference for simpler sentence structure. The fact that these changes are most clearly seen in the *Guardian*, which is on the borderline between up-market and midmarket newspapers, is a sign that the colloquialisation process is now spreading also to such formal writing as the up-market newspaper editorials represent.

References

Primary source

The Corpus of English Newspaper Editorials (CENE). Compiled by Ingrid Westin, Department of English, Uppsala University. For further information, see section 2.2. in the present volume.

Secondary sources

Alexander, L.G. 1988. *Longman English grammar*. London: Longman.

Allerton, David J. 1988. 'Infinitivitis' in English. *Essays on the English language and applied linguistics on the occasion of Gerhard Nickel's 60th birthday*, ed. by Josef Klegraf and Dietrich Niels. 11–23. (Studies in Descriptive Linguistics 18). Heidelberg: Julius Groos Verlag.

Atkinson, Dwight. 1992. The evolution of medical research writing from 1735 to 1985: The case of the *Edinburgh Medical Journal*. *Applied Linguistics* 13: 337–374.

Audit Bureau of Circulations Ltd. Sheets with statistics regarding the circulation figures for the *Guardian*, the *Daily Telegraph*, and *The Times*, 1930–1990.

Axelsson, Margareta Westergren. 1998. *Contractions in British newspapers in the late 20th century*. (Studia Anglistica Upsaliensia 102). Uppsala: Acta Universitatis Upsaliensis.

Bäcklund, Ingegerd. 1986. 'Beat until stiff'. Conjunction-headed abbreviated clauses in spoken and written English. *English in speech and writing*: A *symposium*, ed. by Gunnel Tottie and Ingegerd Bäcklund. 41–55. (Studia Anglistica Upsaliensia 60). Stockholm: Almqvist & Wiksell.

Bauer, Laurie. 1994. *Watching English change*: *An introduction to the study of linguistic change in Standard Englishes in the twentieth century*. New York: Longman.

Beaman, Karen. 1984. Coordination and subordination revisited: Syntactic complexity in spoken and written narrative discourse. *Coherence in spoken and written discourse*, ed. by Deborah Tannen. 45–80. Norwood, New Jersey: Ablex Publishing Corporation.

Bear, M.V. 1927. The length of word as an index of difficulty in silent reading. Unpublished Master's thesis, University of Chicago.

Beckson, Karl and Arthur Ganz. 1990. *Literary terms. A dictionary*. London: André Deutsch.

Bell, Alan. 1984. Language style as audience design. *Language in Society* 13: 145–204.

——— . 1988. The British base and the American connection in New Zealand Media English. *American Speech* 63: 326–344.

———. 1991. *The language of news media.* Oxford: Basil Blackwell.

Besnier, Niko. 1988. The linguistic relationships of spoken and written Nukulaelae registers. *Language* 64: 707–736.

Biber, Douglas. 1985. Investigating macroscopic textual variation through multi-feature/multi-dimensional analyses. *Linguistics* 23: 337–360.

———. 1986. Spoken and written textual dimensions in English: Resolving the contradictory findings. *Language* 62: 384–414.

———. 1987. A textual comparison of British and American writing. *American Speech* 62: 99–119.

———. 1988. *Variation across speech and writing.* Cambridge: Cambridge University Press.

———. 1994. An analytical framework for register studies. *Sociolinguistic perspectives on register,* ed. by Douglas Biber and Edward Finegan. 31–56. New York and Oxford: Oxford University Press.

———. 1995. *Dimensions of register variation: A cross-linguistic comparison.* Cambridge: Cambridge University Press.

———. Biber, Douglas. 2001a. Dimensions of variation among eighteenth-century speech-based and written registers. *Variation in English: Multi-dimensional studies,* ed. by Susan Conrad and Douglas Biber. 200–214. London: Pearson Education.

———. Biber, Douglas. 2001b. Dimensions of variation among university registers: A new MD analysis based on the T2K-SWAL corpus. Paper presented at *The Third North American Symposium on Corpus Linguistics and Language Teaching* in Boston, April 2001.

Biber, Douglas and Edward Finegan. 1988. Drift in three English genres from the 18th to the 20th century: A multi-dimensional approach. *Corpus linguistics, hard and soft. Proceedings of the Eighth International Conference on English Language Research on Computerized Corpora,* ed. by Merja Kytö, Ossi Ihalainen, and Matti Rissanen. 83–101. Amsterdam: Rodopi.

———. 1989. Drift and the evolution of English style: A history of three genres. *Language* 65: 487–517.

———. 1992. The linguistic evolution of five written and speech-based English genres from the 17th to the 20th centuries. *History of Englishes. New methods of interpretations in historical linguistics,* ed. by Matti Rissanen, Ossi Ihalainen, Terttu Nevalainen, and Irma Taavitsainen. 688–704. Berlin and New York: Mouton de Gruyter.

———. 1997. Diachronic relations among speech-based and written registers in English. *To explain the present: Studies in the changing English language in honour of Matti Rissanen,* ed. by Terttu Nevalainen and Leena Kahlas-Tarkka. 253–275. (Mémoires de la Société Néophilologique de Helsinki 52). Helsinki: Société Néophilologique de Helsinki.

Biber, Douglas, Edward Finegan, and Dwight Atkinson. 1994. ARCHER and its challenges: Compiling and exploring a representative corpus of historical English registers. *Creating and using English language corpora. Papers from the Fourteenth International Conference on English Language*

Research on Computerized Corpora, Zürich 1993, ed. by Udo Fries, Gunnel Tottie, and Peter Schneider. 1–13. Amsterdam: Rodopi.

Biber, Douglas and Mohamed Hared. 1994. Linguistic correlates of the transition to literacy in Somali: Language adaptation in six press registers. *Sociolinguistic perspectives on register,* ed. by Douglas Biber and Edward Finegan. 182–214. New York and Oxford: Oxford University Press.

Biber, Douglas, Stig Johansson, Geoffrey Leech, Susan Conrad, and Edward Finegan. 1999. *Longman grammar of spoken and written English.* Harlow: Pearson Education Limited.

Biesenbach-Lucas, Sigrun. 1987. The use of relative markers in modern American English. *Variation in language NWAV-XV at Stanford. Proceedings of the Fifteenth Annual Conference on New Ways of Analysing Variation,* ed. by Kieth M. Denning, Sharon Inkelas, Faye C. McNair-Knox, and John R. Rickford. 13–21. Stanford University, Department of Linguistics.

Bolívar, Adriana. 1994. The structure of newspaper editorials. *Advances in written text analysis,* ed. by Malcolm Coulthard. 276–294. London and New York: Routledge.

Brown, Gillian and George Yule. 1983. *Discourse analysis.* Cambridge: Cambridge University Press.

Burnham, Lord. 1955. *Peterborough Court: The story of the* Daily Telegraph. London: Cassell and Company.

Carrol, John B. 1960. Vectors of prose style. *Style in language,* ed. by Thomas A. Sebeok. 283–292. Cambridge, MA: MIT Press.

Carter, Ronald. 1988. Front pages: Lexis, style and newspaper reports. *Registers of written English: Situational factors and linguistic features,* ed. by Mohsen Ghadessy. 8–16. London: Pinter Publishers.

Chafe, Wallace L. 1982. Integration and involvement in speaking, writing, and oral literature. *Spoken and written language: Exploring orality and literacy,* ed. by Deborah Tannen. 35–53. Norwood, New Jersey: Ablex Publishing Corporation.

——— . 1985. Linguistic differences produced by differences between speaking and writing. *Literacy, language and learning: The nature and consequences of reading and writing,* ed. by David R. Olsen, Nancy Torrance, and Angela Hildyard. 105–123. Cambridge: Cambridge University Press.

———. 1986. Evidentiality in English conversation and academic writing. *Evidentiality: The linguistic coding of epistemology,* ed. by Wallace L. Chafe and Johanna Nichols. 261–272. Norwood, New Jersey: Ablex Publishing Corporation.

Chafe, Wallace L. and Jane Danielewicz. 1987. Properties of written and spoken language. *Comprehending oral and written language,* ed. by Rosalind Horowitz and S. Jay Samuels. 83–113. San Diego: Academic Press.

Chafe, Wallace L. and Johanna Nichols. 1986. Introduction. *Evidentiality: The linguistic coding of epistemology,* ed. by Wallace L. Chafe and Johanna Nichols. vii–xi. Norwood, New Jersey: Ablex Publishing Corporation.

The Chicago manual of style. 1993. 14th ed. Chicago: The University of Chicago Press.

Coates, Jennifer. 1983. *The semantics of the modal auxiliaries.* London and Canberra: Croom Helm.

Collins cobuild English grammar. 1990. London: Collins.

Crystal, David and Derek Davy. 1969. *Investigating English style.* London: Longman.

Cuddon, John Anthony. 1979. *A dictionary of literary terms.* Harmondsworth: Penguin Books.

Dahlqvist, Bengt. 1994. *TSSA: A PC program for text segmentation and sorting.* Uppsala University, Department of Linguistics.

Devito, Joseph A. 1966. Psychogrammatical factors in oral and written discourse by skilled communicators. *Speech Monographs* 33: 73–76.

——— . 1967. Levels of abstraction in spoken and written language. *Journal of Communication* 17: 354–361.

Drieman, G. H. J. 1962. Differences between written and spoken languages: An exploratory study. *Acta Psychologica* 20: 36–57, 78–100.

Evans, Harold, ed. 1974. *News headlines: Editing and design. A five-volume manual of English, typography and layout. Book three.* London: Heinemann.

Fasold, Ralph, Haru Yamada, David Robinson, and Steven Barish. 1990. The language-planning effect of newspaper editorial policy: Gender differences in *The Washington Post. Language in Society* 19: 521–539.

Finegan, Edward. 1994. *Language: Its structure and use.* 2nd ed. Fort Worth: Harcourt Brace College Publishers.

Finegan, Edward and Douglas Biber. 1986. Toward a unified model of sociolinguistic prestige. *Diversity and diachrony,* ed. by David Sankoff. 391–397. Amsterdam: Benjamins.

———. 1994. Register and social dialect variation: An integrated approach. *Sociolinguistic perspectives on register,* ed. by Douglas Biber and Edward Finegan. 315–347. New York and Oxford: Oxford University Press.

——— . 1997. Relative markers in English: Fact and fancy. *From Ælfric to the New York Times: Studies in English corpus linguistics,* ed. by Udo Fries, Viviane Müller, and Peter Schneider. 65–78. Amsterdam: Rodopi.

Floreano, Daniel. 1986. British newspapers and radio news: A study of the differences between "quality" and "popular" news products. Unpublished licentiate thesis. University of Zurich.

Fowler, Roger. 1991. *Language in the news. Discourse and ideology in the press.* London and New York: Routledge.

Francis, W. Nelson and Henry Kučera. 1979. *Manual of information to accompany a standard corpus of present-day edited American English, for use with digital computers.* (1964; revised edition 1979). Providence, Rhode Island: Brown University, Department of Linguistics.

Fries, Udo. 1994. ZEN – Zurich English Newspaper Corpus. *Corpora across the centuries. Proceedings of the First International Colloquium on English*

Diachronic Corpora, ed. by Merja Kytö, Matti Rissanen, and Susan Wright. 17–18. Amsterdam: Rodopi.

Geisler, Christer. 1995. *Relative infinitives in English.* (Studia Anglistica Upsaliensia 91). Uppsala: Acta Universitatis Upsaliensis.

———. 2001. Gender-based variation in formal spoken American English. Paper presented at *Grammatik i fokus,* Lund University, February 2001, and at *the ASLA symposium,* Uppsala University, November 2001.

———. Forthcoming. Investigating register variation in nineteenth-century English. *Using corpora to explore linguistic variation* (working title), ed. by Randi Reppen, Douglas Biber, and Susan Fitzmaurice.

Geisler, Christer and Christine Johansson. 2002. Relativization in formal spoken American English. *Studies in Mid-Atlantic English,* ed. by Marko Modiano.

Ghadessy, Mohsen. 1988. The language of written sports commentary: Soccer – a description. *Registers of written English: Situational factors and linguistic features,* ed. by Mohsen Ghadessy. 17–51. London: Pinter Publishers.

Glasgow University Media Group. 1976. *Bad news.* London: Routledge and Kegan Paul.

———. 1980. *More bad news.* London: Routledge and Kegan Paul.

———. 1993. *Getting the message.* London: Routledge.

Greenbaum, Sidney. 1988. Syntactic devices for compression in English. *Essays on the English language and applied linguistics on the occasion of Gerhard Nickel's 60th birthday,* ed. by Josef Klegraf and Dietrich Niels. 3–10. (Studies in Descriptive Linguistics 18). Heidelberg: Julius Groos Verlag.

Greenbaum, Sidney and Randolph Quirk. 1993. *A student's grammar of the English language.* London and New York: Longman.

Gumpertz, John J., Hannah Kaltman, and Mary Catherine O'Connor. 1984. Cohesion in spoken and written discourse: Ethnic style and the transition to literacy. *Coherence in spoken and written discourse,* ed. by Deborah Tannen. 3–19. Norwood, New Jersey: Ablex Publishing Corporation.

Haan, Pieter de. 1984. Relative clauses compared. *ICAME News* 8: 47–59.

Hackett, Robert A. and Yuezhi Zhao. 1994. Challenging a master narrative: Peace protest and opinion/editorial discourse in the US press during the Gulf War. *Discourse and Society* 5(4): 509–541.

Halliday, M. A. K. 1987. Spoken and written modes of meaning. *Comprehending oral and written language,* ed. by Rosalind Horowitz and S. Jay Samuels. 55–82. San Diego: Academic Press.

Hawes, Thomas and Sarah Thomas. 1996. Rhetorical uses of theme in newspaper editorials. *World Englishes* 15/2: 159–170.

Hetherington, Alastair. 1981. Guardian *years.* London: Chatto and Windus.

Hicks, Wynford. 1993. *English for journalists.* London: Routledge.

Howard, Philip. 1985. *We thundered out: 200 years of* The Times *1785–1985.* London: Times Books.

Hu, Zhuang-Lin. 1984. Differences in mood. *Journal of Pragmatics* 8: 595–606.

Hundt, Marianne, Andrea Sand, and Rainer Siemund. 1998. *Manual of information to accompany The Freiburg–LOB Corpus of British English ('FLOB')*. Albert-Ludwigs-Universität, Englisches Seminar.

Hundt, Marianne, Andrea Sand, and Paul Skandera. 1999. *Manual of information to accompany The Freiburg–Brown Corpus of American English ('Frown')*. Albert-Ludwigs-Universität, Englisches Seminar.

Ilie, Cornelia. 1994. *What else can I tell you? A pragmatic study of English rhetorical questions as discursive and argumentative acts*. (Stockholm Studies in English 82). Stockholm: Almqvist & Wiksell.

Jacobson, Sven. 1989. Some grammatical trends in American newspaper language. *Essays on English language in honour of Bertil Sundby,* ed. by Leiv Egil Breivik, Arnoldus Hille, and Stig Johansson. 145–154. (Studia Anglistica Norvegica 4). Oslo: GCS.

Johansson, Christine. 1995. *The relativizers* whose *and* of which *in present-day English*. (Studia Anglistica Upsaliensia 90). Uppsala: Acta Universitatis Upsaliensis.

Johansson, Christine and Christer Geisler. 1998. Pied piping in spoken English. *Explorations in corpus linguistics*, ed. by Antoinette Renouf. 67–82. Amsterdam: Rodopi.

Johansson, Stig. 1986. *The tagged LOB corpus – user's manual*. Bergen: Norwegian Computing Centre for the Humanities.

Johansson, Stig, Geoffrey Leech, and Helen Goodluck. 1978. *Manual of information to accompany the Lancaster–Oslo/Bergen Corpus of British English, for use with digital computers*. University of Oslo, Department of English.

Jones, Robert L. and Roy E. Carter, Jr. 1959. Some procedures for estimating 'news hole' in content analysis. *Public Opinion Quarterly* 23: 399–403.

Jucker, Andreas H. 1992. *Social stylistics. Syntactic variation in British newspapers*. (Topics in English Linguistics 6). Berlin: Mouton de Gruyter.

Karlsson, Fred, Atro Voutilainen, Juha Heikkilä, and Arto Anttila, eds. 1995. *Constraint grammar. A language-independent system for parsing unrestricted text*. (Natural Language Processing 4). Berlin and New York: Mouton de Gruyter.

Kay, Paul. 1977. Language evolution and speech style. *Sociocultural dimensions of language change*, ed. by Ben G. Blount and Mary Sanches. 21–33. New York: Academic Press.

Kikai, Akio, Mary Schleppegrell, and Sali Tagliamonte. 1987. The influence of syntactic position on relativization. *Variation in language NWAV-XV at Stanford. Proceedings of the Fifteenth Annual Conference on New Ways of Analysing Variation,* ed. by Kieth M. Denning, Sharon Inkelas, Faye C. McNair-Knox, and John R. Rickford. 266–277. Stanford, California: Stanford University, Department of Linguistics.

Kim, Yong-Jin and Douglas Biber. 1994. A corpus-based analysis of register variation in Korean. *Sociolinguistic perspectives on register,* ed. by Douglas Biber and Edward Finegan. 157–181. New York and Oxford: Oxford University Press.

Kiparsky, Paul and Carol Kiparsky. 1970. Fact. *Progress in linguistics. A collection of papers,* ed. by Manfred Bierwisch and Karl Erich Heidolph. 143–173. The Hague and Paris: Mouton.

Klare, G. R. 1963. *The measurement of readability.* Ames, Iowa: Iowa State University Press.

Kress, Gunther. 1983. Linguistic and ideological transformations in news reporting. *Language, image, media,* ed. by Howard Davis and Paul Walton. 120–138. Oxford: Basil Blackwell.

Krippendorff, Klaus. 1980. *Content analysis.* New York: Sage Publications.

Kroll, Barbara. 1977. Combining ideas in written and spoken English. *Discourse across time and space,* ed. by Elinor Ochs Keenan and Tina L. Bennet. 69–108. (Southern California Occasional Papers in Linguistics 5). Los Angeles, California: University of Southern California.

Kytö, Merja and Matti Rissanen. 1988. The Helsinki Corpus of English Texts: Classifying and coding the diachronic part. *Corpus linguistics, hard and soft. Proceedings of the Eighth International Conference on English Language Research on Computerized Corpora,* ed. by Merja Kytö, Ossi Ihalainen and Matti Rissanen. 169–179. Amsterdam: Rodopi.

Leech, Geoffrey N. 1973. *A linguistic guide to English poetry.* London: Longman.

——. 1986. *Principles of pragmatics.* London and New York: Longman.

Ljung, Magnus. 1996. The use of modals in British and American newspapers. *Words. Proceedings of an International Symposium, Lund, 25–26 August, 1995,* ed. by Jan Svartvik. 159–179. (KVHAA Konferenser 36). Stockholm: Almqvist & Wiksell.

——. 1997. Text complexity in British and American newspapers. *Studies in English language and teaching,* ed. by Jan Aarts, Inge de Mönnink, and Herman Wekker. 75–83. Amsterdam: Rodopi.

Longman dictionary of the English language. 1988. 5th edition. London: Longman.

Mair, Christian. 1997. Parallel corpora. A real-time approach to language change in progress. *Corpus-based studies in English. Papers from the Seventeenth International Conference on English Language Research on Computerized Corpora,* ed. by Magnus Ljung. 195–209. Amsterdam: Rodopi.

Mair, Christian and Marianne Hundt. 1997. The corpus-based approach to language change in progress. *Anglistentag 1996. Proceedings,* ed. by Hans Sauer and Uwe Böker. 71–82. Tübingen: Niemeyer.

Mårdh, Ingrid. 1980. *Headlinese: On the grammar of English front page headlines.* (Lund Studies in English 58). Lund: LiberLäromedel/Gleerup.

Mendenhall, William, James T. McClave, and Madelaine Ramey. 1977. *Statistics for psychology.* North Scituate, Massachusetts: Duxbury Press.

Mills, William Haslam. 1921. The Manchester Guardian: *A century of history.* London: Chatto and Windus.

The National Readership Surveys Ltd. 1997. Sheets with statistics regarding circulation and readership for English newspapers, including the *Guardian,* the *Daily Telegraph,* and *The Times,* 1960–1993.

Nilsson, Tore. 2001. Noun phrases in British Travel Texts: A corpus-based study. Ph. D. dissertation. Uppsala University.

Ochs, Elinor. 1979. Planned and unplanned discourse. *Discourse and syntax*, ed. by Talmy Givón. 51–80. New York: Academic Press.

O'Donnell, Roy C. 1974. Syntactic differences between speech and writing. *American Speech* 49: 102–110.

O'Donnell, William Robert and Loreto Todd. 1980. *Variety in contemporary English.* London: Routledge.

Övergaard, Gerd. 1995. *The mandative subjunctive in American and British English in the 20th century.* (Studia Anglistica Upsaliensia 94). Uppsala: Acta Universitatis Upsaliensis.

Perkins, Michael R. 1983. *Modal expressions in English.* London: Frances Pinter.

Poole, Millicent E. and T.W. Field. 1976. A comparison of oral and written code elaboration. *Language and Speech* 19: 305–311.

Quirk, Randolph, Sidney Greenbaum, Geoffrey Leech, and Jan Svartvik. 1985. *A comprehensive grammar of the English language.* London and New York: Longman.

Raumolin-Brunberg, Helena. 1991. *The noun phrase in sixteenth-century English: A study based on Thomas More's writings.* (Mémoires de la Société Néophilologique de Helsinki 50). Helsinki: Société Néophilologique.

Reynolds, Mike and Giovanna Cascio. 1999. It's short and it's spreading: the use of contracted forms in British newspapers: a change under way. *English via various media*, ed. by Hans-Jürgen Diller, Erwin Otto and Gert Stratmann. 179–200. (Anglistik und Englischunterricht 62). Heidelberg: Universitætsverlag C. Winter.

Rissanen, Matti, Merja Kytö, and Minna Palander-Collin. 1993. *Early English in the computer age: Explorations through the Helsinki Corpus.* (Topics in English Linguistics 11). Berlin: Mouton de Gruyter.

Rydén, Mats. 1975. Noun-name collocations in British English newspaper language. *Studia Neophilologica* 47: 14–39.

Rydén, Mats and Sverker Brorström. 1987. *The be/have variation with intransitives in English. With special reference to the Late Modern Period.* (Stockholm Studies in English 70). Stockholm: Almqvist & Wiksell.

Svartvik, Jan. 1966. *On voice in the English verb.* The Hague: Mouton.

Svartvik, Jan, Mats Eeg-Olofsson, Oscar Forsheden, Bengt Oreström, and Cecilia Thavenius. 1982. *Survey of spoken English. Report on research 1975–1981.* (Lund Studies in English 63). Lund: Gleerup.

Svartvik, Jan and Olof Sager. 1983. *Engelsk universitetsgrammatik.* Uppsala: Esselte Herzogs.

Tannen, Deborah. 1982a. The oral/literate continuum in discourse. *Spoken and written language: Exploring orality and literacy,* ed. by Deborah Tannen. 1–15. Norwood, New Jersey: Ablex Publishing Corporation.

——. 1982b. Oral and literate strategies in spoken and written language. *Language* 58: 1–21.

——. 1985. Relative focus on involvement in oral and written discourse. *Literacy, language and learning: The nature and consequences of reading and writing*, ed. by David R. Olsen, Nancy Torrance, and Angela Hildyard. 124–147. Cambridge: Cambridge University Press.

Thompson, Sandra A. 1983. Grammar and discourse: The English detached participial clause. *Discourse perspectives on syntax,* ed. by Flora Klein Andreu. 43–65. New York: Academic Press.

Toolan, Michael. 1988. The language of press advertising. *Registers of written English: Situational factors and linguistic features,* ed. by Mohsen Ghadessy. 52–64. London: Pinter Publishers.

Tottie, Gunnel. 1986. The importance of being adverbial: Focusing and contingency adverbials in spoken and written English. *English in speech and writing: A symposium,* ed. by Gunnel Tottie and Ingegerd Bäcklund. 93–118. (Studia Anglistica Upsaliensia 60). Stockholm: Almqvist & Wiksell.

——. 1988. *No*-negation and *not*-negation in spoken and written English. *Corpus linguistics hard and soft. Proceedings of the Eighth International Conference on English Language Research on Computerized Corpora,* ed. by Merja Kytö, Ossi Ihalainen, and Matti Rissanen. 245–265. Amsterdam: Rodopi.

——. 1991. *Negation in speech and writing*. San Diego: Academic Press.

van Dijk, Teun. 1988a. *News analysis*. Hillsdale, New Jersey: Lawrence Erlbaum Associates.

——. 1988b. *News as discourse*. Hillsdale, New Jersey: Lawrence Erlbaum Associates.

——. 1992. Racism and argumentation: Race riot rhetoric in tabloid editorials. *Argumentation illuminated,* ed. by Frans H. van Eemeren, Rob Grootendorst, J. Anthony Blair, and Charles A. Willard. 243–259. Amsterdam: SICSAT.

Varantola, Krista. 1984. *On noun phrase structures in engineering English.* (Turun Yliopiston Julkaisuja/Annales Universitatis Turkuensis. Sarja-Ser. B 168). Turku: Turun yliopisto.

Wallace, William D. 1977. How registers register: A study in the language of news and sports. *Studies in Linguistic Sciences* 7: 46–78.

Westin, Ingrid. 1997. *The language of English up-market editorials from a 20th century perspective*. (FoU-rapport no. 39). Gävle: Högskolan i Gävle.

——. 2001. The language of English newspaper editorials from a 20th-century perspective. Ph. D. dissertation. Uppsala University.

Westin, Ingrid and Christer Geisler. 2002. A multi-dimensional study of diachronic variation in British newspaper editorials. *ICAME Journal 26*: 115–134.

Woods, Anthony, Paul Fletcher and Arthur Hughes. 1986. *Statistics in language studies*. Cambridge: Cambridge University Press.

Young, George M. 1985. The development of logic and focus in children's writing. *Language and Speech* 28: 115–127.

Appendix

The Appendix presents the statistics for the frequency count of each linguistic feature in the study. The frequency counts are all normalized to a text length of 1,000 words, with the exception of sentence length, word length, and type/token ratio. The statistics show Anova Tables of Variance with F-statistics across Decade and across Paper (one-way analysis of variance). When the F-value is significant, that is, when the probability of the F-value is less than 0.05 (Appx P), a graphical representation of the Newman-Keuls multiple comparison test is reproduced (see Mendenhall et al. 1977:314–320). At the 0.05 significance level, the means of any two groups underscored by the same line are not significantly different. In these representations, the groups are referred to as follows:

Across decades
   Gp 1 refers to DECADE=1900
   Gp 2 refers to DECADE=1910
   Gp 3 refers to DECADE=1920
   Gp 4 refers to DECADE=1930
   Gp 5 refers to DECADE=1940
   Gp 6 refers to DECADE=1950
   Gp 7 refers to DECADE=1960
   Gp 8 refers to DECADE=1970
   Gp 9 refers to DECADE=1980
   Gp 10 refers to DECADE=1993

Across newspapers
   Gp 1 refers to PAPER=The *Daily Telegraph*
   Gp 2 refers to PAPER=The *Guardian*
   Gp 3 refers to PAPER=*The Times*

Terms used in the tables:

Treatment	= Between-group variation
Error	= Within-group variation
S.S	= Sums of Squares
DF	= Degrees of Freedom
MS	= Mean Squares
F	= F-score
Appx P	= Probability associated with a given F-score
R-square	= The amount of variation explained by the dependent variable

R-square values have been calculated by dividing the "Treatment" sums of squares by the "Total" sum of squares: R-square = Treatment / Total

Adverbial amplifiers (section 3.3.1)
Variation across decades

```
Analysis of Variance Table

    Source            S.S.          DF              MS        F          Appx P
-------------------------------------------------------------------------------
    Total           4465.19        863
      Treatment       403.76          9            44.86     9.43        <.001
      Error          4061.43        854             4.76
      R-square (R*R) = 0.09
    Error term used for comparisons = 4.76 with 854 d.f.

Homogeneous Populations, groups ranked
```

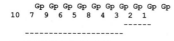

```
              Gp Gp Gp Gp Gp Gp Gp Gp Gp Gp
              10  7  9  6  5  8  4  3  2  1
                                    ------
                   ---------------------
              ---------------------
```

Variation across newspapers

```
Analysis of Variance Table

    Source            S.S.          DF              MS        F          Appx P
-------------------------------------------------------------------------------
    Total           4465.19        863
      Treatment         9.09          2             4.54      .88        0.4162
      Error          4456.1         861             5.18
    Error term used for comparisons = 5.18 with 861 d.f.
```

Agentless passives (section 7.2.1)
Variation across decades

```
Analysis of Variance Table

    Source            S.S.          DF              MS        F          Appx P
-------------------------------------------------------------------------------
    Total          40202.03        863
      Treatment      2364.19          9           262.69     5.93        <.001
      Error         37837.84        854            44.31
      R-square (R*R) = 0.06
    Error term used for comparisons = 44.31 with 854 d.f.

Homogeneous Populations, groups ranked
```

```
              Gp Gp Gp Gp Gp Gp Gp Gp Gp Gp
              10  8  9  2  5  7  3  4  6  1
                        ---------------------
                   ---------
              ---------
```

Variation across newspapers

```
Analysis of Variance Table

    Source            S.S.          DF              MS        F          Appx P
-------------------------------------------------------------------------------
    Total          40202.03        863
      Treatment        72.92          2            36.46      .78        0.4579
      Error         40129.12        861            46.61
    Error term used for comparisons = 46.61 with 861 d.f.
```

Attributive adjectives (section 4.3.1)
Variation across decades

```
Analysis of Variance Table

   Source              S.S.           DF              MS         F         Appx P
----------------------------------------------------------------------------
   Total            212749.5          863
     Treatment        8335.23           9           926.14     3.87          <.001
     Error          204414.3          854           239.36
   R-square (R*R) = 0.04
   Error term used for comparisons = 239.36 with 854 d.f.

Homogeneous Populations, groups ranked

                   Gp Gp Gp Gp Gp Gp Gp Gp Gp Gp
                    1  2  5  4  7  6  3  8  9 10
                    ------------------------
                   ------------------
                                            ---
```

Variation across newspapers

```
Analysis of Variance Table

   Source              S.S.           DF              MS         F         Appx P
----------------------------------------------------------------------------
   Total            212749.5          863
     Treatment        1962.29           2           981.14     4.01         0.0188
     Error          210787.2          861           244.82
   R-square (R*R) = 0.01
   Error term used for comparisons = 244.82 with 861 d.f.

Homogeneous Populations, groups ranked

   Gp  1   refers to PAPER=DT
   Gp  2   refers to PAPER=Gua
   Gp  3   refers to PAPER=Ti

                     Gp Gp Gp
                    2  1  3
                       ------
                   ------
```

By-passives (section 7.2.2)
Variation across decades

```
Analysis of Variance Table

   Source              S.S.           DF              MS         F         Appx P
----------------------------------------------------------------------------
   Total            5838.73          863
     Treatment        57.55            9            6.39      .94         0.4858
     Error          5781.18          854            6.77
   Error term used for comparisons = 6.77 with 854 d.f.
```

Variation across newspapers

```
Analysis of Variance Table

   Source              S.S.           DF              MS         F         Appx P
----------------------------------------------------------------------------
   Total            5838.73          863
     Treatment        26.41            2            13.2      1.96        0.1425
     Error          5812.33          861            6.75
   Error term used for comparisons = 6.75 with 861 d.f.
```

180   *Appendix*

Causative subordination: *because* (section 3.4.5)
Variation across decades

```
Analysis of Variance Table
```

Source	S.S.	DF	MS	F	Appx P
Total	2150.9	863			
Treatment	23.47	9	2.61	1.05	0.4012
Error	2127.43	854	2.49		

Error term used for comparisons = 2.49 with 854 d.f.

Variation across newspapers

```
Analysis of Variance Table
```

Source	S.S.	DF	MS	F	Appx P
Total	2150.9	863			
Treatment	27.48	2	13.74	5.57	0.004
Error	2123.42	861	2.47		

R-square (R*R) = 0.01
Error term used for comparisons = 2.47 with 861 d.f.

```
Homogeneous Populations, groups ranked

    Gp  1  refers to PAPER=DT
    Gp  2  refers to PAPER=Gua
    Gp  3  refers to PAPER=Ti

              Gp Gp Gp
               3  1  2
              ------
                 ---
```

Conditional subordination (section 6.3)
Variation across decades

```
Analysis of Variance Table
```

Source	S.S.	DF	MS	F	Appx P
Total	7518.21	863			
Treatment	172.28	9	19.14	2.23	0.0194
Error	7345.93	854	8.6		

R-square (R*R) = 0.02
Error term used for comparisons = 8.6 with 854 d.f.

```
Homogeneous Populations, groups ranked

          Gp Gp Gp Gp Gp Gp Gp Gp Gp Gp
           5 10  6  1  2  3  8  4  9  7
                 ------------------------
              ---------------------------
```

Variation across newspapers

Analysis of Variance Table

Source	S.S.	DF	MS	F	Appx P
Total	7518.21	863			
Treatment	59.12	2	29.56	3.41	0.0337
Error	7459.09	861	8.66		

R-square (R*R) = 0.01
Error term used for comparisons = 8.66 with 861 d.f.

Homogeneous Populations, groups ranked

    Gp 1 refers to PAPER=DT
    Gp 2 refers to PAPER=Gua
    Gp 3 refers to PAPER=Ti

              Gp Gp Gp
               3 1 2

Conjuncts (section 7.4)
Variation across decades

Analysis of Variance Table

Source	S.S.	DF	MS	F	Appx P
Total	4827.76	863			
Treatment	120.36	9	13.37	2.43	0.0105
Error	4707.4	854	5.51		

R-square (R*R) = 0.02
Error term used for comparisons = 5.51 with 854 d.f.

Homogeneous Populations, groups ranked

       Gp Gp Gp Gp Gp Gp Gp Gp Gp Gp
       10 4 2 1 3 6 5 7 9 8

Variation across newspapers

Analysis of Variance Table

Source	S.S.	DF	MS	F	Appx P
Total	5809.95	863			
Treatment	149.92	2	74.96	11.4	<.001
Error	5660.03	861	6.57		

R-square (R*R) = 0.03
Error term used for comparisons = 6.57 with 861 d.f.

Homogeneous Populations, groups ranked

    Gp 1 refers to PAPER=DT
    Gp 2 refers to PAPER=Gua
    Gp 3 refers to PAPER=Ti

              Gp Gp Gp
               2 3 1

Contractions (section 3.2.5)
Variation across decades

```
Analysis of Variance Table
```

Source	S.S.	DF	MS	F	Appx P
Total	826.63	863			
Treatment	63.02	9	7.	7.83	<.001
Error	763.61	854	.89		

R-square (R*R) = 0.08
Error term used for comparisons = .89 with 854 d.f.

```
Homogeneous Populations, groups ranked
```

```
          Gp Gp Gp Gp Gp Gp Gp Gp Gp Gp
           1  2  5  6  4  3  8  7  9 10
          --------------------------
                                     ---
```

Variation across newspapers

```
Analysis of Variance Table
```

Source	S.S.	DF	MS	F	Appx P
Total	826.63	863			
Treatment	16.95	2	8.47	9.01	<.001
Error	809.69	861	.94		

R-square (R*R) = 0.02
Error term used for comparisons = .94 with 861 d.f.

```
Homogeneous Populations, groups ranked
```

```
Gp  1  refers to PAPER=DT
Gp  2  refers to PAPER=Gua
Gp  3  refers to PAPER=Ti
```

```
          Gp Gp Gp
           3  1  2
          ------
                 ---
```

Demonstrative pronouns (section 3.4.1)
Variation across decades

```
Analysis of Variance Table
```

Source	S.S.	DF	MS	F	Appx P
Total	9210.54	863			
Treatment	330.63	9	36.74	3.53	<.001
Error	8879.91	854	10.4		

R-square (R*R) = 0.04
Error term used for comparisons = 10.4 with 854 d.f.

```
Homogeneous Populations, groups ranked
```

```
          Gp Gp Gp Gp Gp Gp Gp Gp Gp Gp
           5  3  4  6  1 10  2  8  9  7
          --------------------------
          ----------------------
```

Variation across newspapers

```
Analysis of Variance Table
```

Source	S.S.	DF	MS	F	Appx P
Total	9210.54	863			
Treatment	201.87	2	100.93	9.65	<.001
Error	9008.67	861	10.46		

```
  R-square (R*R) = 0.02
Error term used for comparisons = 10.46 with 861 d.f.
```

```
Homogeneous Populations, groups ranked
```

```
Gp  1  refers to PAPER=DT
Gp  2  refers to PAPER=Gua
Gp  3  refers to PAPER=Ti
```

```
        Gp Gp Gp
         3  2  1
            ------
        ---
```

'Detached' past participle clauses (section 7.3.1)
Variation across decades

```
Analysis of Variance Table
```

Source	S.S.	DF	MS	F	Appx P
Total	1284.04	863			
Treatment	30.08	9	3.34	2.28	0.0166
Error	1253.96	854	1.47		

```
  R-square (R*R) = 0.02
Error term used for comparisons = 1.47 with 854 d.f.
```

```
Homogeneous Populations, groups ranked
```

```
        Gp Gp Gp Gp Gp Gp Gp Gp Gp Gp
         8  6  4  7  3  5  2 10  9  1
                        ---------------------------
              ---------------------
```

Variation across newspapers

```
Analysis of Variance Table
```

Source	S.S.	DF	MS	F	Appx P
Total	1284.04	863			
Treatment	1.25	2	.62	.42	0.6584
Error	1282.79	861	1.49		

```
Error term used for comparisons = 1.49 with 861 d.f.
```

Detached' present participle (section 5.4)
Variation across decades

Analysis of Variance Table

Source	S.S.	DF	MS	F	Appx P
Total	2151.99	863			
Treatment	75.02	9	8.34	3.43	<.001
Error	2076.96	854	2.43		

R-square (R*R) = 0.03
Error term used for comparisons = 2.43 with 854 d.f.

Homogeneous Populations, groups ranked

```
Gp Gp Gp Gp Gp Gp Gp Gp Gp Gp
 3  2  6  8  4  9  1  7  5 10
                -----------------
----------------------------
```

Variation across newspapers

Analysis of Variance Table

Source	S.S.	DF	MS	F	Appx P
Total	2151.99	863			
Treatment	6.49	2	3.24	1.3	0.273
Error	2145.5	861	2.49		

Error term used for comparisons = 2.49 with 861 d.f.

Discourse particles
Not tested

Editorial length (section 2.2.2)
Variation across decades

Analysis of Variance Table

Source	S.S.	DF	MS	F	Appx P
Total	89284740.	863			
Treatment	15421796.41	9	1713533.	19.81	<.001
Error	73862940.	854	86490.55		

R-square (R*R) = 0.17
Error term used for comparisons = 86 490.55 with 854 d.f.

```
Gp Gp Gp Gp Gp Gp Gp Gp Gp Gp
 7  8  6 10  5  4  9  3  1  2
                -----------------
----------------------------
                            ---
                        ---
                    ---
```

First person pronouns (section 3.3.3)
Variation across decades

```
Analysis of Variance Table

    Source           S.S.        DF            MS        F        Appx P
    -----------------------------------------------------------------------
    Total          55661.97      863
      Treatment     8747.23        9         971.91    17.69       <.001
      Error        46914.74      854          54.94
      R-square (R*R) = 0.16
    Error term used for comparisons = 54.94 with 854 d.f.

Homogeneous Populations, groups ranked

            Gp Gp Gp Gp Gp Gp Gp Gp Gp Gp
             8 10  9  7  6  4  5  3  1  2
                             ------------
                ------------
                ------------
             ------------
```

Variation across newspapers

```
Analysis of Variance Table

    Source           S.S.        DF            MS        F        Appx P
    -----------------------------------------------------------------------
    Total          55661.97      863
      Treatment      945.28        2         472.64     7.44       <.001
      Error        54716.68      861          63.55
      R-square (R*R) = 0.02
    Error term used for comparisons = 63.55 with 861 d.f.

Homogeneous Populations, groups ranked

    Gp  1  refers to PAPER=DT
    Gp  2  refers to PAPER=Gua
    Gp  3  refers to PAPER=Ti

                Gp Gp Gp
                 3  2  1
                 ------
                 ---
```

General emphatics (section 3.4.7)
Variation across decades

```
Analysis of Variance Table

    Source           S.S.        DF            MS        F        Appx P
    -----------------------------------------------------------------------
    Total          14946.79      863
      Treatment      242.49        9          26.94     1.56      0.1228
      Error         14704.3      854          17.22
    Error term used for comparisons = 17.22 with 854 d.f.
```

Variation across newspapers

```
Analysis of Variance Table

    Source           S.S.        DF            MS        F        Appx P
    -----------------------------------------------------------------------
    Total          14946.79      863
      Treatment       41.5         2          20.75     1.2       0.3025
      Error         14905.29     861          17.31
    Error term used for comparisons = 17.31 with 861 d.f.
```

General hedges (section 3.4.8)
Variation across decades

Analysis of Variance Table

Source	S.S.	DF	MS	F	Appx P
Total	1204.32	863			
Treatment	22.59	9	2.51	1.81	0.0633
Error	1181.73	854	1.38		

R-square (R*R) = 0.02
Error term used for comparisons = 1.38 with 854 d.f.

Variation across newspapers

Analysis of Variance Table

Source	S.S.	DF	MS	F	Appx P
Total	1204.32	863			
Treatment	3.99	2	2.	1.43	0.24
Error	1200.33	861	1.39		

Error term used for comparisons = 1.39 with 861 d.f.

Have to (section 6.6.2)
Variation across decades

Analysis of Variance Table

Source	S.S.	DF	MS	F	Appx P
Total	1737.61	863			
Treatment	36.37	9	4.04	2.03	0.0345
Error	1701.24	854	1.99		

R-square (R*R) = 0.02
Error term used for comparisons = 1.99 with 854 d.f.

Homogeneous Populations, groups ranked

```
      Gp Gp Gp Gp Gp Gp Gp Gp Gp Gp
       1  9  2  6  5  3  4  7 10  8
                -----------------------
          ---------------------------
```

Variation across newspapers

Analysis of Variance Table

Source	S.S.	DF	MS	F	Appx P
Total	1737.61	863			
Treatment	10.48	2	5.24	2.61	0.0745
Error	1727.14	861	2.01		

Error term used for comparisons = 2.01 with 861 d.f.

Imperatives (section 3.2.4)
Variation across decades

```
Analysis of Variance Table
```

Source	S.S.	DF	MS	F	Appx P
Total	2222.96	863			
Treatment	47.43	9	5.27	2.07	0.0307
Error	2175.53	854	2.55		

```
 R-square (R*R) = 0.02
Error term used for comparisons = 2.55 with 854 d.f.
```

```
Homogeneous Populations, groups ranked

          Gp Gp Gp Gp Gp Gp Gp Gp Gp Gp
           8  5  4  3  1  2  6  9  7 10
              ---------------------------
           ---------------------------
```

Variation across newspapers

```
Analysis of Variance Table
```

Source	S.S.	DF	MS	F	Appx P
Total	2222.96	863			
Treatment	3.87	2	1.93	.75	0.4728
Error	2219.09	861	2.58		

```
Error term used for comparisons = 2.58 with 861 d.f.
```

Indefinite pronouns (section 3.4.4)
Variation across decades

```
Analysis of Variance Table
```

Source	S.S.	DF	MS	F	Appx P
Total	3680.91	863			
Treatment	35.91	9	3.99	.93	0.4942
Error	3645.	854	4.27		

```
Error term used for comparisons = 4.27 with 854 d.f.
```

Variation across newspapers

```
Analysis of Variance Table
```

Source	S.S.	DF	MS	F	Appx P
Total	3680.91	863			
Treatment	10.11	2	5.06	1.19	0.3063
Error	3670.8	861	4.26		

```
Error term used for comparisons = 4.26 with 861 d.f.
```

Infinitives (section 6.2)
Variation across decades

```
Analysis of Variance Table

    Source          S.S.        DF            MS        F         Appx P
    ---------------------------------------------------------------------------
    Total          143084.4     863
      Treatment      4150.82       9          461.2    2.83       0.0029
      Error        138933.6      854          162.69
    R-square (R*R) = 0.03
    Error term used for comparisons = 162.69 with 854 d.f.

Homogeneous Populations, groups ranked

              Gp Gp Gp Gp Gp Gp Gp Gp Gp Gp
               3  4  5  2  6  1 10  9  8  7
              ---------------------------
              ---------------------------
```

Variation across newspapers

```
Analysis of Variance Table

    Source          S.S.        DF            MS        F         Appx P
    ---------------------------------------------------------------------------
    Total          143084.4     863
      Treatment       304.96       2          152.48    .92       0.3994
      Error        142779.4      861          165.83
    Error term used for comparisons = 165.83 with 861 d.f.
```

Necessity modals: *must, should, ought to* (section 6.6)
Variation across decades

```
Analysis of Variance Table

    Source          S.S.        DF            MS        F         Appx P
    ---------------------------------------------------------------------------
    Total           11975.02    863
      Treatment       155.89       9           17.32   1.25       0.2612
      Error         11819.13     854           13.84
    Error term used for comparisons = 13.84 with 854 d.f.
```

Variation across newspapers

```
Analysis of Variance Table

    Source          S.S.        DF            MS        F         Appx P
    ---------------------------------------------------------------------------
    Total           11975.02    863
      Treatment        27.53       2           13.76    .99       0.3716
      Error         11947.49     861           13.88
    Error term used for comparisons = 13.88 with 861 d.f.
```

Need to (section 6.6.2)
Variation across decades

```
Analysis of Variance Table

    Source          S.S.        DF            MS        F         Appx P
    ---------------------------------------------------------------------------
    Total            465.72      863
      Treatment        6.43        9            .71    1.33       0.2187
      Error          459.28      854            .54
    Error term used for comparisons = .54 with 854 d.f.
```

Variation across newspapers

```
Analysis of Variance Table

  Source           S.S.          DF              MS       F        Appx P
  -----------------------------------------------------------------------
  Total           465.72        863
    Treatment        .66          2             .33      .61      0.5429
    Error          465.06        861            .54
  Error term used for comparisons = .54 with 861 d.f.
```

Nominalizations (section 8.3)

Variation across decades

```
Analysis of Variance Table

  Source           S.S.          DF              MS       F        Appx P
  -----------------------------------------------------------------------
  Total          148538.2       863
    Treatment       6342.3         9            704.7    4.23      <.001
    Error         142195.9       854            166.51
  R-square (R*R) = 0.04
  Error term used for comparisons = 166.51 with 854 d.f.

Homogeneous Populations, groups ranked

              Gp Gp Gp Gp Gp Gp Gp Gp Gp Gp
               1  5  4  3  2  6  9 10  8  7
              ----------------------------
              ---
```

Variation across newspapers

```
Analysis of Variance Table

  Source           S.S.          DF              MS       F        Appx P
  -----------------------------------------------------------------------
  Total          148538.3       863
    Treatment      1314.59         2            657.29   3.84      0.022
    Error         147223.7       861            170.99
  R-square (R*R) = 0.01
  Error term used for comparisons = 170.99 with 861 d.f.

Homogeneous Populations, groups ranked

  Gp  1  refers to VAR1=DT
  Gp  2  refers to VAR1=Gua
  Gp  3  refers to VAR1=Ti

              Gp Gp Gp
               2  1  3
               ------
              ------
```

No-negation (section 5.3)
Variation across decades

```
Analysis of Variance Table

   Source           S.S.        DF            MS       F        Appx P
----------------------------------------------------------------------
   Total          5926.53       863
     Treatment     144.25         9          16.03    2.37      0.0126
     Error        5782.28       854           6.77
   R-square (R*R) = 0.02
   Error term used for comparisons = 6.77 with 854 d.f.

Homogeneous Populations, groups ranked

           Gp Gp Gp Gp Gp Gp Gp Gp Gp Gp
            8  7 10  9  2  4  6  5  1  3
                     -----------------------
           --------------------------
```

Variation across newspapers

```
Analysis of Variance Table

   Source           S.S.        DF            MS       F        Appx P
----------------------------------------------------------------------
   Total          5926.53       863
     Treatment      20.19         2          10.09    1.47      0.2306
     Error        5906.34       861           6.86
   Error term used for comparisons = 6.86 with 861 d.f.
```

Not-negation (section 3.2.2)
Variation across decades

```
Analysis of Variance Table

   Source           S.S.        DF            MS       F        Appx P
----------------------------------------------------------------------
   Total           904.48       863
     Treatment      18.02         9           2.      1.93      0.046
     Error         886.46       854           1.04
   R-square (R*R) = 0.02
   Error term used for comparisons = 1.04 with 854 d.f.

Homogeneous Populations, groups ranked

           Gp Gp Gp Gp Gp Gp Gp Gp Gp Gp
            5  7  3  2  6  8  4 10  1  9
                     --------------------
           --------------------------
```

Variation across newspapers

```
Analysis of Variance Table

   Source           S.S.        DF            MS       F        Appx P
----------------------------------------------------------------------
   Total           904.48       863
     Treatment       2.2          2           1.1     1.05      0.35
     Error         902.27       861           1.05
   Error term used for comparisons = 1.05 with 861 d.f.
```

Nouns (section 4.2)
Variation across decades

```
Analysis of Variance Table
```

Source	S.S.	DF	MS	F	Appx P
Total	592316.8	863			
Treatment	75293.67	9	8365.96	13.82	<.001
Error	517023.1	854	605.41		

```
R-square (R*R) = 0.13
Error term used for comparisons = 605.41 with 854 d.f.
```

```
Homogeneous Populations, groups ranked
```

```
            Gp Gp Gp Gp Gp Gp Gp Gp Gp Gp
             2  1  3  7  4  6  8  9  5 10
                        -------------------
                  ---------------
            ---------------
                                     ---
```

Variation across newspapers

```
Analysis of Variance Table
```

Source	S.S.	DF	MS	F	Appx P
Total	592316.8	863			
Treatment	1531.55	2	765.78	1.12	0.3284
Error	590785.2	861	686.16		

```
Error term used for comparisons = 686.16 with 861 d.f.
```

Past participle WHIZ-deletion (section 7.3.2)
Variation across decades

```
Analysis of Variance Table
```

Source	S.S.	DF	MS	F	Appx P
Total	9025.88	863			
Treatment	87.87	9	9.76	.93	0.496
Error	8938.01	854	10.47		

```
Error term used for comparisons = 10.47 with 854 d.f.
```

Variation across newspapers

```
Analysis of Variance Table
```

Source	S.S.	DF	MS	F	Appx P
Total	9025.88	863			
Treatment	29.69	2	14.84	1.42	0.2425
Error	8996.19	861	10.45		

```
Error term used for comparisons = 10.45 with 861 d.f.
```

Past tense verbs (section 5.2)
Variation across decades

```
Analysis of Variance Table
```

Source	S.S.	DF	MS	F	Appx P
Total	130282.4	863			
Treatment	2769.52	9	307.72	2.06	0.0314
Error	127512.9	854	149.31		

R-square (R*R) = 0.02
Error term used for comparisons = 149.31 with 854 d.f.

```
Homogeneous Populations, groups ranked

            Gp Gp Gp Gp Gp Gp Gp Gp Gp Gp
             8  7  6 10  3  9  2  5  4  1
            ---------------------------
             ---------------------------
```

Variation across newspapers

```
Analysis of Variance Table
```

Source	S.S.	DF	MS	F	Appx P
Total	130282.5	863			
Treatment	833.99	2	417.	2.77	0.0634
Error	129448.5	861	150.35		

R-square (R*R) = 0.01
Error term used for comparisons = 150.35 with 861 d.f.

```
Homogeneous Populations, groups ranked

   Gp  1  refers to PAPER=DT
   Gp  2  refers to PAPER=Gua
   Gp  3  refers to PAPER=Ti

            Gp Gp Gp
             1  3  2
             ------
             ------
```

Perfect aspect verbs (section 5.5)
Variation across decades

```
Analysis of Variance Table
```

Source	S.S.	DF	MS	F	Appx P
Total	40541.06	863			
Treatment	409.1	9	45.46	.97	0.4663
Error	40131.96	854	46.99		

Error term used for comparisons = 46.99 with 854 d.f.

Variation across newspapers

```
Analysis of Variance Table
```

Source	S.S.	DF	MS	F	Appx P
Total	40541.06	863			
Treatment	12.36	2	6.18	.13	0.877
Error	40528.7	861	47.07		

Error term used for comparisons = 47.07 with 861 d.f.

Pied piping (section 8.2.2)
Variation across decades

Analysis of Variance Table

Source	S.S.	DF	MS	F	Appx P
Total	4354.86	863			
Treatment	254.79	9	28.31	5.9	<.001
Error	4100.07	854	4.8		

R-square (R*R) = 0.06
Error term used for comparisons = 4.8 with 854 d.f.

Homogeneous Populations, groups ranked

```
        Gp Gp Gp Gp Gp Gp Gp Gp Gp Gp
        8 10  9  5  6  7  2  4  3  1
                  ----------------------
        ------------------
```

Variation across newspapers

Analysis of Variance Table

Source	S.S.	DF	MS	F	Appx P
Total	4354.86	863			
Treatment	4.	2	2.	.4	0.6737
Error	4350.86	861	5.05		

Error term used for comparisons = 5.05 with 861 d.f.

Possibility modals (section 3.4.2)
Variation across decades

Analysis of Variance Table

Source	S.S.	DF	MS	F	Appx P
Total	17886.29	863			
Treatment	332.18	9	36.91	1.8	0.0666
Error	17554.12	854	20.56		

Error term used for comparisons = 20.56 with 854 d.f.

Variation across newspapers

Analysis of Variance Table

Source	S.S.	DF	MS	F	Appx P
Total	17886.29	863			
Treatment	25.22	2	12.61	.61	0.545
Error	17861.08	861	20.74		

Error term used for comparisons = 20.74 with 861 d.f.

Predictive modals (section 6.5)
Variation across decades

Analysis of Variance Table

Source	S.S.	DF	MS	F	Appx P
Total	31665.13	863			
Treatment	202.88	9	22.54	.61	0.7873
Error	31462.24	854	36.84		

Error term used for comparisons = 36.84 with 854 d.f.

Variation across newspapers

```
Analysis of Variance Table
```

Source	S.S.	DF	MS	F	Appx P
Total	31665.12	863			
Treatment	219.	2	109.5	3.	0.0508
Error	31446.12	861	36.52		

```
   R-square (R*R) = 0.01
   Error term used for comparisons = 36.52 with 861 d.f.

Homogeneous Populations, groups ranked

   Gp  1  refers to PAPER=DT
   Gp  2  refers to PAPER=Gua
   Gp  3  refers to PAPER=Ti

            Gp Gp Gp
             1  3  2
             ------
             ------
```

Prepositions (section 4.3.2)
Variation across decades

```
Analysis of Variance Table
```

Source	S.S.	DF	MS	F	Appx P
Total	269585.	863			
Treatment	31977.65	9	3553.07	12.77	<.001
Error	237607.4	854	278.23		

```
   R-square (R*R) = 0.12
   Error term used for comparisons = 278.23 with 854 d.f.

Homogeneous Populations, groups ranked

            Gp Gp Gp Gp Gp Gp Gp Gp Gp Gp
             8 10  9  7  6  5  2  1  4  3
                         ---------------
                        ---------------
                      ------
                ------------
```

Variation across newspapers

```
Analysis of Variance Table
```

Source	S.S.	DF	MS	F	Appx P
Total	269585.	863			
Treatment	7763.24	2	3881.62	12.76	<.001
Error	261821.8	861	304.09		

```
   R-square (R*R) = 0.03
   Error term used for comparisons = 304.09 with 861 d.f.

Homogeneous Populations, groups ranked

   Gp  1  refers to PAPER=DT
   Gp  2  refers to PAPER=Gua
   Gp  3  refers to PAPER=Ti

            Gp Gp Gp
             2  1  3
             ---
                ---
                   ---
```

Present participle WHIZ- deletion (section 4.3.3)
Variation across decades

Analysis of Variance Table

Source	S.S.	DF	MS	F	Appx P
Total	3008.	863			
Treatment	98.93	9	10.99	3.23	<.001
Error	2909.07	854	3.41		

R-square (R*R) = 0.03
Error term used for comparisons = 3.41 with 854 d.f.

Homogeneous Populations, groups ranked

```
Gp Gp Gp Gp Gp Gp Gp Gp Gp Gp
 5  8  3  2  1  4  6  9  7 10
                          ------
---------------------------
```

Variation across newspapers

Analysis of Variance Table

Source	S.S.	DF	MS	F	Appx P
Total	3008.	863			
Treatment	13.18	2	6.59	1.89	0.1515
Error	2994.82	861	3.48		

Error term used for comparisons = 3.48 with 861 d.f.

Present tense verbs (section 3.2.1)
Variation across decades

Analysis of Variance Table

Source	S.S.	DF	MS	F	Appx P
Total	160537.2	863			
Treatment	4862.88	9	540.32	2.96	0.0019
Error	155674.4	854	182.29		

R-square (R*R) = 0.03
Error term used for comparisons = 182.29 with 854 d.f.

Homogeneous Populations, groups ranked

```
Gp Gp Gp Gp Gp Gp Gp Gp Gp Gp
 5  1  3  4 10  9  6  7  2  8
             -----------------------
---------------------------
```

Variation across newspapers

```
Analysis of Variance Table

    Source            S.S.        DF            MS        F       Appx P
    ----------------------------------------------------------------------
    Total           160537.2      863
      Treatment       2280.27       2         1140.13    6.2      0.0022
      Error          158257.      861          183.81
    R-square (R*R) = 0.01
    Error term used for comparisons = 183.81 with 861 d.f.

Homogeneous Populations, groups ranked

    Gp  1  refers to PAPER=DT
    Gp  2  refers to PAPER=Gua
    Gp  3  refers to PAPER=Ti

              Gp Gp Gp
               3  1  2
               ------
               ---
```

Private verbs (section 3.3.2)
Variation across decades

```
Analysis of Variance Table

    Source            S.S.        DF            MS        F       Appx P
    ----------------------------------------------------------------------
    Total            28012.61     863
      Treatment        875.49       9           97.28    3.06     0.0014
      Error          27137.12     854           31.78
    R-square (R*R) = 0.03
    Error term used for comparisons = 31.78 with 854 d.f.

Homogeneous Populations, groups ranked
```

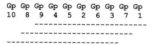

```
              Gp Gp Gp Gp Gp Gp Gp Gp Gp Gp
              10  8  9  4  5  2  6  3  7  1
                  ------------------------
                  ------------------------
              ------------------------
```

Variation across newspapers

```
Analysis of Variance Table

    Source            S.S.        DF            MS        F       Appx P
    ----------------------------------------------------------------------
    Total            28012.61     863
      Treatment         26.01       2           13.       .4       0.6705
      Error          27986.6      861           32.5
    Error term used for comparisons = 32.5 with 861 d.f.
```

Pronoun *it* (section 3.3.4)
Variation across decades

```
Analysis of Variance Table
```

Source	S.S.	DF	MS	F	Appx P
Total	54009.7	863			
Treatment	1337.61	9	148.62	2.41	0.0111
Error	52672.09	854	61.68		

R-square (R*R) = 0.02
Error term used for comparisons = 61.68 with 854 d.f.

```
Homogeneous Populations, groups ranked
```

```
        Gp Gp Gp Gp Gp Gp Gp Gp Gp Gp
        10  1  5  7  9  3  8  6  4  2
           --------------------------
        -----------------------
```

Variation across newspapers

```
Analysis of Variance Table
```

Source	S.S.	DF	MS	F	Appx P
Total	54009.71	863			
Treatment	642.19	2	321.1	5.18	0.0059
Error	53367.51	861	61.98		

R-square (R*R) = 0.01
Error term used for comparisons = 61.98 with 861 d.f.

```
Homogeneous Populations, groups ranked
```

```
Gp  1  refers to PAPER=DT
Gp  2  refers to PAPER=Gua
Gp  3  refers to PAPER=Ti
```

```
        Gp Gp Gp
         3  1  2
        ------
           ---
```

Public verbs (section 5.6)
Variation across decades

```
Analysis of Variance Table
```

Source	S.S.	DF	MS	F	Appx P
Total	15057.47	863			
Treatment	156.94	9	17.44	1.	0.4394
Error	14900.53	854	17.45		

Error term used for comparisons = 17.45 with 854 d.f.

Variation across newspapers

```
Analysis of Variance Table
```

Source	S.S.	DF	MS	F	Appx P
Total	15057.47	863			
Treatment	65.47	2	32.74	1.88	0.1536
Error	14992.	861	17.41		

Error term used for comparisons = 17.41 with 861 d.f.

Questions (section 3.2.3)
Variation across decades

Analysis of Variance Table

Source	S.S.	DF	MS	F	Appx P
Total	6383.56	863			
Treatment	183.05	9	20.34	2.8	0.0032
Error	6200.51	854	7.26		

R-square (R*R) = 0.03
Error term used for comparisons = 7.26 with 854 d.f.

Homogeneous Populations, groups ranked

```
        Gp Gp Gp Gp Gp Gp Gp Gp Gp Gp
         5  2  4  3  1  6 10  9  7  8
            ---------------------------
         ---------------------------
```

Variation across newspapers

Analysis of Variance Table

Source	S.S.	DF	MS	F	Appx P
Total	6383.56	863			
Treatment	143.51	2	71.75	9.9	<.001
Error	6240.05	861	7.25		

R-square (R*R) = 0.02
Error term used for comparisons = 7.25 with 861 d.f.

Homogeneous Populations, groups ranked

```
Gp  1  refers to PAPER=DT
Gp  2  refers to PAPER=Gua
Gp  3  refers to PAPER=Ti

        Gp Gp Gp
         3  1  2
            ------
         ---
```

Relative *that*-clauses (section 8.2.2)
Variation across decades

Analysis of Variance Table

Source	S.S.	DF	MS	F	Appx P
Total	5329.53	863			
Treatment	115.66	9	12.85	2.1	0.0276
Error	5213.87	854	6.11		

R-square (R*R) = 0.02
Error term used for comparisons = 6.11 with 854 d.f.

Homogeneous Populations, groups ranked

```
        Gp Gp Gp Gp Gp Gp Gp Gp Gp Gp
         7  6  9  3 10  8  2  4  1  5
               ----------------------
            ---------------------------
```

Variation across newspapers

Analysis of Variance Table

Source	S.S.	DF	MS	F	Appx P
Total	5329.53	863			
Treatment	69.3	2	34.65	5.67	0.0037
Error	5260.23	861	6.11		

R-square (R*R) = 0.01
Error term used for comparisons = 6.11 with 861 d.f.

Homogeneous Populations, groups ranked

```
Gp  1  refers to VAR1=DT
Gp  2  refers to VAR1=Gua
Gp  3  refers to VAR1=Ti

        Gp Gp Gp
         1  2  3
         ------
         ---
```

Relative *wh*-clauses (section 8.2.1)
Variation across decades

Analysis of Variance Table

Source	S.S.	DF	MS	F	Appx P
Total	22343.54	863			
Treatment	2886.83	9	320.76	14.08	<.001
Error	19456.72	854	22.78		

R-square (R*R) = 0.13
Error term used for comparisons = 22.78 with 854 d.f.

Homogeneous Populations, groups ranked

```
     Gp Gp Gp Gp Gp Gp Gp Gp Gp Gp
      8 10  9  6  7  5  1  3  4  2
                            ------------
            ------------
            ------------
      ------------
```

Variation across newspapers

Analysis of Variance Table

Source	S.S.	DF	MS	F	Appx P
Total	22343.55	863			
Treatment	2.93	2	1.46	.06	0.9451
Error	22340.62	861	25.95		

Error term used for comparisons = 25.95 with 861 d.f.

Second person pronouns (section 3.4.3)
Variation across decades

Analysis of Variance Table

Source	S.S.	DF	MS	F	Appx P
Total	10415.1	863			
Treatment	158.29	9	17.59	1.46	0.1582
Error	10256.81	854	12.01		

Error term used for comparisons = 12.01 with 854 d.f.

Variation across newspapers

```
Analysis of Variance Table

 Source            S.S.        DF          MS       F       Appx P
 -----------------------------------------------------------------------
 Total            7901.49      863
   Treatment        26.38        2         13.19    1.44     0.2374
   Error          7875.11      861          9.15
 Error term used for comparisons = 9.15 with 861 d.f.
```

Sentence length (section 4.5.1)
Variation across decades

```
Analysis of Variance Table

 Source            S.S.        DF          MS       F       Appx P
 -----------------------------------------------------------------------
 Total             390.23       29
   Treatment       297.45        9         33.05    7.12     <.001
   Error            92.79       20          4.64
 R-square (R*R) = 0.76
 Error term used for comparisons = 4.64 with 20 d.f.
```

```
Homogeneous Populations, groups ranked

           Gp Gp Gp Gp Gp Gp Gp Gp Gp Gp
           10  8  9  7  6  5  3  4  2  1
```

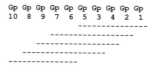

Variation across newspapers

```
Analysis of Variance Table

 Source            S.S.        DF          MS       F       Appx P
 -----------------------------------------------------------------------
 Total             390.23       29
   Treatment        43.99        2         21.99    1.72     0.199
   Error           346.24       27         12.82
 Error term used for comparisons = 12.82 with 27 d.f.
```

Suasive verbs (section 6.4)
Variation across decades

```
Analysis of Variance Table

 Source            S.S.        DF          MS       F       Appx P
 -----------------------------------------------------------------------
 Total           10415.1       863
   Treatment       158.29        9         17.59    1.46     0.1582
   Error         10256.81      854         12.01
 Error term used for comparisons = 12.01 with 854 d.f.
```

Variation across newspapers

```
Analysis of Variance Table

 Source            S.S.        DF          MS       F       Appx P
 -----------------------------------------------------------------------
 Total           10415.1       863
   Treatment         8.24        2          4.12     .34     0.7114
   Error         10406.86      861         12.09
 Error term used for comparisons = 12.09 with 861 d.f.
```

Subordination (section 4.5.2)
Variation across decades

```
Analysis of Variance Table

    Source            S.S.        DF          MS        F        Appx P
    ------------------------------------------------------------------------
    Total          58910.81      863
      Treatment     2271.37        9        252.37     3.81       <.001
      Error        56639.44      854         66.32
    R-square (R*R) = 0.04
    Error term used for comparisons = 66.32 with 854 d.f.

Homogeneous Populations, groups ranked

              Gp Gp Gp Gp Gp Gp Gp Gp Gp Gp
              10  9  5  8  3  6  7  2  4  1
                 ---------------------------
              ---
```

Variation across newspapers

```
Analysis of Variance Table

    Source            S.S.        DF          MS        F        Appx P
    ------------------------------------------------------------------------
    Total          58910.82      863
      Treatment      470.03        2        235.01     3.46       0.0321
      Error        58440.79      861         67.88
    R-square (R*R) = 0.01
    Error term used for comparisons = 67.88 with 861 d.f.

Homogeneous Populations, groups ranked

    Gp  1  refers to PAPER=DT
    Gp  2  refers to PAPER=GUA
    Gp  3  refers to PAPER=TI

              Gp Gp Gp
               3  2  1
                 ------
              ------
```

Subordinators having multiple functions (section 7.5)
Variation across decades

```
Analysis of Variance Table

    Source            S.S.        DF          MS        F        Appx P
    ------------------------------------------------------------------------
    Total           3798.05      863
      Treatment       57.38        9          6.38     1.46       0.1617
      Error         3740.67      854          4.38
    Error term used for comparisons = 4.38 with 854 d.f.
```

Variation across newspapers

```
Analysis of Variance Table

    Source            S.S.        DF          MS        F        Appx P
    ------------------------------------------------------------------------
    Total           3798.05      863
      Treatment        .41         2           .21      .05       0.9543
      Error         3797.64      861          4.41
    Error term used for comparisons = 4.41 with 861 d.f.
```

Third person pronouns (section 5.7)
Variation across decades

Analysis of Variance Table

Source	S.S.	DF	MS	F	Appx P
Total	157990.8	863			
Treatment	2836.3	9	315.14	1.73	0.0786
Error	155154.5	854	181.68		

Error term used for comparisons = 181.68 with 854 d.f.

Variation across newspapers

Analysis of Variance Table

Source	S.S.	DF	MS	F	Appx P
Total	157990.8	863			
Treatment	1260.41	2	630.21	3.46	0.0321
Error	156730.4	861	182.03		

R-square (R*R) = 0.01
Error term used for comparisons = 182.03 with 861 d.f.

Homogeneous Populations, groups ranked

Gp 1 refers to PAPER=DT
Gp 2 refers to PAPER=Gua
Gp 3 refers to PAPER=Ti

```
Gp Gp Gp
 2  1  3
    ------
------
```

Type/token ratio (section 4.4.2)
Variation across decades

Analysis of Variance Table

Source	S.S.	DF	MS	F	Appx P
Total	16857.51	864			
Treatment	1744.62	9	193.85	10.97	<.001
Error	15112.89	855	17.68		

R-square (R*R) = 0.10
Error term used for comparisons = 17.68 with 855 d.f.

Homogeneous Populations, groups ranked

```
Gp Gp Gp Gp Gp Gp Gp Gp Gp Gp
 2  3  4  1  7  5  6  8  9 10
          ------------------
       ----------------
    ------
------
                       ---
```

Variation across newspapers

```
Analysis of Variance Table

    Source              S.S.        DF          MS        F        Appx P
    ------------------------------------------------------------------------
    Total            16857.51       864
      Treatment       1499.57         2       749.78    42.08        <.001
      Error          15357.95       862        17.82
      R-square (R*R) = 0.09
    Error term used for comparisons = 17.82 with 862 d.f.

Homogeneous Populations, groups ranked

    Gp  1  refers to VAR1=DT
    Gp  2  refers to VAR1=GUA
    Gp  3  refers to VAR1=TI

              Gp Gp Gp
               3  2  1
              ---
                 ---
                    ---
```

Wh-questions (section 3.2.3)
Variation across decades

```
Analysis of Variance Table

    Source              S.S.        DF          MS        F        Appx P
    ------------------------------------------------------------------------
    Total             1792.57       863
      Treatment         48.64         9         5.4     2.65        0.0053
      Error           1743.93       854        2.04
      R-square (R*R) = 0.03
    Error term used for comparisons = 2.04 with 854 d.f.

          Gp Gp Gp Gp Gp Gp Gp Gp Gp Gp
           5  1  2  6  4  3  7  9 10  8
                    ------------------------
          ---------------------------
```

Variation across newspapers

```
Analysis of Variance Table

    Source              S.S.        DF          MS        F        Appx P
    ------------------------------------------------------------------------
    Total             1792.57       863
      Treatment         14.47         2        7.23     3.5         0.0308
      Error           1778.1        861        2.07
      R-square (R*R) = 0.01
    Error term used for comparisons = 2.07 with 861 d.f.

Homogeneous Populations, groups ranked

    Gp  1  refers to VAR2=DT
    Gp  2  refers to VAR2=Gua
    Gp  3  refers to VAR2=Ti

              Gp Gp Gp
               3  1  2
              ------
                 ---
```

Word length (section 4.4.1)
Variation across decades

```
Analysis of Variance Table
```

Source	S.S.	DF	MS	F	Appx P
Total	.23	29			
Treatment	.18	9	.02	9.69	<.001
Error	.04	20	.		
R-square (R*R) = 0.09					

```
Homogeneous Populations, groups ranked

              Gp Gp Gp Gp Gp Gp Gp Gp Gp Gp
               3  1  5  2  4  7  6  9  8 10
                               ---------
                          ---------------
                   ---------------------
```

Variation across newspapers

```
Analysis of Variance Table
```

Source	S.S.	DF	MS	F	Appx P
Total	.23	29			
Treatment	.02	2	.01	1.56	0.2281
Error	.2	27	.01		

```
Error term used for comparisons = .01 with 27 d.f.
```

Yes-no questions (section 3.2.3)
Variation across decades

```
Analysis of Variance Table
```

Source	S.S.	DF	MS	F	Appx P
Total	3101.69	863			
Treatment	66.73	9	7.41	2.09	0.0292
Error	3034.95	854	3.55		
R-square (R*R) = 0.02					

Variation across newspapers

```
Analysis of Variance Table
```

Source	S.S.	DF	MS	F	Appx P
Total	3101.69	863			
Treatment	67.2	2	33.6	9.53	<.001
Error	3034.49	861	3.52		
R-square (R*R) = 0.02					

```
Error term used for comparisons = 3.52 with 861 d.f.

Homogeneous Populations, groups ranked

     Gp  1  refers to VAR2=DT
     Gp  2  refers to VAR2=Gua
     Gp  3  refers to VAR2=Ti

              Gp Gp Gp
               3  1  2
                  ------
               ---
```